Trade, Jobs and Wages

Trade, Jobs and Wages

Hian Teck Hoon

Associate Professor, Department of Economics, National University of Singapore, Singapore

Edward Elgar Publishing Ltd

Cheltenham, UK • Northampton, MA, USA

Published by
Edward Elgar Publishing Limited
Glensanda House
Montpellier Parade
Cheltenham
Glos GL50 1UA
UK

Edward Elgar Publishing, Inc.
136 West Street
Suite 202
Northampton
Massachusetts 01060
USA

A catalogue record for this book
is available from the British Library

Library of Congress Cataloguing in Publication Data

Hoon, Hian Teck.
Trade, jobs and wages / Hian Teck Hoon.
Includes index.
I. Foreign trade and employment. 2. Unemployment. 3. Wages.
4. Equilibrium (Economics) I. Title.

HD5710.7.H66 2000
331.1—dc21

00–029413

ISBN 1 85898 7121

Printed and bound in Great Britain by MPG Books Ltd, Bodmin, Cornwall

Contents

Figures

Tables

Preface

It is estimated that in 1960, the year after Singapore obtained self-rule from Britain, its rate of unemployment stood at 13.5 per cent. Over the next four decades, the unemployment rate steadily declined to reach an average of just over 2.5 per cent in the 1990s. This downward trend in the movement of the unemployment rate has been accompanied by low inflation rates over the same period (except for the episodes of the two oil shocks in the seventies). Price stability is to a great extent the result of a monetary policy that is centred on maintaining an exchange rate target. Via a deliberate policy choice of allowing a gradual appreciation of the Singapore dollar, Singapore's domestic inflation has been kept below foreign inflation. With an exchange-rate-based monetary policy, Singapore has been able to maintain a stable and low rate of inflation. Since monetary policy has not been used to generate short-run booms, the resulting price stability has provided an economic environment within which real factors have played an important part in reducing the huge amount of joblessness that existed in Singapore at independence and in raising its workers' real purchasing power, which saw an increase by a factor of three from the early sixties to the late nineties.

To make sense of the shifts of the average unemployment rate over four decades, it seems reasonable to abstract from monetary factors and concentrate on non-monetary shocks and propagation mechanisms. It also seems important to model unemployment as having the feature that, in equilibrium, identical workers who are unemployed cannot go to a firm and promise to work for it at a lower than prevailing wage. We want to generate endogenous job rationing in general equilibrium with those who are employed being unambiguously better off than those who are not. Over the past fifteen years or so, a body of work has developed that provides a framework for thinking about the determinants of the natural rate of unemployment. Unlike the earlier Keynesian literature, which focused on deviations from an exogenous natural rate, there has emerged a theory of an endogenous natural rate.

My own exposure to this line of work began as a graduate student at Columbia University in the late eighties. At that time, Professor Edmund Phelps was reworking macroeconomic theory to provide an account of the decadal rise in unemployment in Europe since the early seventies. His early

1968 paper had provided a labour-turnover model in a monetary setting. Later, Steven Salop developed a prototypical general-equilibrium model of quitting that was stripped of monetary complications. Subsequently, the companion shirking model was given a general-equilibrium characterisation by Carl Shapiro and Joseph Stiglitz. Phelps brought together elements from the asymmetric information view of the labour market and intertemporal dimensions of firms' labour demand to develop an intertemporal general-equilibrium theory of the natural rate. I participated in his project as a PhD student and attempted to extend the original Salop model to incorporate explicitly the forward-looking behaviour of firms, giving the real interest rate a key role in shaping the evolution of the path of equilibrium unemployment.

Coming from a country that is so integrated into the world economy, whose value of trade is three times greater than its GDP, the theory that Professor Phelps was then developing seemed appealing to me as just the right framework for thinking about Singapore's long-term unemployment and wage performance provided that it could be extended to the global economy. Data gathered on the experience of the other three highly open East Asian economies of Hong Kong, South Korea and Taiwan also showed a steady decline of the unemployment rate from the early sixties accompanied by steady rises in the real wage. It seemed to me that traditional trade models – running from Ricardian to Heckscher–Ohlin to monopolistically competitive models – were missing something important by assuming full-employment at the outset. In the traditional models, international trade can affect real factor rewards but not aggregate unemployment. This conclusion is problematic especially when thinking about the influence of trade on jobs and wages in small open economies whose trade share out of GDP is high. Since integration into the global economy represents such a major economic shock to these countries, affecting both the wages that firms can afford to pay as well as the bundle of goods that workers are able to purchase with their pay, surely the equilibrium amount of joblessness must be affected *along with* changes in the real factor rewards structure.

This book represents my attempt at showing how both aggregate equilibrium unemployment and real wages are endogenously affected by trade in different theoretical settings. In undertaking this enterprise, the book makes a departure from the conventional treatment of unemployment in the international economics literature. In contrast to standard pure trade-theoretic models, the natural rate of unemployment is not exogenous – it moves in response to economic shocks; and in contrast to open economy macroeconomics, the focus is on structural unemployment rather than on cyclical unemployment. By focusing on the determinants of the natural rate of unemployment, the theory places an emphasis on real (as opposed to monetary) factors in accounting for long-run movements in wages and unemployment. The theory is micro-foundation based, being built up from optimisation problems solved by decision-making workers and firms. The crucial new element that is introduced to standard full-employment trade models is the informational asymmetric problem arising from the difficulty that firms have in monitoring the effort levels of workers.

I owe a great debt to Professor Phelps for my intellectual capital accumulated over many years and for his encouragement. However, I bear sole responsibility for any errors and shortcomings in this book. Finally, I wish to dedicate this book to my wife, Lian Leck, whose commitment and integrity in her work have set an example for me.

1. Introduction

1.1 WHY WORK?

Work is central to one's life. Through work, one earns a living wage to support a certain lifestyle and, for many, a family as well. It is true that one can tide over a period of unemployment through various means in order to maintain some semblance of a normal quality of life: by drawing down on current assets – the result of accumulation of past savings; by turning to the state for financial support if welfare payments are made in the event of job loss; or by turning to friends, relatives and other community support systems. But that period of unemployment cannot be prolonged. When joblessness becomes a long-term experience, economic hardship generally sets in unless the welfare system provides a cushion indefinitely. So, generally, one needs to hold a job in order to sustain a certain type of consumption activity and to enjoy a circle of social relationships.

But work does not bring only pecuniary rewards. There are many non-pecuniary rewards as well. One's self-esteem, for example, tends to be very much tied up with one's ability to tackle the challenges that the workplace throws up. There is a sense of accomplishment that comes from being able to size up a problem and to marshall the available resources to solve the problem. When one's contribution to solving a problem at work is acknowledged, even if only tacitly, it boosts self-confidence and encourages greater initiative. Even when a particular kind of job is mundane, the worker feels a sense of self-worth from earning the bread he eats. Another benefit of work is that it gives a certain structure to one's life. Work helps us to organise our time. Many goals that we set are work-related and these serve to give us a sense of purpose as we begin each new day. When we are absorbed in our work, time flies. On the other hand, there is a certain listlessness that accompanies prolonged joblessness. Many meaningful relationships are also developed at our workplace. This is partly due to the fact that the production process in modern enterprises is a collaborative effort requiring teamwork. As we work along with colleagues to achieve common goals and contribute jointly to problem-solving, we develop a social bond and a sense of belonging that are important for our emotional health.

There are external benefits from gainful employment as well, especially when that is the normal experience of most of the members of a community or country. A child growing up in such a community is motivated to work hard at school, believing that it is a common experience to land a suitably-paid job with the educational qualification he or she attains. In such an environment, parents can teach their children that personal achievement and financial independence can be attained through hard work by personal example or by pointing to other models in the community. When other members of one's community are largely employed and can afford a broadly similiar pattern of consumption, there are also common facilities – a good library, a common garden and so on – that they can share and feel a shared responsibility to protect. In an environment where income disparities are not too large, it is more likely that there will be a healthy respect for property rights and property crimes would be correspondingly lower.

Since work, as just argued, holds such a central position of importance in one's life, the loss of a job, especially when it leads to long-term unemployment, has severe consequences not only for the worker concerned but also for others. The loss of a regular source of income means that the consumption sets of the worker and his dependents are reduced, perhaps substantially, requiring the forgoing of certain consumption items that it might have been normal to have possessed prior to unemployment. In countries where there are no state-mandated unemployment benefits as is the case in the East Asian economies, workers who lose their jobs draw down their past savings or turn to relatives and friends in order to provide the basic necessities of life such as paying for their children's education. The enjoyment of various leisure activities such as a holiday abroad would now be deemed to be extravagant. Family members would have to adjust to a lower standard of living.

Initially, when a worker is laid off, there may be a hope that the period of job loss is only temporary. However, as each job application and job interview turn out to be unsuccessful, a mood of pessimism and general boredom set in. Clark and Oswald (1994), in their study of 6000 British workers in 1991, show that mental stress is twice as high among the unemployed as among those who have work. Interestingly, they find that the worst thing about becoming unemployed is not the drop in take-home income; it is the non-pecuniary distress (see Oswald, 1997). Relationships become strained when one is enveloped in a cloud of defeatism. Other family members bear the brunt of the unemployed worker's frustration and the quality of family relationships generally suffers. This is accentuated by the fact that a deep sense of helplessness sometimes leads to alcoholism, gambling and drug-taking. The health of the unemployed worker also suffers. Research has shown that there is a positive relationship between unemployment and poor health. After controlling for the effects of smoking and animal fat consumption, both of which increase the risk of heart disease, Brenner (1987) found a positive association between unemployment and increased heart disease mortality in nine industrialised countries between 1954 and 1978 (cited in Kates, Grieff and Hagen, 1990).[1]

When joblessness is concentrated in a particular geographical area, there could be adverse community effects as well, extending beyond the family. These manifest themselves in higher crime rates and a preponderance of drug-related problems and prostitution. The plight of children in such an environment in South-east Asia has been highlighted recently in the wake of the Asian financial crisis. Piriyarangsan (1999) reports on the findings of a study on the poor and the unemployed in Thailand done by the Northeast Development Association. One finding is that as a result of the increased incidence of joblessness brought about by the economic crisis in 1997, children were found to be at greater risk of committing drug-related crimes and of being subject to sexual abuse.

1.2 A GENERAL-EQUILIBRIUM MODEL OF JOBLESSNESS

The economist can contribute to our understanding of joblessness – how it is determined and what factors influence the amount – by developing a macroeconomic model of unemployment. In this book, we adopt a particular approach to the general-equilibrium determination of the natural rate of unemployment. The basic idea goes back to Phelps (1968), where an incentive-wage (or efficiency-wage) story is used to generate a labour-market equilibrium locus exhibiting job rationing under correct expectations. Using some notations, suppose that W is the log of nominal wage being set, W_{-1} is the log of nominal wage set last period, W^e is the expected wage, and $\phi(u)$ is a function of the unemployment rate, u. Then, we can write the Phillips curve as:

$$W - W_{-1} = \phi(u) + W^e - W_{-1}.$$

Under correct expectations, where $W = W^e$, we have a value of u, denoted u^*, that makes the function $\phi(u)$ equal to zero. This value, u^*, is in general non-zero and we call it the natural rate of unemployment.

The original Phelps (1968) paper generated the $\phi(u)$ function by drawing upon a quitting or labour-turnover story in a monetary setting. Salop (1979) did away with the monetary complications and worked instead with a non-monetary model of the natural rate of unemployment. In that model, newly hired employees receive firm-specific training, which is a form of investment undertaken by the firms. However, these trained employees are prone to quit to find employment elsewhere for pecuniary and non-pecuniary reasons. In order to combat quitting, each firm reasons that up to a point an increase in its own wage, given wages expected elsewhere, can lower the quit rate sufficiently to make the saving on training of replacements cover the higher cost. Since all firms think likewise, no firm will actually create a wage premium over its competitors in a symmetric equilibrium scenario. Instead, the economy-wide wage is bidded up above the level that corresponds to market-clearing thus resulting in unemployment. A feature of the unemployment thus generated is that it is involuntary in the sense that identical workers who are unemployed cannot go to the firm and promise to work for it at a lower than prevailing wage. The firm would reckon that at the lower wage the apparently similiar worker offers to work, his quit propensity would be higher. That could not be an optimal trade-off for the firm since it had already chosen the wage to reach an optimum on its wage-quitting opportunity locus.

In more familiar terms, the choice of the optimal wage by firms under correct expectations leads to a wage curve that is upward-sloping in the employment rate–real wage plane. At the optimum, the cost saving per employee from raising the real wage by one unit is exactly equal to one. In the convenient case of a constant marginal training cost, say T, this cost saving is equal to T multiplied by the marginal decline in the quit propensity. This condition pins down a unique size of the real wage differential, which, following Calvo (1979), we can write as $w - w^e$, where w^e is the real wage expected elsewhere. If we approximate w^e by $(1 - u)w$, that is, the wage offered elsewhere adjusted by the probability of obtaining a job (proxied by the employment rate), it is immediately clear that as the employment rate rises (or unemployment rate declines) the real wage must rise to generate the optimal wage differential. Thus we obtain a positively-sloped wage curve.

General equilibrium in the stationary state with a zero rate of time discount is obtained by positing a downward-sloping labour demand curve that is juxtaposed against the upward-sloping wage curve. A tighter labour market induces higher quits, which makes the wage that the firm can afford to pay fall. In the constant-returns-to-scale case with no capital, this fact alone is enough to generate a downward-sloping labour demand curve.

There are three comments that can be made about the basic model of the endogenous natural rate model just sketched. Firstly, the model, in focusing on the stationary state, does not give adequate attention to the role played by the real interest rate. This shortcoming is corrected to some extent in Hoon and Phelps (1992), which provides a more complete analysis of the intertemporal problem solved by the firm. A whole book-length treatment has now been supplied by Phelps (1994), which puts the real rate of interest at centre stage in the analysis of the long swings of economic activity.

Secondly, the quitting or labour-turnover story is not the only one that generates a wage curve that is serviceable for a general-equilibrium analysis of equilibrium unemployment. A rather parallel story comes from the shirking or supervision perspective. In this model, supervision of workers is costly and there is an upper bound on the type of punishment that can be meted out on workers for substandard performance. A worker who is caught shirking on the job can be suspended or fired but typically imprisonment or cash fines are not feasible. The firm instead uses wages as an incentive device. In this model, market clearing cannot be an equilibrium since workers would then face zero cost from being caught shirking and losing their job – they will simply be rehired in another firm. There would be rampant shirking at full employment. As in the quitting story, each firm raises its wage above the market-clearing level. In a symmetric equilibrium, no firm succeeds in creating a relative wage improvement. Instead, equilibrium unemployment results. A fully micro-theoretic model of the shirking story is provided by Shapiro and Stiglitz (1984), which supplies us with a wage curve that is also called a no-shirking constraint.

Yet another approach to the modelling of the labour market, providing a wage curve, rests on the bargaining power of workers (see Mortensen and Pissarides, 1998). This power comes from the fact that it is costly for the firm to find replacement for workers who decide to leave. The amount of bargaining power a worker has depends on the attributes of the job. Apart from job characteristics, however, labour-market conditions have an effect on workers' bargaining power. The firm will find it more difficult to find a suitable replacement when the labour market is tight, at a low rate of unemployment. This in turn will increase the bargaining power of employed workers, who will then be able to secure higher wages. It is much easier to find good replacements when the unemployment rate is high. In this situation employed workers have less bargaining power, and they may be forced to settle for lower wages. Such an argument leads, once again, to the existence of an upward-sloping wage-setting curve in the employment rate–real wage plane.

Thirdly, notice that the labour demand curve is derived from a one-good aggregative model under the assumption of perfect competition. In fact, a much richer specification of product market conditions can give rise to a demand–wage relation that we can juxtapose against the wage curve. This includes the consideration of multi-sectors and the possibility of imperfect competition in the product market. Thus, we open for consideration a much wider set of factors – the relative price structure, the size of the market, and the degree of product-market competition, for example – that can affect the determination of the natural rate of unemployment.

In short, there is now a model of the equilibrium rate of unemployment involving product-market equilibrium and labour-market equilibrium. Our objective in this book is to use this model to study the role that trade plays in jointly determining the equilibrium amount of joblessness and workers' remunerations. In doing so, we abstract from the short-run movements of the unemployment rate arising from expectational disequilibrium, and focus instead exclusively on the movements of the equilibrium rate of unemployment and real prices.

It should be pointed out, however, that although prolonged unemployment is an important source of poverty in many societies, and has many other negative consequences for both the affected workers as well as their families, the inability to earn more than a very *low wage* is thought to be another important source of poverty and is at the centre of both academic and policy interest in the advanced economies, especially in the USA. Two sorts of models emphasise the determination of absolute and relative pay levels of low-wage workers in a general-equilibrium framework. The first sort of model generates a wage premium between identical workers employed in two different sectors – a primary sector and a secondary sector – within a dual labour market set-up. The other sort of model introduces workers with different skill levels. In the simplest set-up, there are only two types of workers – high-skilled and low-skilled workers. The wage premium between the two types of workers is endogenously determined.

1.3 WHY TRADE?

Once we have a model of the equilibrium rate of unemployment, we want to know what the economic factors are that determine the amount of joblessness and wages that prevail in a country. Trade is clearly one major shock that would have an effect on an economy's structure of relative commodity prices unless the country is so large that total exports and imports are a negligible share of its gross domestic product. (This statement should be qualified. As we show in a model in Chapter 5, even when no trade flows actually occur, the increased product–market competition in an integrated world economy affects the wage that firms can afford to pay and consequently affects the natural rate.) Since trade affects the structure of relative prices in an economy – whether relative commodity prices or wages relative to product prices – an analysis using a model of the natural rate would show that the amount of joblessness as well as workers' pay are both jointly affected by international trade.

It should not escape the reader's attention that this is *not* the traditional view of unemployment determination in the international economics literature. The development of the field of international economics has proceeded very much along the micro/macro divide with pure trade theory studying the determination of relative prices and real factor rewards under full employment and open-economy macroeconomics studying, among other things, the determination of unemployment. Open-economy macroeconomics, however, treats the natural rate of unemployment as invariant and exogenous and so its focus is on cyclical unemployment – deviations from the natural rate. In pure trade theory, trade among nations, even though it affects real factor rewards through changing relative prices and enlarging the effective size of the market, has ultimately no effect on jobs. Since nations benefit from trade through changing the composition of the products it consumes and produces, there might be frictional unemployment resulting from a re-allocation of factors across sectors. In the medium to long term, however, the amount of joblessness is presumed, in standard trade theory, to be unaffected as workers displaced from a shrinking sector find employment in an expanding sector. The framework we develop, however, leads us to the conclusion that quite apart from frictional unemployment, there is a structural unemployment that is affected by trade. The framework also allows for the shocks typically studied in pure trade theory – policy shocks, technological shocks, terms of trade shocks and so on – to have an effect on aggregate equilibrium unemployment. It is plausible that over the medium to long term, such shocks in the global economy have large effects on structural unemployment and thereby have greater welfare significance than the shocks that are typically analysed in open-economy macroeconomics, which only produce cyclical movements of unemployment around an invariant natural rate.

The view that we need a theory of how international trade affects the natural rate of unemployment endogenously is fortified by the experience of the East Asian economies of Hong Kong, Singapore, South Korea and Taiwan, which turned to trade as part of their development efforts in the sixties. Despite the recent economic crisis that saw the unemployment rates in some of these countries go up sharply, it should be pointed out that the average decadal unemployment rates of the East Asian Newly Industrialising Countries (NICs) since the sixties actually underwent a steady decline. Data compiled by Fields (1984) show Singapore's unemployment rate decline from 9.1 per cent in 1965 (the year it gained independence) to 3.5 per cent in 1980, South Korea's unemployment rate decline from 8.2 per cent in 1963 to 4.1 per cent in 1981 and Taiwan's unemployment rate decline from 6.3 per cent in 1955 to 1.3 per cent in 1981. At the same time, real wages have increased by three to four times over this period.

We would like to be able to interpret the steady decline of average joblessness together with a steady rise in real wages in these countries within the framework of a natural rate model and, in particular, will examine the Singapore experience in some detail in Chapter 2.

The basic approach of this book can be illustrated with a simple Ricardian model with two goods, X and Y. Let the wage curve be represented by

$$\frac{w}{p_x^{\alpha} p_y^{1-\alpha}} = h(1-u;z);\; h_{1-u} > 0,$$

where the left-hand side of the equation gives the real consumption wage (the worker being assumed to have a Cobb–Douglas utility function with α the share of the budget going to good X and $1-\alpha$ the share going to good Y) and the right-hand side gives a function of the rate of employment (that is, one minus the rate of unemployment). The symbol z represents other factors that affect the wage curve. Note that it is the real consumption wage – what the wage can buy in terms of goods consumed – that matters to a worker, and that can be re-expressed as $(w/p_x)(p_x/p_y)^{1-\alpha}$. In a closed economy with the Ricardian structure, both goods are produced. The zero-profit condition gives rise to

$$w = \frac{p_x}{a_x} = \frac{p_y}{a_y},$$

where a_x and a_y are the unit labour input requirements in sectors X and Y, respectively. Equating the demand wage to the supply wage, we can derive a labour–market equilibrium locus relating the relative price, p_x/p_y, to the rate of employment, $1-u$:

$$a_x^{-1}\left(\frac{p_x}{p_y}\right)^{1-\alpha} = h(1-u;\, z).$$

This is shown as the positively-sloped schedule in Figure 1.1.

Assuming that workers have identical Cobb–Douglas tastes, product–market equilibrium requires that

$$\frac{p_x}{p_y} = \frac{a_x}{a_y}.$$

We show this as a horizontal line in Figure 1.1. The intersection of the labour–market equilibrium locus and the product–market equilibrium locus gives the unique natural rate of unemployment.

Consider the effect of trade. Suppose, for simplicity, that under trade this is a small open economy that takes the world relative price, $(p_x/p_y)^f$, as given. If, without loss of generality, $(p_x/p_y)^f > (a_x/a_y)$, the country becomes

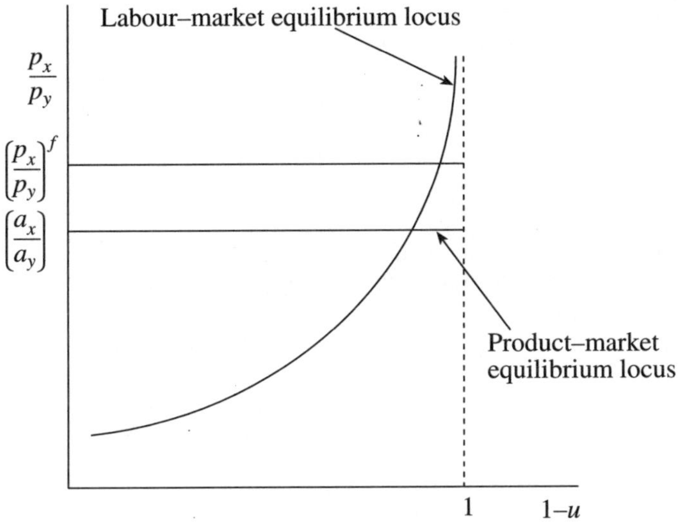

Figure 1.1 Labour– and product–market equilibrium

a net exporter of good X and completely specialises in producing good X. In Figure 1.1, the line giving the world relative price lies above the autarkic relative price, with the result that the natural rate of unemployment declines as a result of trade. In terms of the production possibilities frontier diagram shown in Figure 1.2, we see that trade not only expands the consumption possibilities set (the conventional result) but it also shifts out the production possibilities frontier itself.

In the Ricardian model, the essential mechanism through which participation in international trade leads to a decline in the natural rate of unemployment, and consequently to an outward shift of the production possibilities frontier, is the increase in the stake of holding a job as the constant real product wage (that is, the wage in terms of the export good) earned by an employed worker now translates into a higher real consumption wage. The higher real consumption wage is obtained as the result of trade based upon comparative advantage, which ensures that the import good can be bought from abroad at a lower relative price than in autarky. As workers value their jobs more under trade, the incentive wage that firms are *required* to pay is equated to the demand wage that firms can *afford* to pay at a lower equilibrium rate of unemployment. In a two-country world where trade leads to complete specialisation, workers in both countries enjoy higher real purchasing power under trade despite the fact that their real product wages remain constant given the constant marginal (and

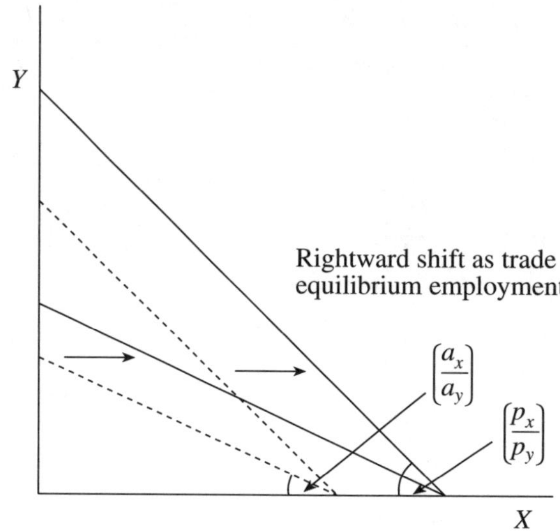

Figure 1.2 Trade and shift of PPF

average) labour productivities. So the natural rate of unemployment declines in both countries.

The effect of trade on the natural rate of unemployment is, however, different in the Heckscher–Ohlin model where trade is based upon differences in relative factor endowments. In that model, the real product wage both in terms of the export good as well as the import good is increased under trade if the country is relatively labour abundant but is decreased if the country is relatively capital abundant. Consequently, regardless of how the worker divides his expenditure between the export and the import good, the real consumption wage is raised by international trade in the former but lowered in the latter. As work incentives are strengthened in the labour abundant country, trade lowers its natural rate; however, trade weakens work incentives in the capital abundant country, which therefore suffers a rise in its natural rate of unemployment.

In the Ricardian and Heckscher–Ohlin models, international trade affects work incentives through changing the relative goods price, lowering the natural rate in both participating economies in the former model but raising the natural rate in the capital abundant country in the latter model. With perfectly competitive goods markets, changes in the natural rate of unemployment brought about by trade are linked directly to changes in the relative goods price. Work in the trade area since the late seventies, however, suggests that international trade at a fundamental level enlarges the effective size of the market and increases the degree of product–market competition even in the absence of relative goods price changes. The larger market size has a positive effect on the consumption-based measure of a worker's real factor reward through two channels: by increasing the range of the varieties of differentiated consumer products; and by increasing labour productivity, and hence, the real demand wage through having access to a wider range of intermediate inputs. By increasing the degree of product–market competition, the price–marginal cost mark-up is reduced, which translates once again into an increase in the real demand wage. In a set-up which abstracts from movements in the relative goods price, an enlarged market size and increased competition under trade lead unambiguously to a rise in the consumption-based measure of a worker's real wage in all participating economies. This increases a worker's stake in holding on to a job and consequently expands equilibrium employment in every trading nation.

When both relative factor endowment differences and the enjoyment of product diversity resulting from a larger effective market size form the basis for international trade, and when trade increases product–market competition in an imperfectly competitive setting, it is possible that trade will lower the natural rate in the capital abundant country as well, despite the job-depressing effect of the relative price movement it faces. To capture the various channels through which trade affects the natural rate of unemployment, it is useful to depict the general equilibrium in the Marshallian employment rate–real wage plane, where the natural rate is obtained at the intersection of a positively-sloped wage-setting curve and a horizontal real demand–wage relation. We represent the real supply wage, more generally, as

$$\left(\frac{w}{p_x}\right)^s = h\left(1-u; \frac{p_x}{p_y}, z\right),$$

and the real demand–wage relation as

$$\left(\frac{w}{p_x}\right)^d = g\left(\frac{p_x}{p_y}, 1+\mu, n_m\right).$$

The real supply wage increases as the labour market tightens (unemployment rate falls) and the cost of being caught shirking decreases. Alternatively, as the unemployment rate falls, the bargaining position of the firm weakens and workers are emboldened to ask for higher wages. For a given wage in terms of good X, a rise in the relative goods price, p_x/p_y, translates into a higher real consumption wage. This makes workers value their jobs more and so be willing to accept a lower product wage at any rate of unemployment without shirking. Alternatively, the bargaining position of the

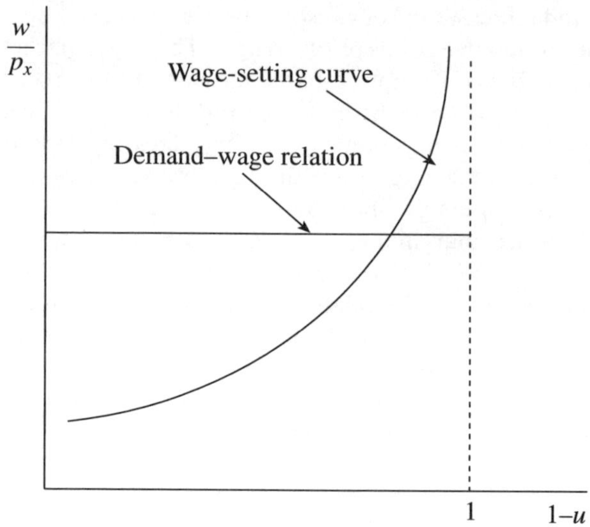

Figure 1.3 Marshallian employment rate–real wage diagram

firm strengthens and they are able to force on workers a lower supply wage in terms of good X. In other words, an increase in p_x/p_y shifts the wage-setting curve in Figure 1.3 to the right. In Chapter 6, workers are assumed to have a 'love for variety' utility function. Consequently, when the number of monopolistically competitive consumption goods is increased, workers value their jobs more as any given expenditure level can now be divided over a wider range of goods, which raises utility. We now include in z the range of differentiated consumption goods. When that increases, the wage-setting curve shifts right.

The real demand wage increases with an increase in the relative goods price, p_x/p_y, if good X is relatively labour-intensive but is inversely related to p_x/p_y if good X is relatively capital-intensive under Heckscher–Ohlin assumptions. It decreases when there is an increase in the size of the price-marginal cost mark-up, $1 + \mu$, which in the simple model of Chapter 5, is simply inversely related to the number of oligopolistically competitive firms. Greater international product–market competition implies a fall in the mark-up, which raises the real demand wage. Finally, in the model of Chapter 6, labour productivity is increased when the range of monopolistically competitive intermediate goods represented by n_m is increased. Thus an increase in n_m raises the real demand wage. Figure 1.3 is a useful diagram for thinking through how international trade affects the natural rate of unemployment in each trading nation.

If we believe that the integration of an economy into the global goods market represents a major economic shock, the analysis presented in this book leads us to predict that trade has an influence on both the natural rate as well as the real factor rewards structure. Consequently, when an economy moves from autarky to free trade, the welfare effects of trade may be greater than what traditonal trade theory with an exogenous natural rate would predict. The ability of Singaporean workers to buy a wide range of consumption goods with their pay had positive work incentive effects, and the ability of firms to buy a wide range of intermediate inputs raised the real demand wage that firms could afford to pay. Both channels acted to lower the natural rate. Moreover, in the sixties and early seventies, Singapore, as well as the other East Asian economies, relied on exporting labour-intensive products such as textiles, garments and simple assembly-line electronics into the world market, which added to labour demand and further reduced the natural rate. These channels may now play important roles in alleviating the unemployment problem of the newly-emerging economies, provided the international trading system remains open.

There is another channel through which international trade can affect the natural rate, based upon the recent findings of Coe, Helpman and Hoffmaister (1997) (see also Bayoumi, Coe and Helpman, 1996) that increased international trade by a nation allows it to enjoy substantial international R&D spillovers. The basic idea is that through foreign trade, and also through foreign investment, a nation is able to learn from its trading partners' production methods, product design, organisational methods and product market conditions. In addition, trade flows provide a channel for follower-countries to copy foreign technologies in leader-countries and to adapt them for domestic use. According to this hypothesis, the decision of the East Asian economies to integrate with the world trading system in the sixties combined with the fact that they were then far behind the world knowledge frontier made it possible for these countries to experience significant technological catch-up. In this view, total factor productivity improvements occurred rapidly along with physical and human capital accumulation in the East Asian economies. Indeed, if we accept the Nelson–Phelps (1966) view that increased education enables economic agents to learn new technologies, the fact that human capital accumulation occurred at a tremendous pace in the East Asian economies particularly equipped them to learn from their trading partners. The high productivity growth experienced by these small open economies, at given world interest rates, prompted firms to raise labour demand. With wages pulled up relative to wealth, wage pressures were also reduced. The result was a steady decline of the equilibrium rate of unemployment.

We want a trade model exhibiting an endogenous natural rate for another reason. In conventional trade models exhibiting an exogenous natural rate, we are apt to conclude that there is little basis for arguing that protectionism, even when practised on a large scale, as occurred in the interwar years when international trade collapsed, cannot lead to massive joblessness. This is, for example, the view expressed by Krugman (1994a, pp. 123–4):

> Although most policymakers in Washington are convinced that protectionism is a bad thing, few of them have any clear idea why. In popular arguments against protectionism, the usual warning is that protectionism threatens our jobs – the Smoot–Hawley tariff of 1931, we are told, caused the Depression, and history can repeat itself.
>
> Although protectionism *is* [emphasis in original] usually a bad thing, it is worth pointing out that it isn't as bad as all that. Protectionism does not cost our economy jobs, any more than the trade deficit does: US employment is essentially determined by supply, not demand. The claim that protectionism caused the Depression is nonsense; the claim that future protectionism will lead to a repeat performance is equally nonsensical.
>
> The real harm done by protectionism is much more modest and mundane: It reduces the efficiency of the world economy. To the extent that countries limit each other's exports, they block the mutually beneficial process by which nations specialize in producing goods for which their knowledge and resources are particularly well fitted. They also fragment markets, preventing firms and industries from realizing economies of scale. A protectionist country is usually less productive and thus poorer than it would have been under free trade; a protectionist world economy almost always so . . .

The perspective developed in this book suggests a channel through which protectionism can, indeed, lead to a world-wide collapse in output and rise in unemployment as occurred in the interwar years. While the *cause* of the Great Depression in the United States is unlikely to be due to the implementation of the Smoot–Hawley tariffs, trade being such a small share of US GDP in 1929, the setting up of tariff barriers by the largest economy in the world at the time and the accompanying retaliatory trade barriers put up by the other economies led to a collapse of world trade. In the framework developed here, the fragmentation of markets and the removal of the gains from trade must shift upwards the wage curve and downwards the aggregate labour demand curve, with the end result that the collapse of world trade must be accompanied by a rise in equilibrium unemployment. Such a perspective does away with any role for Keynesian effective demand but relies on real supply-side factors to understand the link between trade and the volume of joblessness. Within this framework, we can not only ask how protectionist policies affect jobs and wages in the economies of trading partners, but also study the effects of a number of other shocks in the contemporary world economy on the medium- to long-term unemployment and wage performance of nations. What are the effects on wages and joblessness in the developed economies that follow from the integration of labour-abundant economies? What are the effects of technical catch-up in East Asia on the rest of the world?

1.4 ORGANISATION OF THE BOOK

In Chapter 2, we provide an account of the evolution of wages and unemployment of the Singapore economy over the past four decades. We document that over this period, there has been a fairly steady decline in the unemployment rate, interrupted only by the sharp rise in unemployment during the mid-eighties recession, and the real wage saw a larger than threefold increase. We interpret the decadal decline in Singapore's unemployment rate as primarily a story of the downward shift of its natural rate of unemployment.

The basic Ricardian model of trade with an endogenous natural rate developed in Chapter 3 gives a first pass at the problem of how trade affects the equilibrium amount of joblessness. The main insight we obtain here is that under trade, workers have an increased stake in job-holding as the real consumption wage is increased. Consequently, an integration into the world economy leads to a lowering of the natural rate of unemployment for all participating economies except for the large country whose relative price is unaffected by trade. For the large country, trade has no influence on its natural rate. Some basic economic shocks are also studied in an integrated two-country Ricardian world economy. In such a world, trade wars lead to a reduction in economic welfare as trade volume shrinks and equilibrium unemployment rises for all the countries engaged in economic warfare. More generous unemployment benefits supported by higher payroll taxes lead to higher unemployment in the policy-active country as firms there face higher after-tax wage costs of hiring an additional worker, and employees enjoy increased fall-back incomes in the event that they lose their jobs. This has the consequence of exporting a slump to the rest of the world through a deterioration in the latter's terms of trade. A level increase in worker productivity in the export sector of the home country must benefit its trading partner by raising foreigners' welfare through raising their employment prospects and their real consumption wages although it is theoretically possible that the country experiencing the productivity improvement may actually face a rise in unemployment and suffer a decline in real incomes. An expansion of one country's labour force lowers unemployment in the rest of the world but raises joblessness in the expanding country. Labour standards naturally rise as incomes are raised through trade, and employment prospects improve. In turn, the higher labour standards raise the value of job-holding, further expanding aggregate employment.

The Heckscher–Ohlin model with an endogenous natural rate developed in Chapter 4 presents a very different vision of how trade affects jobs and wages. Here it is shown how trade leads to a rise in the natural rate of unemployment in the capital abundant country although it must lead to a decline in the natural rate in the labour abundant country. In theory, the capital abundant country can overall suffer a welfare decline under trade. There are, however, two other forces that can strengthen the basic messsage of the Ricardian model – that *all* trading partners can gain from trade. These are the pro-competitive effects of trade explored in Chapter 5, and the scale effects of trade explored in Chapter 6. When these two effects are incorporated into a relative factor-endowment differences model, it is possible that all trading countries, including the capital abundant country, experience a decline in joblessness as well as an increase in real consumption wages under trade.

Two sorts of models emphasise the determination of absolute and relative pay levels of low-wage workers in a general-equilibrium framework. In Chapter 7, we explore a model which generates a wage premium between identical workers employed in two different sectors – a primary sector and a secondary sector – within a dual labour market set-up. A key result we obtain here is that integration among industrial economies dominated by intra-industry trade leads to the expansion of high-wage premium jobs along with a narrowing of the wage gap in all participating economies. This stands on its head the popular supposition that globalisation widens the wage gap. Then Chapter 8 explores a model where there are two types of workers – high-skilled and low-skilled workers. The wage premium between the two types of workers is endogenously determined. We show that trade can raise the real returns to both factors of production when scale economies are sufficiently important.

Chapter 9 introduces wealth in a neoclassical model of perfect information to derive results about the influence of intertemporal trade and capital mobility on wages and labour force participation. One result we obtain is that higher growth in open economies leads to higher labour force participation, a fact observed about the East Asian economies. We also discuss the role of wealth in determining the natural rate, and explore the influence that trade has on jobs through the beneficial effects of international R&D spillovers. Finally, Chapter 10 explores a classical model of trade whose structure is drawn from Ricardo's *Essay on Profits*. We show that under free trade, the relatively land abundant country experiences a decline in its growth rate – correspondingly, a decline in the rate at which employment grows. When we introduce an intermediate goods sector that produces a variety of fertilizer inputs, giving rise in effect to increasing returns to scale, we show that intra-industry trade allows all participating countries to experience a rise in the rate of employment expansion. Chapter 11 concludes with a synthesis of some of the major themes of the book.

NOTES

1. Sen (1999) stresses the loss of freedom and capability associated with long-term unemployment. He argues: '[U]nemployment is not merely a deficiency of income that can be made up through transfers by the state (at heavy fiscal cost that can itself be a very serious burden); it is also a source of far-reaching debilitating effects on individual freedom, initiative, and skills. Among its manifold effects, unemployment contributes to the "social exclusion" of some groups, and it leads to losses of self-reliance, self-confidence and psychological and physical health.' (p. 21)

2. Factors shaping Singapore's wages and unemployment

2.1 INTRODUCTION

Against a near three-fold increase in the level of unemployment in much of Western Europe in the past three decades, the decline in Singapore's unemployment rate from an estimated 13.5 per cent in 1960 to an average of just over 2.5 per cent in the 1990s must be regarded as nothing short of dramatic.[1] Moreover, this downward trend in the movement of the unemployment rate has been accompanied by low inflation rates during the past four decades (except for the episodes of the two oil shocks). Price stability is to a great extent the result of a monetary policy that is centred on maintaining an exchange rate target.[2] Being a highly open economy that takes world prices as given, external conditions have a large influence on domestic prices. According to the estimates of two Singapore central bankers, Teh and Shanmugaratnam (1992), for every 1 per cent increase in import prices, consumer prices will increase by about 0.7 per cent. This means that a 5 per cent rate of import price inflation translates into a 3.5 per cent rate of CPI inflation, in the absence of any independent domestic source of inflation. Via a deliberate policy choice of allowing a gradual appreciation of the Singapore dollar, Singapore's domestic inflation has been kept below foreign inflation. With an exchange-rate-based monetary policy, Singapore has been able to maintain a stable and low rate of inflation. Since monetary policy has not been used to generate short-run booms, the resulting price stability has provided an economic environment within which real factors have played an important part in reducing the huge amount of joblessness that existed in Singapore at independence.[3]

Romer and Romer (1998) recently obtained cross-sectional evidence from a large sample of countries which showed that low inflation and stable aggregate demand growth are associated with improved well-being of the poor in the long run. The Singapore story can be interpreted as one where, in an environment of price stability and other conditions such as political stability and good infrastructural support, foreign investors were attracted to come to Singapore bringing with them a demand for workers and offering jobs to Singaporean workers.[4] The commitment, not only to liberal rules on flows of foreign direct investments, but also to unhindered international flows of goods and services, provided workers with the opportunity to purchase with their pay the whole range of consumer goods available in the world economy. Since the means to buy goods derived largely from the ability of workers to hold on to a job, the gains from increased product diversity under free trade made holding on to a job more worthwhile. This acted to shift down the wage curve. Firms were also free to purchase the whole range of intermediates available in the world economy for use in the production process. Moreover, in the early stage of economic development, many of the foreign direct investments were in labour-intensive industries such as garments and textiles as well as simple assembly-line electronics. The ability to enjoy scale economies arising from an international division of labour in intermediates, and the ability to produce and sell labour-intensive goods in the world market both raised the wage that firms could afford to pay. These shifts – in the wage curve and the affordable wage schedule – led to a decline in the volume of joblessness.

With continued inflows of foreign direct investments and steady increases in the stock of human capital, Singapore's relative factor endowments have changed over time. As a result, the economy has undergone major structural transformations, with higher value-added industries becoming more competitive and replacing lower value-added ones. While this factor is apt to raise the amount of frictional unemployment, we have not actually witnessed a rise in average unemployment over the eighties and nineties. What has been at work is that the ability to sell into the world market goods that are increasingly higher up the value-added chain means that the new firms have been able to afford to pay increasingly higher real wages. Insofar as wages have kept ahead of wealth for a significant fraction of the workforce, due, for example, to credit market imperfections, the structural unemployment rate would tend to decline and offset the rise in frictional unemployment. Another force was apparently at work if we accept the important findings of David Coe and Elhanan Helpman, and their co-authors (see Coe and Helpman, 1995; Coe, Helpman and Hoffmaister, 1997; and Bayoumi, Coe and Helpman, 1996) that increased trade openness and high levels of educational attainments lead to substantial international R&D spillovers. The decision to launch an industrialisation programme based on inviting multinational corporations to produce in Singapore to sell into the world market, and the public investment in raising the educational attainment of the workforce, enabled the country to learn new production methods, product designs and organisational forms needed to compete in the world market. The resulting improvements in total factor productivity led firms to raise labour demand, while the growth of productivity ahead of wealth kept down wage pressures. Consequently, equilibrium unemployment declined (see Hoon and Phelps, 1997).

The data show that the real product wage of the manufacturing sector, proxied by the real export wage, was roughly unchanged during the seventies but began to rise in the early eighties. However, as the export price was rising relative to the GDP deflator since the early seventies, a more comprehensive measure of the real wage that is relevant for consumer welfare, namely, the real consumption wage, has also been on the increase since the early seventies. In this chapter, we take the premise that the Singapore story is primarily one of a shifting natural rate of unemployment. We then seek to uncover the forces that have driven up real wages on the one hand, and lowered the natural rate of unemployment on the other. We also attempt to place the influence of the National Wages Council (NWC) on the joint determination of the real wage and unemployment rate in this framework. The NWC comprises representatives of employees, employers and the government, and, since 1972, has issued annual wage guidelines. Although the wage guidelines are not mandatory in nature, they have been implemented in the public sector and are closely followed in the private sector as well. Faced with negative external shocks to the small open economy, the NWC, as a tripartite body, has brought national consensus on accepting wage guidelines recommending broad real wage reductions such as during the oil crisis years as well as more recently during the Asian financial crisis. The NWC is therefore an institution that has a major influence on the position of the wage curve as we shall argue and has played the role of conflict management in the face of external shocks. The need for an institutional framework to manage conflict in countries that choose to be integrated into the global economy has recently been emphasised by Rodrik (1999).

The chapter is organised as follows. In Section 2.2, we examine the empirical facts. We then present in Section 2.3 a theoretical structure within which to explain the facts highlighted in Section 2.2. Concluding remarks are contained in Section 2.4.

2.2 EMPIRICAL FACTS

Figure 2.1(a) shows the steady decline of Singapore's unemployment rate from 8.9 per cent in 1966 to less than 2.5 per cent in 1997, interrupted only by the sharp recession year of 1985 when the unemployment rate shot up momentarily to over 6 per cent. In contrast, Figure 2.1(b) shows, for selected European Union countries, the persistent rise in unemployment over the decades of the seventies and eighties. Figure 2.1(c) shows the rise of manufacturing wage deflated by the consumer price index over nearly

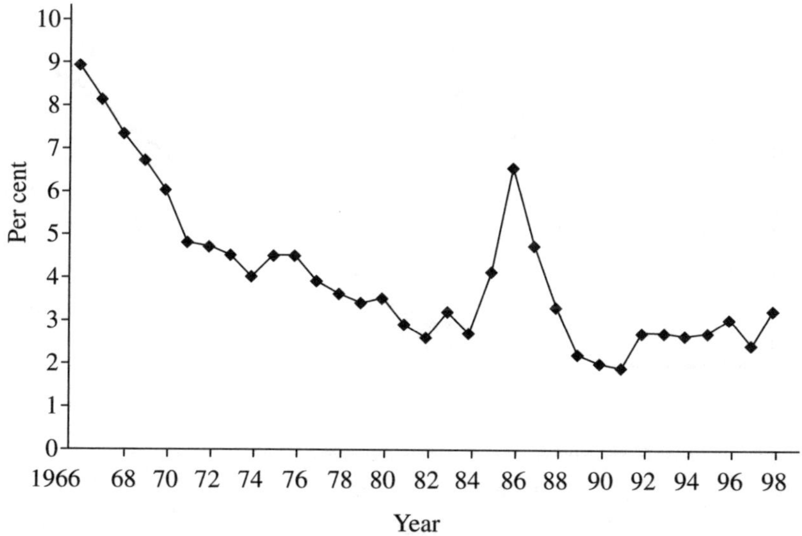

Source: *Yearbook of Statistics*, Singapore, various issues

Figure 2.1(a) Singapore's unemployment rate, 1966–98

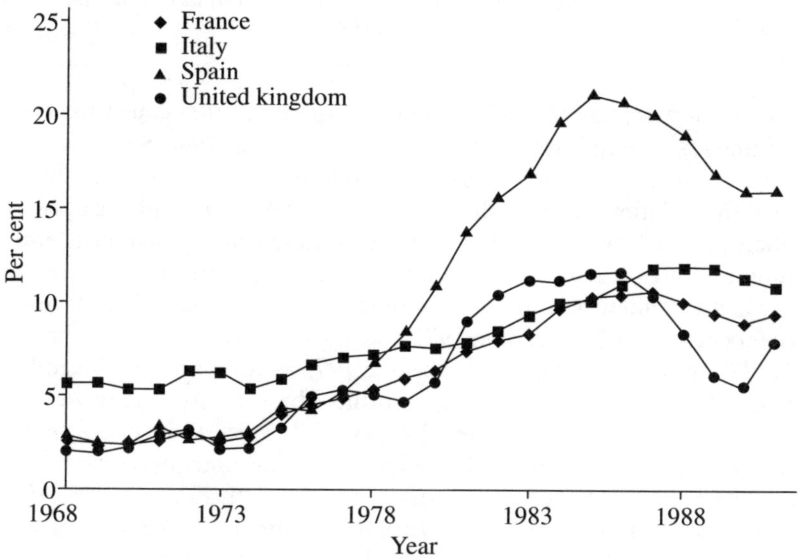

Source: OECD (1993), *Labour Force Statistics*

Figure 2.1(b) Unemployment rate of some OECD countries

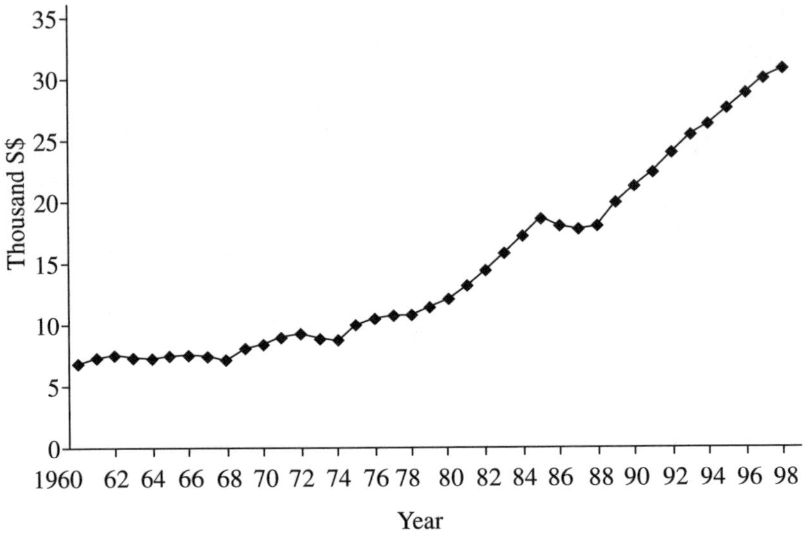

Source: *Report on the Census of Industrial Production*, Singapore, various issues
Note: Base year is October 1992 to September 1993

Figure 2.1(c) Real annual remuneration per worker in manufacturing, 1960–98

four decades. A scatter plot of Singapore's inflation rate against the contemporaneous unemployment rate over the period 1966–93 shown in Figure 2.2 fails to reveal any statistically significant negative relationship between the inflation rate and the unemployment rate. Instead, we observe that there is a fairly wide variation in the unemployment rate at consistently low inflation rates, leaving out the outliers. The latter correspond to the two years when the inflation rate in Singapore rose to unusually high levels – 19.6 per cent and 22.3 per cent in 1973 and 1974, respectively. According to Lee (1987), the CPI rose by 17.7 per cent in 1973 as compared to November 1972. Of the five categories of expenditure, the increase was most pronounced in food prices, reaching 31.4 per cent. Since food prices had a weight of 49 per cent in the CPI, the increase in average food prices contributed 87 per cent of the increase in the general CPI. A large proportion of the increase in food prices was in turn due to the rise in the price of rice and other cereals of 83 per cent in 1973, which had a weight of 21.6 per cent in food. Most of the food, and practically all of rice, was imported. Thus it was the escalation of food and especially rice prices in the world which was the major cause of inflation in 1973.

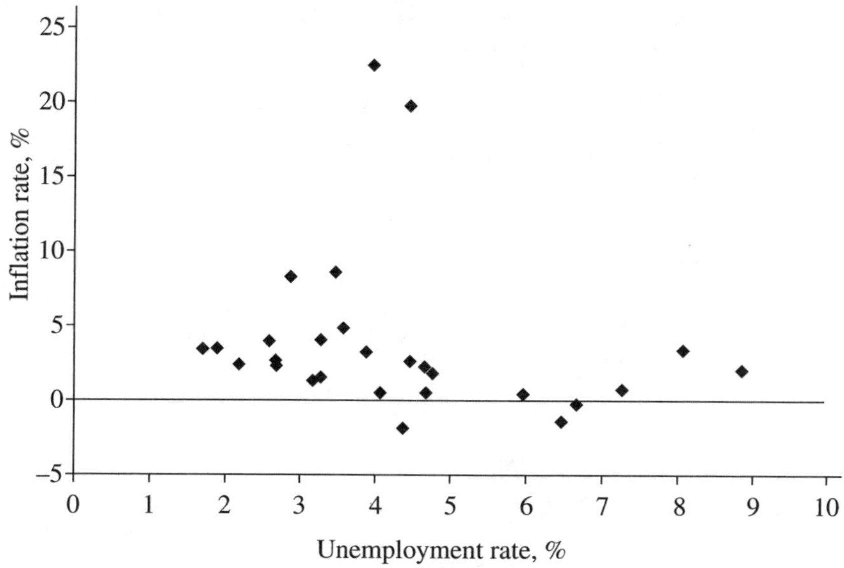

Source: *Yearbook of Statistics*, Singapore, various years

Figure 2.2 Singapore's plot of inflation rate against unemployment rate, 1966–93

Inflation in food prices also contributed 56 per cent to overall inflation in 1974. The increase in the price of public road transport and to a lesser extent of petrol were the main causes of the increase in the price of transport and communications of 37.6 per cent, which contributed some 4 percentage points to overall inflation that year. These increases were primarily the result of the four-fold increase in oil prices which occurred in late 1973. In 1974 as in 1973, therefore, inflation was mainly due to the inflation in imported foods and energy, the latter causing inflation in the prices of such commodities as domestic transport and fuel and light costs (see Lee, 1987).

A simple ordinary least squares regression of the inflation rate on the unemployment rate reported in Table 2.1 reveals an estimated coefficient that is not statistically significantly different from zero. These observations, we argue, are consistent with a shifting 'natural' or inflation-invariant rate of unemployment.[5] In the standard Keynesian view of the economics of booms and recessions, nominal price rigidity and expectational disequilibrium lead to short-term fluctuations of the unemployment rate around a largely invariant natural rate as the economy is subject to various shocks and economic impulses. In Singapore's experience, we have argued that

Table 2.1 Regression line relating Singapore's inflation rate to unemployment rate

Dependent variable	:	Inflation rate
Sample	:	1966–93
Method	:	OLS
R-squared	:	0.029302

Parameters	Estimates	t-statistic
Constant	5.84127	2.24134
Slope coefficient	−0.497953	−0.885917

Source: *Yearbook of Statistics*, Singapore, various years

Table 2.2 Singapore's average unemployment rate

Period	Average unemployment rate %
1966–70	7.4
1971–75	4.5
1976–80	3.74
1981–85	3.1
1986–90	3.68
1991–95	2.52

Sources: *Yearbook of Statistics*, Singapore, various years; *Economic Survey of Singapore*, 1995

monetary policy has not been used as an active short-run stabilisation tool. Fiscal policy, in the sense of large government investment expenditure in building infrastructure and developing industrial sites over a fairly long period, has nevertheless been active. The effects of fiscal policy, however, seem to have been largely on the supply side, there being little inflationary pressure. In order to abstract from cyclical movements of the unemployment rate, we take five-year averages of annual unemployment rates and show how the average semi-decadal unemployment rates have changed over the past three decades or so. As is evident from examining Table 2.2, there has indeed been a decline in Singapore's average five-year unemployment rates, from a high of 7.4 per cent in the second half of the sixties to 2.5 per cent in the first half of the nineties. This evidence is suggestive of a decline

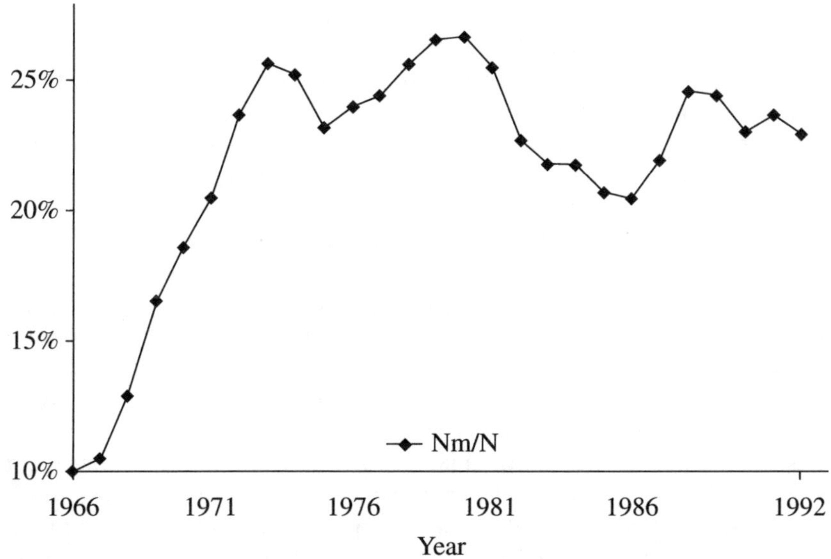

Notes:
Nm: Number of workers in the manufacturing sector
N: Total employment of the economy
Source: *Yearbook of Statistics*, Singapore, various years

Figure 2.3 Manufacturing sector's share of total employment, 1966–92

in the natural rate of unemployment. In the parlance of conventional macroeconomics, the Singapore economy seems to have experienced a leftward shift of the vertical long-run Phillips curve in the span of the last three to four decades.

Consistent with the process of industrialisation, the manufacturing sector has been a net absorber of the labour force. Thus, while job opportunities have generally increased in the overall economy over the past four decades, the manufacturing sector has contributed a disproportionately large number of job openings. In Figure 2.3, we see that whereas the manufacturing sector absorbed about 10 per cent of all workers employed in the mid-sixties, by the early seventies, its share had increased to over 25 per cent. Its share then hovered around that level, reaching 27 per cent in 1979 and 1980 before receding in the next few years to a level just above 20 per cent.

What part does international trade play in fuelling the expansion of the manufacturing sector? The answer is: Quite a big part. According to the *Singapore Input–Output Tables 1988*, the value of export of the manufacturing sector made up about 75 per cent of the total vaule of export of the whole economy. In terms of its size, the manufacturing sector, however, contributed only to about 29 per cent of total real output in that year. Thus, the manufacturing sector's contribution to total export far exceeds its relative economic size and it can be regarded primarily as an export sector. In this sense, trade has been a propeller of jobs in Singapore's recent economic history. In contrast, the following sectors, Utility, Construction, Commerce, Transport and Communications, Financial and Business Services, and Other Services contributed 0.13 per cent, 0 per cent, 8.6 per cent, 12.8 per cent, 3.5 per cent and 0.19 per cent, respectively, to the total value of the economy's export. These sectors' relative contributions to total export were not commensurate with their economic size. Their share of total real output in 1988 amounted to 2 per cent, 5.8 per cent, 17.8 per cent, 14.1 per cent, 25.3 per cent, and 10.9 per cent, respectively.[6]

As the manufacturing sector is largely an export sector, it is convenient to construct (as a measure of the true opportunity cost of labour) an index of the real export wage. In other words, the real export wage can be used here as a proxy for the real product wage of the manufacturing sector, namely, the wage in terms of the output produced by workers. This is distinct from, though related to, the real consumption wage, which is the wage deflated by the consumer price index. The latter gives the wage in terms of the basket of goods consumed by the worker. The former measure is useful when thinking through how production and demand conditions affect the determination of the equilibrium cost of hiring labour, while, obviously, it is the latter measure that is relevant for consumer welfare. In this chapter, with an eye to understanding how various production and demand conditions have shaped the adjustment of wages and employment, we work directly with the real export wage. Nevertheless, we show how the real consumption wage can be inferred from our real export wage series.

Figures 2.4(a) and 2.4(b) show the indices of the real export wage in selected industry groups in the manufacturing sector over the period 1971–92. The nominal wage, which includes basic salary, employer's and employee's contributions to the Central Provident Fund (Singapore's fully-funded social security system), bonuses, pension paid by employer (where applicable) and other benefits provided, is deflated by the GDP deflator for the exports of goods and services. (Altogether the share of the 16 selected industry groups in the total gross value added of the manufacturing sector is 94.4 per cent in 1992.) Before 1980, the real export wage rate was somewhat constant for about a decade. However, the real export wage rates were increasing by the early eighties. The largest increase is seen in Paper and paper products, industry group 341, for which the real export wage in 1992 was about 3.5 times its level in 1971. In contrast, Petroleum refineries and

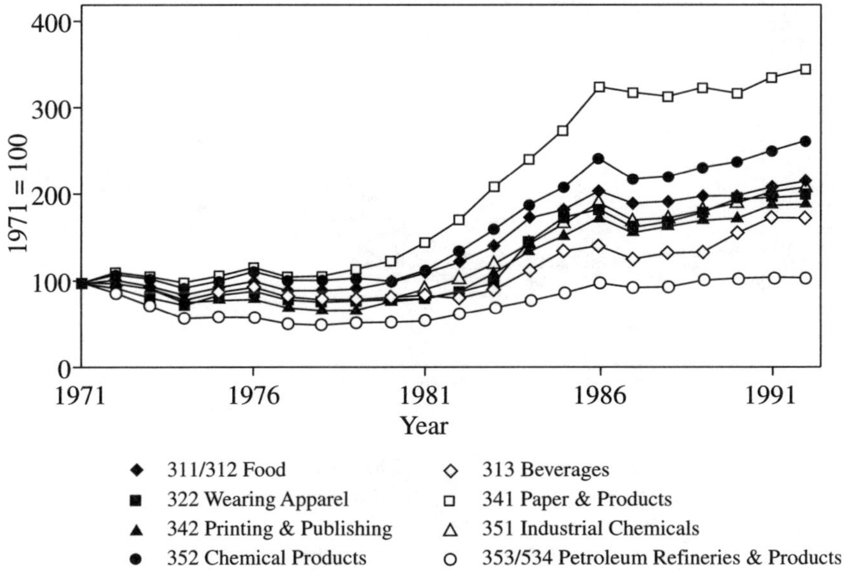

Sources: Computed from *Yearbook of Statistics*, Singapore, various years; *Report on the Census of Industrial Production*, Singapore, various years; Economic Development Board, unpublished data

Figure 2.4(a) Plot of real export wage index by selected major industry groups

products, industry group 353/354, saw the smallest rise in its real export wage of less than 1.2 times over the same period. Electronic products and components, industry group 384, which accounted for most of manufacturing exports and employment had, in 1992, a real export wage rate that was about twice the level in 1971.

What factors determine the equilibrium values of the real export wage? As we will see in the next section, the equilibrium real export wage is determined jointly with the equilibrium employment rate in a diagram that juxtaposes a downward-sloping labour demand curve against an upward-sloping wage curve. Although the Shapiro–Stiglitz effort-elicitation model, which adopts a zero-one effort decision rule, leads to a horizontal demand-wage schedule, it is more realistic, for empirical purposes, to assume a variable effort function. Since such an effort function, under consistent-expectations equilibrium, would depend negatively on the equilibrium employment rate, assuming a variable effort function would lead to a

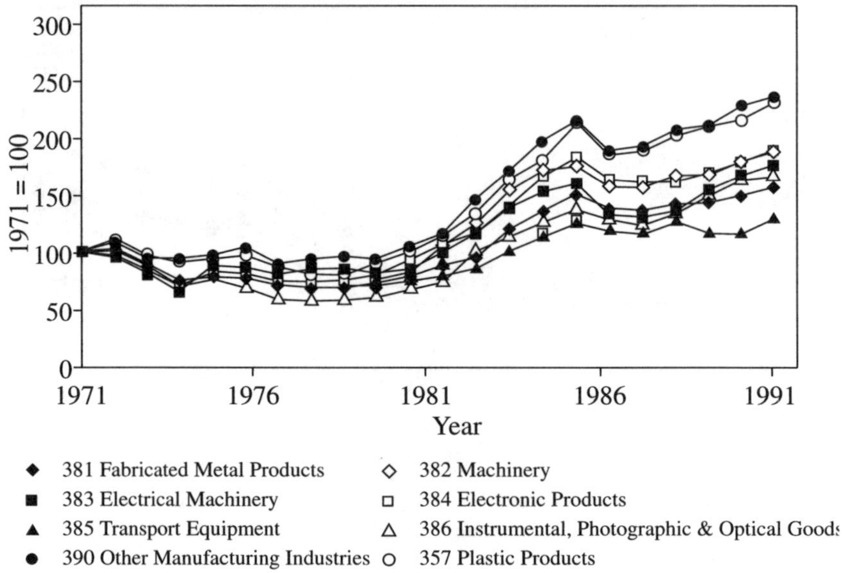

Sources: As in Figure 2.4(a)

Figure 2.4(b) Plot of real export wage index by selected major industry groups

downward-sloping demand-wage schedule. Essentially, as the labour market tightens, workers are prone to exert less effort thus making hiring an additional worker less profitable. Consequently, the affordable wage declines as the unemployment rate falls. A quitting story of the labour market would also give rise to a downward-sloping labour demand curve, as a tighter labour market induces higher quits. *Ceteris paribus*, factors that shift the wage curve to the right lower the equilibrium real export wage and expands equilibrium employment; factors that shift the labour demand curve to the right raise both the equilibrium real export wage as well as the equilibrium employment rate.

There are three factors that can shift the labour demand curve: relative goods price, technological improvements and capital deepening. In Figure 2.6 below, we show that the export price has risen relative to the price of nontradables since the early seventies. Under some assumptions about relative factor intensities, we can infer how these relative price changes affect the position of the labour demand curve. Next, if we accept the empirical findings of Coe, Helpman and co-authors that trade integration and openness to inflows of foreign direct investments have been an important con-

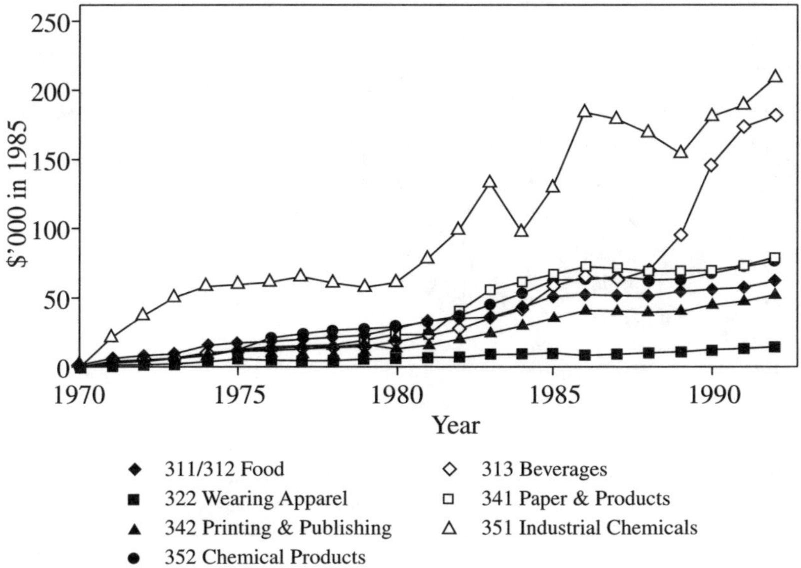

Sources: As in Figure 2.4(a)

Figure 2.5(a) Physical capital–labour ratio by selected major industry groups

tributory factor to acquiring new technologies in the East Asian economies, the total factor productivity growth of Singapore's sectors would also act to raise labour demand. Thirdly, capital deepening is another prime candidate for explaining the rightward shift of the labour demand curve.[7] In Figures 2.5(a) and 2.5(b), we show that over the period 1970–92, all the selected manufacturing industry groups illustrated in Figures 2.4(a) and 2.4(b) moved towards more capital-intensive methods of production. (Industry group 353/354, Petroleum refineries and products, saw its capital intensity rising to unusually high levels compared to the other industry groups by the early eighties, and has not been included in the figures.) Juxtaposed against a given wage curve, the rightward shift of labour demand results in a rise in the real export wage.

While the real export wage measures the marginal cost of hiring facing an export firm, it is the real consumption wage that is relevant for measuring consumer welfare. We have shown that since about 1980, the real export wage has increased and noted that in the seventies, although the real export wage was roughly constant, the export price was rising relative to the price of non-tradables. What can we say about the behaviour of the real

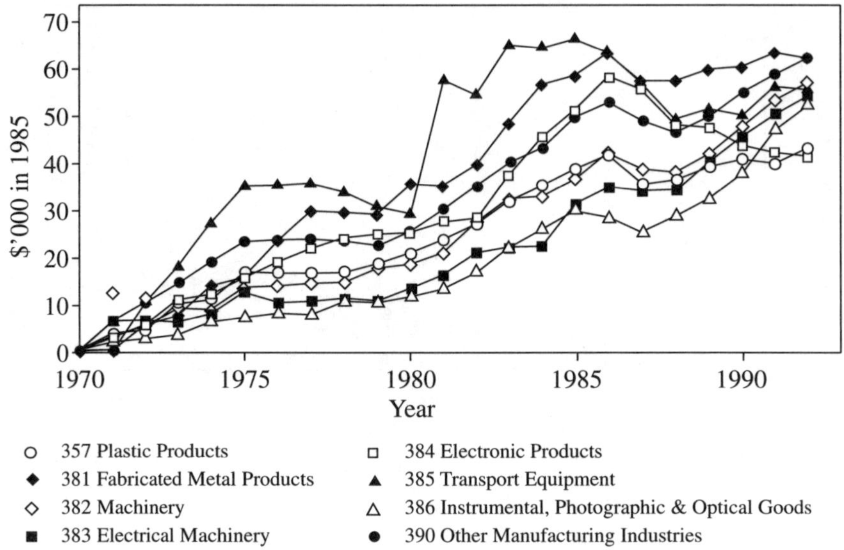

Sources: As in Figure 2.4(a)

Figure 2.5(b) Physical capital–labour ratio by selected major industry groups

consumption wage? To illuminate the analysis, some mathematical symbols will be helpful. Suppose, for simplicity, that we can classify the economy's goods into two categories: manufacturing (which we can regard as tradable) and others (which we can broadly regard as non-tradable). Under 'others', we have in mind items like housing and transport. Let w represent the nominal wage rate, p_x the manufacturing price index, and p_n the non-traded good price index. In this terminology, w/p_x represents the real export wage. Defining the consumer price index as p, where $p \equiv p_x^{\alpha} p_n^{1-\alpha}$, α being the share of manufacturing good in the worker's consumption basket and $1-\alpha$ the corresponding share of the non-tradable in the worker's consumption basket, we can write the real consumption wage, w/p, as $w/p = (w/p_x)(p_x/p_n)^{1-\alpha}$.

It is now clear that the real consumption wage, w/p, can rise for three reasons: (i) a rise in w/p_x; (ii) a rise in p_x/p_n; and (iii) a rise in $1-\alpha$, *ceteris paribus*. We have already shown that the real export wage, w/p_x, was somewhat constant in the decade before 1980 but has risen since about 1980. In Figure 2.6, we show how the ratio of the export price to non-traded good price, p_x/p_n, has changed over the period 1966–92. We see that over the

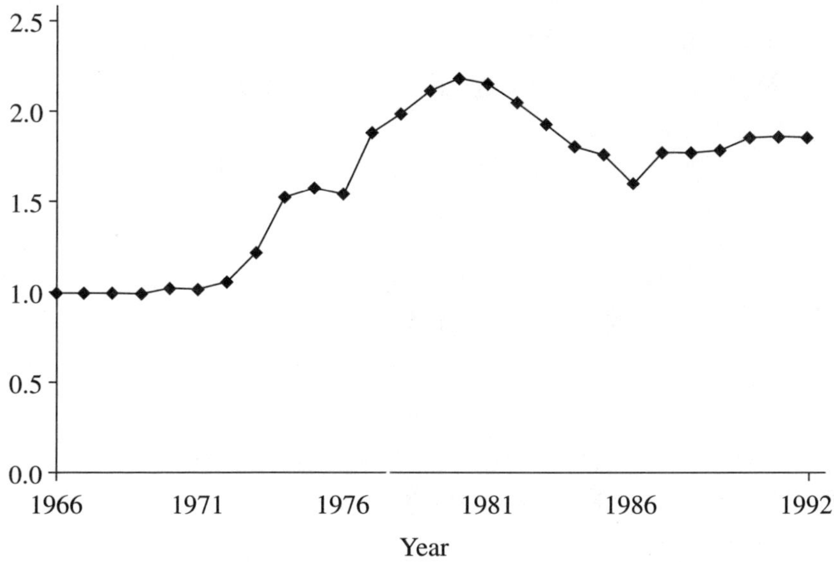

Source: *Yearbook of Statistics*, Singapore, various years

Figure 2.6 Trend of export price relative to non-traded good price, 1966–92

1970s, there was a fairly sharp rise in p_x/p_n before it declined somewhat after the early 1980s. The ratio, however, has remained higher compared to the starting year of 1966. Thus, broadly speaking, the change in p_x/p_n has contributed to a rise in the real consumption wage. Finally, we see that a rise in the share of the non-traded good in the worker's consumption basket, $1 - \alpha$, magnifies the contribution of the rise in p_x/p_n to a rising real consumption wage index. In Figure 2.7, we show that the share of housing and transport combined, increased from slightly above 27 per cent in 1972/73 to over 39 per cent in 1992/93. Taking the perspective of the two and a half decades, there seems, indeed, to have been a rise in Singapore's real consumption wage.[8]

In the next section, we seek to provide a theoretical framework within which to explain the empirical facts highlighted in this section.

2.3 THEORETICAL FRAMEWORK

A set of stylised facts of the Singapore economy now comes into view. Caught with high structural unemployment at independence, the economy

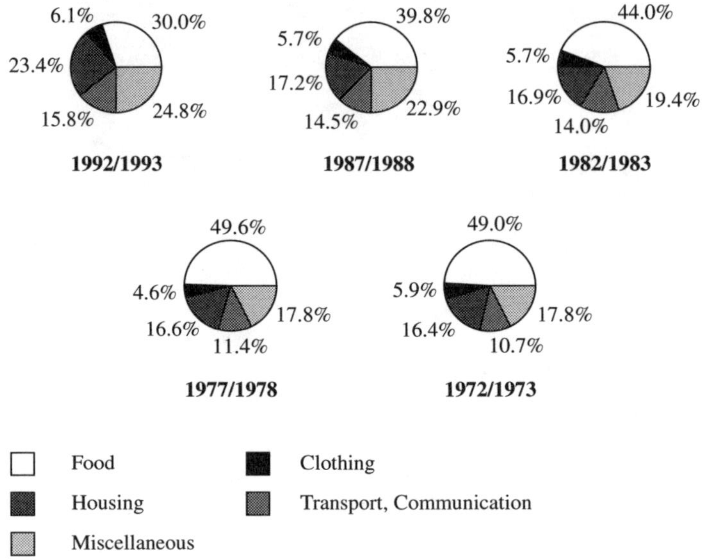

Source: *Consumer Price Index*, Department of Statistics, Singapore, various years

Figure 2.7 The expenditure share of major components in consumption basket

launched into an industrialisation programme based on production for sale in the world economy. With more factories being built to produce and sell labour-intensive goods such as garments, textiles and simple assembly-line electronics into the world market in the early stage of industrialisation, demand for workers was raised in the manufacturing sector. The upward shift of the labour demand curve along a given wage curve led to a decline in the natural or equilibrium rate of unemployment.

This wage curve is generated by the requirement that at each rate of equilibrium unemployment, firms must pay an adequate wage in order to induce the right amount of effort from workers, avoid too high a rate of absenteeism, and prevent too high a rate of labour turnover. This required wage, it can be argued, rises as the equilibrium rate of unemployment declines since at a lower rate of unemployment, it is somewhat less costly to lose a job. The worker, figuring that he can soon enough find a new job in a tight labour market, is induced to quit more frequently and slacken in his current job. Accordingly, firms must pay more in order to stimulate work effort and induce workers to value their jobs more highly as the unemployment rate declines.[9]

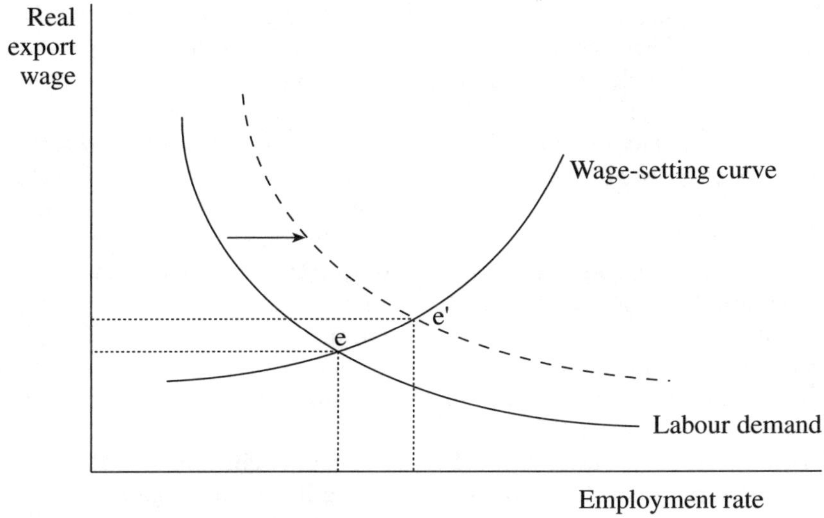

Figure 2.8 Marshallian diagram

The above argument gives rise to an upward-sloping wage curve, which we can depict in Figure 2.8. It is arguable that in the atmosphere of the sixties, with very high unemployment, the relevant section of the wage curve was also somewhat flat, that is, the increase in the required wage was small with each percentage decrease in the unemployment rate. As we moved into the early eighties, and the unemployment rate came down to the 2 to 3 per cent region, labour turnover became a major problem. As workers saw that they were increasingly in a sellers' market, with firms fighting to retain their workers, they were emboldened to ask for a better deal with the threat of quitting. Rampant quitting would serve a blow to firms since the money spent to orientate workers when they were raw recruits would now be lost without the benefits reaped as the workers became experienced members of the firms' workforce. It is arguable that in the atmosphere of the eighties, with very low unemployment, the wage curve was also somewhat steep, that is, the increase in the required wage was large with each percentage decrease in the unemployment rate. Thus, the wage-setting curve can be shown as gently-sloping in the region of high unemployment but steeply-sloping in the region of low unemployment.

Turning to the production side of the model, we can imagine an export-oriented manufacturing sector alongside another aggregative sector that is to a large extent non-traded. The manufacturing sector should be thought of as consisting of a potential range of goods that can be ranked by their relative capital intensity, with simple standardised garments as very labour-intensive and pharmaceuticals as more capital-intensive, for example. With garments and textiles as well as simple assembly-line electronics dominating the manufacturing sector in the sixties, this sector can be thought of as being relatively labour-intensive compared to the non-traded good sector early in Singapore's post-independence development. Firms in each sector express a demand for labour, setting the demand wage equal to the value of marginal product. The demand wage is the affordable wage that firms are able to pay and depends on the value of output that their workers produce. In the simple setting of the labour-turnover model, the demand wage schedule or labour demand curve is downward-sloping in Figure 2.8 – as the rate of unemployment declines, each worker's propensity to quit rises, raising the marginal cost of hiring an additional worker, and dampening the wage that firms can afford to pay.

The intersection between the labour demand schedule and the wage curve gives the joint determination of the equilibrium or natural rate of unemployment and the equilibrium real export wage. How might we explain the decline in the equilibrium unemployment rate through the sixties? The early stage of industrialisation was mainly propelled by foreign direct investments into textiles and garments, as well as simple assembly-line electronics. As the factories being built and equipment and machines being added to factory floors were employed mainly in the production of labour-intensive goods to sell into the world market based upon comparative advantage, the increased value of the marginal productivity of labour in manufacturing led firms to raise their demand for workers to co-operate with their machines in production. Manufacturing firms signalled their increased demand for labour by raising the real demand wage they were willing to pay. In other words, the labour demand curve shifted to the right. However, as the economy operated along the rather flat portion of the wage curve in Figure 2.8, the economy experienced a decline in the equilibrium rate of unemployment without a significant rise in the equilibrium real export wage. The upward pressure on the real demand wage was translated instead into more job openings. At the original relative price ratio, the non-traded good sector shrank in order to release workers to work with more machines in the manufacturing sector. Therefore, the expansion of the manufacturing sector not only reduced the pool of the jobless but also drew workers from the other sub-sectors of the economy.

How should we interpret the introduction of the National Wages Council (NWC) in the early seventies as a national institution that brought together representatives from government, private sector employers and employees to recommend annual wage guidelines? To understand its role, we need to understand the problem that firms face in reducing labour turnover. Notice that by the early seventies, a decade of industrialisation had succeeded in lowering the equilibrium rate of unemployment to the 5 per cent level. The problem of high labour turnover became more severe in the modern setting of a free-enterprise market economy. To combat the problem of having workers quit after firms have injected money into providing them with firm-specific training, each firm has an incentive to outpay other firms. Each firm reasons that, up to a point, a payment above the rate that other firms are paying for similiar workers would induce its workers to value their jobs at the firm more highly and thus to stay loyal to the firm. However, since all firms think likewise, any attempt by a single firm to raise its own wage rate above that which other firms are paying is frustrated. No firm is better placed than any of its rivals in offering a higher relative wage; instead, the competitive bidding to retain its workforce succeeds only in driving up the marginal factor cost of hiring an additional worker. The required wage is pushed up but workers are by no means more loyal or productive; accordingly, the number of workers that each firm can afford to hire is reduced.

To put the matter in another way, firms have to face the problem of retaining the workers they have invested in. A means available to them is to offer a more attractive pay package. However, one firm's action to raise its own wage offer frustrates other firms' attempts to retain their workers by giving them attractive offers; if firm A raises its wage by a dollar, then firm B, which has just raised its wage offer by a dollar, finds that it is in no apparent advantageous position. With wages already raised, however, no firm would want to lower its wage offer initially without losing good workers. We have here a case of a prisoners' dilemma. If firm B does not raise its wage offer, firm A will benefit by raising its own wage offer since it will then be able to retain its own experienced workers. Should firm B raise its wage offer, firm A must do so as well just to maintain status quo. The argument carries through when applied from firm B's point of view. Thus, whatever my rival firm does, I benefit from raising my own wage when acting unilaterally. The decentralised solution leads to the worst possible outcome – both firms pay too much without any gain in the form of reduced quitting. In general equilibrium, this translates into the affordable wage being equated to the required wage at a higher equilibrium rate of unemployment.

What the National Wages Council does is to co-ordinate the wage-setting behaviour of firms. By bringing together employers, one function that the NWC fulfils is to internalise the negative externality pointed to in the preceding paragraph. Each firm, when choosing its own wage policy, now recognises that other firms will aim at the same broad guidelines set down by the NWC. In the langauge of the prisoners' dilemma problem, both firms

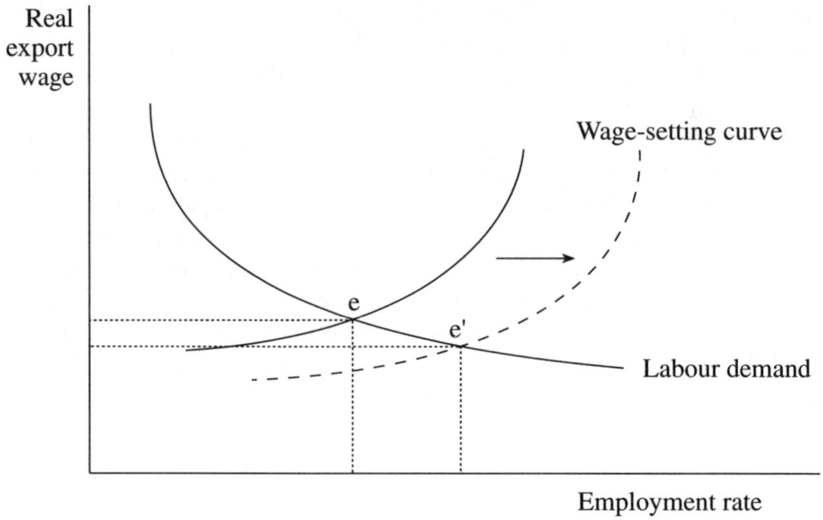

Figure 2.9 Effect of NWC on wage-setting curve

A and B agree to choose the co-operative solution. In terms of Figure 2.9, the negotiations done through the NWC act to shift down the wage-setting curve. Notice that this has an expansionary influence on employment, although a dampening effect on the real export wage.

Apart from the role of internalising the negative externality of a firm bidding up the required wage, the National Wages Council, through bringing together employers, labour unions and the public sector representatives, could have served to contribute to the decline in equilibrium unemployment in another way. In particular, the NWC has served to highlight critical factors that matter for overall macroeconomic management, especially in the face of negative external shocks, and has brought these factors to bear on the wage-setting process of firms. An example is how the oil shock of 1973 affected wage setting.

To see this, notice that by the early seventies, the unemployment rate had fallen somewhat from the high levels of the sixties so that the economy would have moved in a north-easterly direction along the lower wage-setting curve in Figure 2.9 as capital accumulation proceeded, fuelled not only by high domestic savings but also by strong inflows of direct foreign investment. Technological catch-up is another factor pulling up labour demand. Moreover, the rise of the export price relative to the non-traded good price in the seventies would exert upward pressure on the real demand wage if we assume that the manufacturing sector in those years was still rel-

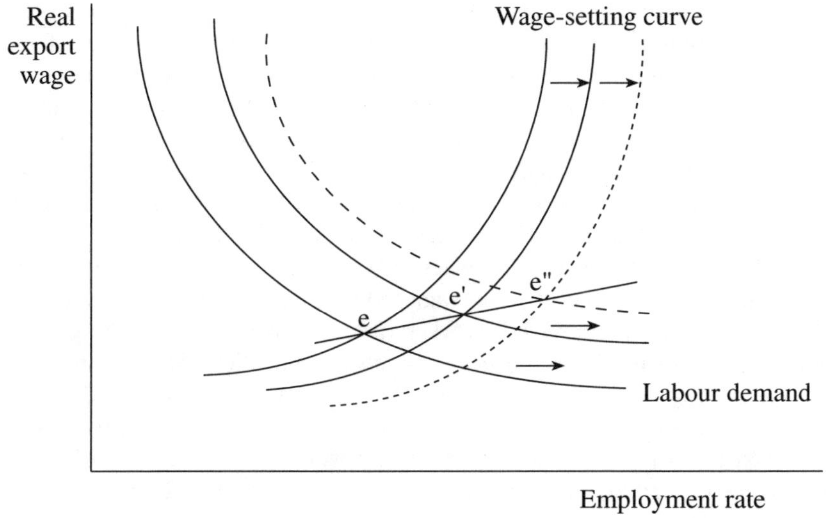

Figure 2.10 Trend of wage-employment equilibrium with shifting labour demand and wage-setting curves

atively labour-intensive compared to the non-traded good sector. The result would have been declining equilibrium unemployment along with rising real export wages. Instead, what we observe is that through the seventies, the unemployment rate continued to fall but real export wages were somewhat stagnant.

Why did real export wages not increase along with declining unemployment rates in the 1970s? A possible explanation lies in the fact that the economy was hit by the world-wide recession prompted by the first oil shock in 1973, leading to the National Wages Council recommending greater caution in the pace of wage-setting amidst increased economic uncertainty. In terms of Figure 2.10, the upward shift of the labour demand schedule occurred in tandem with a downward shift of the wage-setting curve, tracing out a set of intersection points giving somewhat constant real export wages along with declining unemployment.[10]

Rodrik (1999) has emphasised the importance of national institutions in the task of conflict resolution as whole societies face negative external shocks in the process of international economic integration. In Singapore, the National Wages Council has played a very important role in forging a national consensus on wage matters by bringing together representatives from workers, employers and the public sector in closed-door meetings. The result of the meetings is the issue of annual wage guidelines which take into account the nature of shocks facing the economy. Most recently, when the Asian financial crisis led to a recession and an expected slowdown of the economy's medium-term growth, the National Wages Council made recommendations for a fairly substantial reduction in the employers' share of the social security contributions accruing to the employed workforce. The recommendations were accepted and speedily implemented. Just as in the earlier response to the recessionary shocks of 1985, and earlier on in the response to the oil shocks, the NWC has been able to bring about what is in effect a rightward shift of the wage curve. Part of the reason why labour has been willing to accept these wage reductions during bad times is that when the economy recovered, workers have enjoyed compensating wage increases. For example, a major policy response to the 1985 recession was a 15-percentage point cut in employers' Central Provident Fund (CPF) contributions from an original 25 per cent. Employees' CPF contributions remained at 25 per cent. As the economy recovered by the end of 1986, employers' contribution rates were gradually increased to 20 per cent and workers' contributions were reduced from 25 to 20 per cent hence increasing their take-home pay. These were the prevailing rates until the contagion effects from the Asian financial crisis adversely hit the economy and employers' CPF contribution rates were again cut.

Another study by Rodrik (1997) based on international cross-sectional data has argued that in economies subject to external risks as a result of trade opening, government consumption spending, especially income transfers, has been especially high. Rodrik interprets this finding to mean that economies that have been open to trade have found it necessary to develop a welfare state partly as an insurance against external shocks. Within the endogenous natural rate framework developed here, the rise of the welfare state would act to shift leftwards the wage curve as job attachments are weakened, and absenteeism and the propensity to shirk increase with workers' fall-back incomes enlarged. Ultimately, this must lead to a higher equilibrium rate of unemployment. In the Singapore case, there has, in fact, *not* been a simultaneous increase in welfare spending as the economy opened up to foreign trade and investment. Instead, the setting up of the Central Provident Fund, a fully-funded social security system, is a key pillar of the government social policy. Under this scheme, monthly contributions are made by both employers and employees to the workers' social security accounts only when the workers are employed, the savings being allowed to be drawn out to pay for medical expenses subject to certain limits and to pay for housing mortgages. Being fully funded, the scheme does not have work disincentive effects found in unemployment benefit schemes. The bulk of government expenditures instead goes to education and defence.

It might also be asked why the share of employment in manufacturing did not continue its upward drift after the mid-seventies. A possible explanation might be found in the fact that a greater convergence occurred between the capital intensities of the non-traded good sector and the manufacturing sector from the mid-seventies onwards so that the non-traded good sector could afford to pay matching wages to retain its workers. Moreover, the increasing demand for the non-traded good accompanying the economy's rapid growth could have served to expand the non-traded good sector's demand for workers.

Through the late eighties and first half of the nineties, the continued rise in capital–labour ratio along with higher educational attainment and technological progress continue to shift up the demand wage schedule. Within the manufacturing sector, there is a shift towards more capital-intensive lines of production, which is to say, higher value-added goods. In terms of Figure 2.8, we can show an upward movement along the somewhat steep portion of the wage-setting curve, with equal successive outward shifts of the labour demand curve leading to successively large increments of wage and small decrements of the unemployment rate. In other words, labour demand shifts now trace out intersection points giving sharper rises in real export wages with smaller declines in the equilibrium unemployment rates.

Notice a change in the way reliance on selling into the world market as a small open economy helped to create jobs for Singapore workers from the sixties to the nineties. In the early days of industrialisation, trade helped to reduce joblessness and raise real wages via the ability to sell relatively labour-intensive goods into the world market. Through the Stolper–Samuelson channel, the ability to export the relatively labour-intensive good raised the relative price of the labour-intensive good and so raised the wage that firms could afford to pay. Juxtaposed against the wage curve, this implies a fall in equilibrium unemployment. Later on, partly because of the high quality of the institutions that facilitated capital accumulation – the so-called 'social infrastructure', the term used by Hall and Jones (1999) – the economy's relative factor endowment position shifted towards greater relative capital abundance. In a multi-good rather than a two-good framework, the changing capital–labour ratio in a small open economy led to structural transformation as higher value-added industries expanded and lower value-added industries such as garments and textiles contracted at given world prices. Correspondingly, the higher value-added industries could afford to pay higher wages, implying an upward shift of the labour demand curve. What about the wage curve? Let me suggest an alternative interpretation of the behaviour of the wage curve in terms of private wealth. It is plausible that in the two decades or so after independence, wages got ahead of wealth, so that shifts in labour demand produced huge declines in unemployment along a largely invariant wage curve. However, as workers' private wealth caught up in the eighties and nineties among a fraction of the workforce – with workers owning more consumer durables and other non-human assets – the successive outward shifts in labour demand competed with upward shifts of the wage curve. As workers became wealthier, the incentive wage that firms had to pay to combat quitting at any given rate of unemployment increased, implying upward shifts of the wage curve. Thus, in the latter two decades, we observe steady increases in the real wage without large movements in the natural rate.

2.4 CONCLUDING REMARKS

In this chapter, we have attempted to provide an account of the evolution of wages and unemployment of the Singapore economy over the past three to four decades, abstracting from expectational disequilibrium that may play a part in short-run fluctuations. We have documented that over the past four decades, there has been a fairly steady decline in the unemployment rate, interrupted only by the sharp rise in unemployment during the mid-eighties recession. We interpret the decadal decline in Singapore's unemployment rate as primarily a story of the downward shift of its natural rate of unemployment. This shift of the natural rate has occurred along with roughly constant real export wages up to the early eighties and fairly steady increase since then. Since the export price was rising relative to the non-traded good price since the early seventies, however, the real consumption wage has enjoyed an increase since the early seventies. We also provide evidence that the process of capital deepening has occurred across all the major industry groups in the manufacturing sector.

Our story of the joint determination of wages and unemployment is interpretable within the context of a quasi-Marshallian diagram involving the intersection between an upward-sloping wage curve and a downward-sloping labour demand curve. The slope of the wage curve is argued to be gentle at high rates of unemployment and steep at very low rates of unemployment. Later on, as wealth increased, there was also pressure for the wage curve to be shifted up. In the sixties, the ability to export labour-intensive goods into the world market shifted the labour demand schedule along the gentle portion of the wage-setting curve. In the seventies, the introduction of the NWC led to a rightward shift of the wage-setting curve for two reasons: Firstly, by internalising the problem of upward bidding of wages by firms acting unilaterally, and secondly, by highlighting economy-wide macroeconomic factors and bringing them to bear on the wage-negotiation process especially in the face of negative external shocks, the required wage needed to induce the optimal level of work effort and quit rate was reduced at each rate of unemployment. The continued rightward shift of the labour demand schedule on account of capital deepening, technological catch-up and rising relative export price now intersected with rightward shifts of the wage curve, giving rise to declining unemployment and roughly constant real export wages. Finally, in the eighties and early nineties, the labour demand schedule continued its rightward shift, propelled by increased human capital accumulation as well as technological progress along the steep portion of the wage curve. In addition, with wealth rising among a larger fraction of the workforce, wage pressures also increased. The result was a rise in real export wages with a roughly constant natural rate of unemployment.

NOTES

1. This chapter draws on Hoon and Kee (1998).
2. The Monetary Authority of Singapore, Singapore's *de facto* central bank, manages the exchange rate of the Singapore dollar against a trade-weighted basket of currencies of its major trading partners and competitors. The trade-weighted Singapore dollar is allowed to float within an undisclosed target band, according to two Singapore central bankers, Teh and Shanmugaratnam (1992).
3. Singapore, a former British colony, obtained self-rule from Britain in 1959 but was part of the Malaysian peninsula until it broke away and became an independent city-state in 1965.
4. The share of foreign net investment commitments in total manufacturing investment was 80 per cent in 1972 and 71 per cent in 1996. Most of the output produced by foreign-owned firms is exported into the world market. Hoon and Ho (1999) provide a more detailed discussion of the role of multinational corporations in Singapore.
5. This is the unemployment rate at which the actual rate of inflation is equal to the expected rate of inflation.
6. Up to the mid-eighties, Singapore ran a deficit on its current account balance. In recent years, however, the current account balance has been in surplus as the balance of services has generated surpluses that have more than offset the merchandise trade deficit. Included in the services account is net investment income, which is made up of net earnings on investment abroad, that is, earnings on assets abroad owned by Singapore residents less payments on assets in Singapore owned by foreigners. The combination of a high national savings rate and an active regionalisation drive can be expected to beef up the services account.
7. Krugman (1994b) and Young (1992) have emphasised the dominant role played by factor accumulation in accounting for Singapore's output growth. There are, however, others who have emphasised a larger role played by total factor productivity. Apart from the work of Coe, Helpman and co-authors (see Coe, Helpman and Hoffmaister, 1997 and Bayoumi, Coe and Helpman, 1996) emphasising the positive link between trade and international R&D spillovers, Hsieh (1998) and Nelson and Pack (1999) argue that total factor productivity growth in Singapore has been somewhat higher than estimated by Young (1992 and 1995). Hsieh (1998) exploited a dual approach to growth accounting, whereby the Solow residual is computed from growth rates of factor prices rather than factor quantities, to redo Young's (1995) estimates of total factor productivity growth for the four East Asian economies. Strikingly, his estimate for Singapore's total factor

productivity growth changes from the primal estimate of around zero found by Young to a dual estimate of 2.2 per cent per year.

8. Our results are corroborated in Table 2 of Lim (1998) and in Figure 2.1(c).
9. The quitting story of an endogenous natural rate of unemployment is developed in Salop (1979) and put into macroeconomic use in Hoon and Phelps (1992).
10. There is another factor that might be responsible for shifting down the wage curve in the employment rate–real export wage plane in the seventies. As we note from Figure 2.6, there was a steady rise in the export price relative to the non-traded good price in that decade implying that a decline in the real export wage would be required to achieve a given level of real consumption wage. Since what matters for the worker's decision to quit is the worker's real consumption wage, this implies a rightward and hence downward shift of the wage curve in the Marshallian plane drawn with the real export wage on the vertical axis.

3. The Ricardian model with an endogenous natural rate

3.1 INTRODUCTION

In Chapter 1, we made the point that there appear to be two traditions in the treatment (or non-treatment) of unemployment in the international economics literature. On the real side of international economics, *full employment* is typically assumed though there is a small amount of literature dealing with the effects of minimum wages (see, for example, Brecher, 1974). Efficiency wages have also been introduced into a Ricardian economy by Copeland (1989), whose model nevertheless generates an endogenous wage gap among identical workers without generating equilibrium unemployment. On the monetary side of international economics, the prevailing paradigm is that of Keynesian economics applied to the open economy. The result is the Mundell–Fleming model.[1] We can rationalise this division by alluding to the classical dichotomy. In the short run – the domain covered by the monetary side of international economics – the price level is somewhat rigid or sticky. Consequently, unemployment, which is viewed from this perspective as cyclical in character, fluctuates in response to various economic shocks. In the long run – the domain covered by the real side of international economics – the price level is completely flexible, and the economy settles at the natural level of employment or unemployment.

Thus the theory has explanatory power for improving our understanding of what causes unemployment to deviate from the natural level. However, the economic forces that lead countries to exchange goods and services with one another and that affect the real incomes of factors of production under international exchange do not affect the natural rate of unemployment itself. In other words, the natural rate of unemployment is treated in standard trade models as essentially *exogenous*. While not necessarily a constant, the natural rate of unemployment is unaffected by the economic forces under study.[2]

The neglect of unemployment in trade theory, however, seems inappropriate in the light of some evidence collected over the past two to three decades of the role that international trade has played in lowering the equilibrium rate of unemployment in a number of developing economies.[3] Moreover, the development of theories of an endogenous equilibrium rate of unemployment in macroeconomics points to a set of real factors that can impinge on the natural rate along with real factor rewards. The latter development has largely been spurred by the persistent rise of unemployment in many of the OECD countries in the past two decades or so, especially in the European Union (see Lindbeck and Snower (1988) for insider–outsider models; McDonald and Solow (1981) and Layard, Nickell and Jackman (1991) for wage bargaining models; and Hoon and Phelps (1992) and Phelps (1994) for efficiency-wage models).

In Hoon and Phelps (1992), we integrate some early work pointing to a new paradigm in the economics of the long swings in economic activity to show rigorously how the natural rate of unemployment is endogenised.[4] In particular, we draw upon the incentive-wage theory of the labour market to derive an equilibrium wage curve, which, in the Marshallian employment rate–real wage plane, is an upward-sloping schedule. By taking into account the structure of the goods market, we show how an economy-wide labour demand locus can be derived, which, juxtaposed against the equilibrium wage locus, determines the unique general-equilibrium rate of unemployment. Various real factors are shown to impinge upon the evolution of wages and the natural rate of unemployment.

Looking at the economic experience of the East Asian economies, there seems to be some supporting evidence of such a moving natural rate theory at the global level since the secular decline of the rates of unemployment of the Newly Industrialising Countries (NICs) in the last three decades must surely be largely a decline of the equilibrium rate of unemployment. Fields (1985) examined the employment effects of outward orientation in the East Asian economies. He found that between the early 1960s and the early 1980s unemployment rates declined from 8 to 10 per cent to less than 4 per cent in Hong Kong, Singapore, South Korea and Taiwan. Moreover, real wages rose by as much as a factor of four and inequality levels have fallen to low to moderate levels. He concludes that '[A]n important force contributing to improvement in labour market conditions and income distribution is the expansion of foreign trade and foreign investment'. (p. 371)

Empirical work that has studied the favourable employment performance of various developing economies invariably alludes to the importance of an export-led growth based upon selling into the world market. For example, in a comparative study of eight developing countries, Krueger (1983) found that considerable employment gains were obtained through a shift from import substitution to export orientation. Using labour input coefficients for individual sectors, these employment gains were found to vary between 21 and 107 per cent, with the results for Indonesia and Thailand exceeding 100 per cent (see Balassa, 1989). A plausible hypothesis is that international trade has served to raise wages and lower equilibrium unemployment in these economies.

While such is the impression of the remarkable macroeconomic performance of these open economies, conventional trade theory has no predictive power regarding the effect of free trade on the equilibrium rate of unemployment since it assumes at the outset *full employment*. There are a number of issues in the global economy, however, for which a theory explaining the endogenous response of wages and equilibrium unemployment is needed. What is the effect, for example, of tariff escalation on jobs and wages? How does a major technological catch-up in one part of the world affect wages and equilibrium unemployment in the rest of the world? How does the dismantling of the welfare state affect the prospects of jobs and wages for those in the home country and for those abroad?

Concerned with the need to understand the general-equilibrium implications of free trade and protection for wages and unemployment, Blinder (1988), in his Richard T. Ely lecture, issued a call for international trade economists to develop microfoundation-based models to re-evaluate trade theorems in the context of endogenous unemployment. Such work is of some current importance as well since recent discussions of trade liberalisation in Europe, for example, occurs in the context of high unemployment.

In this chapter, we draw upon the effort elicitation model of Shapiro and Stiglitz (1984), augmented to include dynamics as in Kimball (1994), to generate endogenous involuntary unemployment in a Ricardian global economy.[5] Section 3.2 develops the basic model and studies the welfare effects of free trade. A crucial point that the model makes is the following: when workers rely on the ability to hold on to a job in order to satisfy consumption, there being no non-wage income, trade based upon comparative advantage produces a positive work incentive effect as the pay workers earn allows them to achieve an enlarged consumption set. As Keynes (1920, p. 9) wrote, reflecting upon the benefits of free trade in Europe before the war, 'The inhabitant of London could order by telephone, sipping his morning tea in bed, the various products of the whole earth, in such quantity as he might see fit, and reasonably expect their early delivery upon his doorstep . . .' The consumption set of the 'inhabitant of London' would be greatly circumscribed were England completely closed to trade and had to produce every good and service itself! In the two-good model here with Ricardian technologies, the constant real product wage translates into a higher real consumption wage, which is what matters for work incentives. In the employment rate–real product wage plane, trade leads to a rightward shift of the wage curve, and hence a lower natural rate of unemployment. Section 3.3 studies a series of economic shocks in the basic model, while Section 3.4 discusses some generalisations of the basic model. Section 3.5 discusses the robustness of some key results of the chapter, and Section 3.6 concludes.

3.2 THE BASIC MODEL

3.2.1 Worker's Decision

We assume that a worker's utility function is given by the Cobb–Douglas form, $c_x^{\alpha}c_y^{1-\alpha}$, $0<\alpha<1$. Given an income level, I, and the prices of goods X and Y, p_x and p_y, respectively, the indirect utility function is given by $Ap_x^{-\alpha}p_y^{-(1-\alpha)}I$, where $A\equiv\alpha^{\alpha}(1-\alpha)^{1-\alpha}$. Since all income in this model comes from work remuneration, we write $I\equiv w$, where w is the pay level. Consequently, the indirect utility function can be expressed as $A[w/(p_x^{\alpha}p_y^{1-\alpha})]$, which makes clear that indirect utility is directly related to the real consumption wage.

Next, we consider the decision problem of a worker hired at firm i whether to shirk or not when he is employed. To work towards the fundamental asset equation for the worker in each state, we solve a simple dynamic programming problem. Let $V_{es}^i(t)$, $V_{en}^i(t)$ and $V_u(t)$ denote, respectively, the expected present value of utility in the case of an employed worker at firm i who shirks, of one who does not shirk, and of an unemployed worker at time t. For the employed worker at firm i who does not shirk, his Bellman equation is given for the time interval $(0,t)$ by

$$V_{en}^i(0)=A\left[\frac{w^i}{p_x^{\alpha}p_y^{1-\alpha}}\right]t-e+(1-\rho t)[btV_u(t)+(1-bt)V_{en}^i(t)]$$

$$=A\left[\frac{w^i}{p_x^{\alpha}p_y^{1-\alpha}}\right]t-e+(1-\rho t)[bt(V_u(0)+t\dot{V}_u)+(1-bt)(V_{en}^i(0)+t\dot{V}_{en}^i)].$$

Rearranging, and applying L'Hopital's rule, we obtain

$$\rho V_{en}^i=A\left[\frac{w^i}{p_x^{\alpha}p_y^{1-\alpha}}\right]-e+b(V_u-V_{en}^i)+\dot{V}_{en}^i, \tag{3.1}$$

where, for notational simplicity, we have left out the time subscripts. If the worker performs at the customary level of effort for his job, that is, he does not shirk, firm i pays him the wage w^i and he retains his job until exogenous factors cause a separation to occur. In choosing the optimal incentive wage to pay, the firm treats the goods prices, p_x and p_y, as given. By a similiar procedure, we can obtain the fundamental asset equation for the employed worker at firm *i* who shirks:

$$\rho V^i_{es} = A\left[\frac{w^i}{p_x^{\alpha} p_y^{1-\alpha}}\right] + (b+g)\,(V_u - V^i_{es}) + \dot{V}^i_{es}. \tag{3.2}$$

In equations (3.1) and (3.2), *e* is the exogenously specified positive level of effort exerted; ρ is the subjective discount rate; *b* is the separation rate (due to exogenous reasons other than shirking) and is assumed to be the same for all firms; and *g* is the probability of being caught if shirking (also assumed to be exogenous). Here, $\dot{V}^i_{es}$ and $\dot{V}^i_{en}$ represent the time derivatives of V^i_{es} and V^i_{en}, respectively. The fundamental asset equations (3.1) and (3.2) are of the form 'interest rate times asset value equals flow benefits (dividends) plus expected capital gains (or losses)'. The flow benefit in equation (3.1) is the flow utility from consumption, $A[w^i/(p_x^{\alpha} p_y^{1-\alpha})]$, minus effort; the expected capital gain (actually loss) is the probability of job loss for a non-shirker *b* times the amount of utility lost by becoming unemployed, $V_u - V^i_{en}$, plus the rate of change of V^i_{en} itself, $\dot{V}^i_{en}$. Equation (3.2) has a similiar interpretation.

In order for it not to be worthwhile for the worker to shirk, it is necessary that $V^i_{es} \leq V^i_{en}$. From equations (3.1) and (3.2), this condition can be stated as

$$A\left[\frac{w^i}{p_x^{\alpha} p_y^{1-\alpha}}\right] \geq \rho V_u + g^{-1}(b+\rho+g)e + g^{-1}(b+\rho)\dot{V}^i_{es} - g^{-1}(b+\rho+g)\dot{V}^i_{en}. \tag{3.3}$$

There is no reason for the firm to pay more than necessary to prevent shirking. Thus equation (3.3) holds with equality, and no worker shirks. We have

$$A\left[\frac{w^i}{p_x^{\alpha} p_y^{1-\alpha}}\right] = \rho V_u + g^{-1}(b+\rho+g)e + g^{-1}(b+\rho)\dot{V}^i_{es} - g^{-1}(b+\rho+g)\dot{V}^i_{en}, \tag{3.4}$$

which is equivalent to the condition that

$$V^i_{es} = V^i_{en},\ \forall t. \tag{3.5}$$

Thus, we also have

$$\dot{V}^i_{es} = \dot{V}^i_{en},\ \forall t. \tag{3.6}$$

Using equations (3.5) and (3.6), we can combine equations (3.1) and (3.2) to yield

$$V^i_{en} = g^{-1}e + V_u, \forall t. \tag{3.7}$$

Since g and e are both constants, we also have

$$\dot{V}^i_{en} = \dot{V}_u, \forall t. \tag{3.8}$$

The expected discounted value of utility for an unemployed worker V_u must obey the 'asset' equation:

$$\rho V_u = a(V_{en} - V_u) + \dot{V}_u, \tag{3.9}$$

where a is the accession rate and V_{en} is the expected present discounted value of utility of a worker being employed in a representative firm in the economy. V_{en} is in turn given by

$$\rho V_{en} = A\left[\frac{w}{p_x^{\alpha} p_y^{1-\alpha}}\right] - e + b(V_u - V_{en}) + \dot{V}_{en},$$

where w is the wage paid by the representative firm. Solving for V_u, we obtain

$$\rho V_u = \left(\frac{a}{\rho + b + a}\right)\left(A\left[\frac{w}{p_x^{\alpha} p_y^{1-\alpha}}\right] - e\right) + \left(\frac{a}{\rho + b + a}\right)(\dot{V}_{en} - \dot{V}_u) + \dot{V}_u. \tag{3.10}$$

Substituting equation (3.10) into equation (3.4), and using equations (3.6) and (3.8), we obtain

$$A\left[\frac{w^i}{p_x^{\alpha} p_y^{1-\alpha}}\right] = \left(\frac{a}{\rho + b + a}\right)\left(A\left[\frac{w}{p_x^{\alpha} p_y^{1-\alpha}}\right] - e\right) + \left(\frac{a}{\rho + b + a}\right)(\dot{V}_{en} - \dot{V}_u) + \frac{(b + \rho + g)e}{g}. \tag{3.11}$$

Equation (3.11) gives the wage chosen by firm i as an increasing function of the aggregate wage, w, of the accession rate, a, and of the differential $\dot{V}_{en} - \dot{V}_u$.

In the general equilibrium with all firms identical, we have $w^i = w$ and $\dot{V}^i_{en} = \dot{V}_{en}$. By virtue of equation (3.8), $\dot{V}_{en} = \dot{V}_u$. Hence, from equation (3.11), we obtain

$$A\left[\frac{w}{p_x^{\alpha} p_y^{1-\alpha}}\right] = \frac{(a + b + \rho)e}{g} + e, \tag{3.12}$$

which is an expression for the representative firm's optimal supply wage. It is higher the greater is the required effort, the higher is the job acquisition rate, the higher is the exogenous separation rate and the higher is the rate of time discount. On the other hand, the greater the likelihood of being detected if shirking, the lower is the optimal supply wage. Note also that the optimal supply wage is increasing in the consumer price index, $p_x^{\alpha}p_y^{1-\alpha}$.

The job acquisition rate, a, can itself be related to more fundamental parameters in the model. Out of steady state, the accession rate can be obtained from the expression that gives the flow rate of employment:

$$\dot{L} = a(\overline{L} - L) - bL, \tag{3.13}$$

where $\overline{L}$ is the exogenously given fixed labour force size, and L is total employment. Rewriting equation (3.13), we have

$$a = \frac{\dot{L} + bL}{\overline{L} - L}. \tag{3.14}$$

Note that at a given rate of increase of employment, $\dot{L}$, the higher is the job acquisition rate the lower is the equilibrium rate of unemployment. Similarly, at a given rate of unemployment, the higher is the job acquisition rate the faster is the increase in employment. Substituting equation (3.14) into equation (3.12), we finally obtain our aggregate no-shirking constraint (NSC):

$$A\left[\frac{w^s}{p_x^{\alpha}p_y^{1-\alpha}}\right] = \left[1 + \frac{b+\rho}{g} + \frac{\dot{L} + bL}{g(\overline{L} - L)}\right]e, \tag{3.15}$$

where we use the superscript s to emphasise that this is the optimal supply wage. The NSC says that the higher is the level of employment, and thus the shorter the expected time spent in unemployment if fired, the less costly it is to be fired and the more tempting it is to shirk. To avoid this, firms must pay a higher wage. Similarly, the faster is the increase in employment, the higher is the exit rate from unemployment, and so the higher is the supply wage that must be paid to maintain a motivated workforce.

Expressing the rate of increase in employment as a function of the real consumption wage and the current level of employment, we obtain from equation (3.15)

$$\dot{L} = \left[ge^{-1}\left(A\left[\frac{w^s}{p_x^{\alpha}p_y^{1-\alpha}}\right] - e\right) - \rho\right][\overline{L} - L] - b\overline{L}. \tag{3.16}$$

Assuming that the size of the labour force, $\overline{L}$, is constant, an alternative characterisation of equation (3.16) expresses it in terms of the rate of employment, $1-u$, namely,

$$(\dot{\overline{1-u}}) = \left[ge^{-1}\left(A\left[\frac{w^s}{p_x^{\alpha}p_y^{1-\alpha}}\right] - e\right) - \rho\right][1 - (1-u)] - b. \tag{3.17}$$

Expressed in this way, the left-hand side of equation (3.17) tells us the maximum rate of increase in employment corresponding to the supply wage (at a given rate of unemployment) that is consistent with non-shirking behaviour. At a given rate of unemployment, a rise in the rate of increase of employment requires a rise in the supply wage if work incentives are not to be weakened.

3.2.2 Production Side and Autarkic Equilibrium

To close the model, let us first examine an economy in autarky. Let a_x and a_y denote the labour input requirements per unit of output in the production of goods X and Y, respectively. Then the production functions are given by $X = a_x^{-1} eL_x$ and $Y = a_y^{-1} eL_y$. With both goods being demanded, and hence produced, the following conditions hold:

$$\frac{wa_x}{e} = p_x, \tag{3.18}$$

$$\frac{wa_y}{e} = P_y. \tag{3.19}$$

Product–market equilibrium can simply be expressed by the condition that the autarkic relative price of good X in terms of Y, $p \equiv p_x / p_y$, is given by $p = a_x / a_y$. This is represented by the horizontal line in Figure 3.1.

The demand wage, that is, the wage that firms can afford to pay, can be expressed as $w^d = ea_x^{-1} p_x = ea_y^{-1} p_y$, where the use of the superscript d emphasises that it is the demand wage. Equating the demand wage to the supply wage in equation (3.15), we obtain our labour–market equilibrium condition:

$$A\left[\frac{1}{a_x}\left(\frac{p_x}{p_y}\right)^{1-\alpha}\right] = \left[1 + \frac{b+\rho}{g} + \frac{\dot{L} + bL}{g(\bar{L} - L)}\right]. \tag{3.20}$$

Note that the left-hand side of equation (3.20) can also be replaced by $A[a_y^{-1}(p_x/p_y)^{-\alpha}]$ since, by equations (3.18) and (3.19),

$$\frac{w}{p_x^{\alpha} p_y^{1-\alpha}} = \left(\frac{e}{a_x}\right)\left(\frac{p_x}{p_y}\right)^{1-\alpha} = \left(\frac{e}{a_y}\right)\left(\frac{p_x}{p_y}\right)^{-\alpha}.$$

Hence the labour–market equilibrium condition can also be expressed as

$$A\left[\frac{1}{a_y}\left(\frac{p_x}{p_y}\right)^{-\alpha}\right] = \left[1 + \frac{b+\rho}{g} + \frac{\dot{L} + bL}{g(\bar{L} - L)}\right]. \tag{3.21}$$

The steady-state labour–market equilibrium locus described by equation (3.20) with $\dot{L} = 0$ can be depicted as the positively-sloped schedule in Figure 3.1. The arrows of motion are indicated.

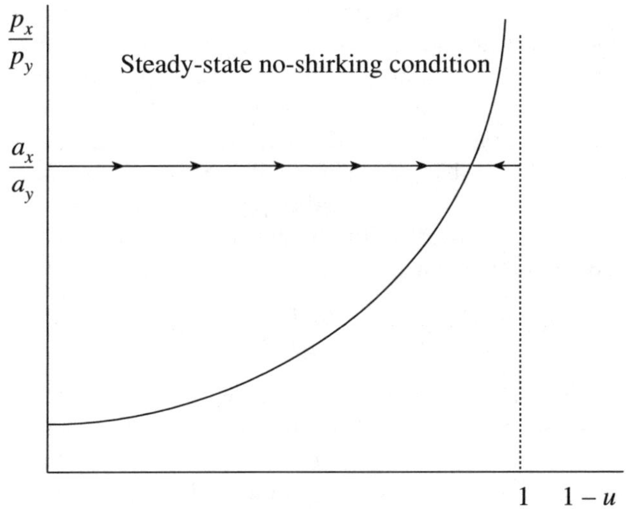

Figure 3.1 Dynamics in a closed economy

Combining the product–market equilibrium condition ($p_x/p_y = a_x/a_y$) with the labour–market equilibrium condition (represented either by equation (3.20) or (3.21)) yields a dynamic first-order differential equation in $(1-u)_t$:

$$(1 \dot{-} u)_t = [g(Aa_x^{-\alpha}a_y^{-(1-\alpha)} - 1) - \rho]\,[1-(1-u)_t] - b. \qquad (3.22)$$

Figure 3.1 shows the dynamic evolution of $(1-u)_t$ towards its steady state. The system is dynamically stable.[6]

3.2.3 Opening up to Trade

To examine the effects of international trade, let us suppose that there is another country, called Foreign, whose variables are denoted by an asterisk. We assume that tastes and the parameters b and g are identical across both countries. Its labour input requirements are denoted as a_x^* and a_y^*. Let us suppose that Home has comparative advantage in good X so that we write $a_x/a_y < a_x^*/a_y^*$. Under trade, assuming complete specialisation, Home ends up as the net exporter of good X. In general, the equilibrium free trade relative price, denoted p_f, must lie between the two countries' autarkic relative prices, $p_a = a_x/a_y$ and $p_a^* = a_x^*/a_y^*$, respectively. In particular, $p_a < p_f < p_a^*$.

In autarky, the indirect utility from consumption of a worker in Home can be expressed as $Ap_a^{1-\alpha}ea_x^{-1}$. Under free trade, it is given by $Ap_f^{1-\alpha}ea_x^{-1}$. Since $p^f > p_a$, it follows that the indirect utility from consumption rises under trade. In Foreign, the autarkic indirect utility from consumption is given by $Ap_a^{*-\alpha}ea_y^{*-1}$. Under free trade, it is given by $Ap_f^{-\alpha}ea_y^{*-1}$. Since $p_f < p_a^*$, it follows that the foreign indirect utility from consumption also rises under free trade. To obtain the precise value of the equilibrium relative price under free trade, we can use the condition that the relative price must equal the marginal rate of substitution in consumption and the condition that world goods markets must clear. Hence,

$$p_f = \left[\frac{\alpha}{1-\alpha}\right]\left[\frac{a_x}{a_y^*}\right]\left[\frac{(1-u^*)\overline{L}^*}{(1-u)\overline{L}}\right]. \tag{3.23}$$

Since the rate of employment is not a jumpy variable, the goods' relative price at the point of opening up to free trade in equation (3.23) is solved by substituting the autarkic levels of employment on the right-hand side. Since the purchasing power of wages that workers command is increased by trade, thus increasing their stake in holding on to their current jobs, firms are induced to increase the pace of hiring without weakening work incentives. Consequently, the aggregate employment rate begins to rise. To study where the new steady state of the model is, set $(1 \dot{-} u) = 0$ in equation (3.17) and use $w^d = Ap_f^{1-\alpha}ea_x^{-1}$ and $w^s = w^d$ to obtain

$$(1-u) = 1 - \frac{b}{g[Ap_f^{1-\alpha}a_x^{-1} - 1] - \rho}. \tag{3.24}$$

A similiar procedure applied to Foreign yields

$$(1-u^*) = 1 - \frac{b}{g[Ap_f^{-\alpha}a_y^{*-1} - 1] - \rho}. \tag{3.25}$$

Using equations (3.24) and (3.25) in equation (3.23), we have one equation in one unknown, the relative price p_f. Diagrammatically (not shown), we can depict the left-hand side of the resulting equation as a forty-five degree line. Since $(1-u^*)$ is decreasing in p_f while $(1-u)$ is increasing in p_f, the right-hand side of the resulting equation is downward sloping. Hence we obtain a unique intersection point.

An alternative characterisation of the world trading equilibrium in terms of $1-u$ and $1-u^*$ is instructive. Since equation (3.23) must be satisfied at each point in time, we can use that expression in the two equations giving the dynamic evolution of $1-u$ and $1-u^*$. From equation (3.23), we write $p_f = \Phi(1-u, 1-u^*; \overline{L}, \overline{L}^*, a_x, a_y^*)$. Using this in equations (3.24) and (3.25), we obtain two schedules in Figure 3.2 giving the loci of $(1 \dot{-} u) = 0$ and $(1 \dot{-} u^*) = 0$. As shown in Appendix 3.1, the locus of $(1 \dot{-} u) = 0$ is gentler than the locus of $(1 \dot{-} u^*) = 0$. If we let E_1 represent the initial point of

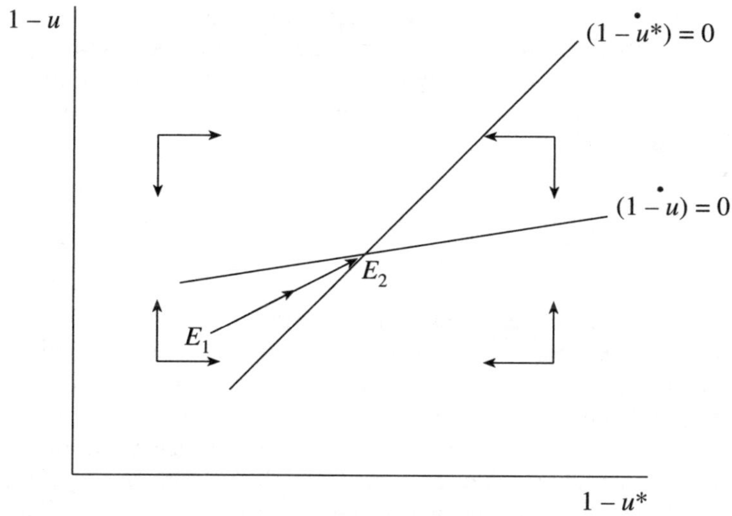

Figure 3.2 Global stability

autarky, the effect of opening up to trade is to move the world economy gradually in a northeasterly direction to point E_2. That the $(1 \dot{-} u) = 0$ locus must lie above point E_1 is clear. As argued before, trade raises the indirect utility from consumption. Consequently, at the autarkic $1-u^*$, the free trade $1-u$ must lie above Home's autarkic level. (From equation (3.24), since $p_a < p_f$, it follows that the free trade level of $1-u$ must lie above the autarkic level.) By the same reasoning, the $(1 \dot{-} u^*) = 0$ locus must lie to the right of point E_1. (At the autarkic $1-u$, the free trade $1-u^*$ must lie above Foreign's autarkic level using $p_f < p_a^*$ in equation (3.25).) Along the adjustment path, $(1 \dot{-} u) > 0$ and $(1 \dot{-} u^*) > 0$. From equation (3.15) and the Foreign counterpart, we infer that along the transition paths and in the new steady state, indirect utilities in Home and Foreign are both higher than their respective autarkic values.

The welfare effects of opening up to trade are easily calculated. Consider a worker in Home. His welfare can be represented by his expected indirect utility, $(1-u)A[w/(p_x^{\alpha} p_y^{1-\alpha})]$. In autarky, this can be written as $(1-u_a)Ap_a^{1-\alpha}ea_x^{-1}$, where $1-u_a$ is the autarkic rate of employment. At the moment of opening up to trade, employment $1-u_a$ is unchanged but the real consumption wage jumps up, so expected utility rises, on impact, to $(1-u_a)Ap_f^{1-\alpha}ea_x^{-1}$, where, as noted before, $p_f > p_a$. Along the transition path $1-u$ rises to reach a higher level in the new steady state. Since $p_f > p_a$, the real consumption wage under trade is also higher than in autarky along the transition path as well as in the new steady state. Consequently, trade unambiguously raises welfare both through creating jobs as well as through raising the real consumption wage. By the same token, the expected utility of a worker in Foreign is increased through trade via the expansion of wages and employment.

3.3 ECONOMIC SHOCKS

There are five economic shocks that we will use the model to analyse. We first study the consequences of tariff protection by both Home and Foreign. We show that the proliferation of trade barriers as occurred during the interwar years not only has an immiserising effect on real consumption wages but also raises global unemployment. Then we ask how trade affects wages and unemployment when one country introduces an unemployment compensation system financed by payroll taxes. A policy to transfer a fraction of the unemployment benefits to finance an employment subsidy is then analysed. We also study the effect of a level increase in productivity in the export sector of one country. Then we look at the effects of an increase in the size of the labour force in one country. Finally, we incorporate an endogenous labour standard into the model and show that trade itself leads to a rising labour standard as well as declining equilibrium unemployment.

3.3.1 Tariff Protection

Let t_r be the *ad valorem* tariff rate imposed by Home on its imports of good Y and t_r^* be the *ad valorem* tariff rate imposed by Foreign. From Home's point of view, the domestic price of good Y is $(1+t_r)p_y^f$, where the superscript f denotes international price. Hence Home's domestic relative price of good X is $p_f/(1+t_r)$, where $p_f \equiv p_x^f/p_y^f$ is the international terms of trade. Analogously the domestic price of good X from Foreign's point of view is $(1+t_r^*)p_x^f$. Hence Foreign's domestic relative price of good X is $(1+t_r^*)p_f$.

Letting I_n and I_n^* now denote incomes inclusive of lump-sum tariff rebates, the trade balance equilibrium condition at international prices becomes

$$\frac{(1-\alpha)I_n}{1+t_r} = \frac{\alpha I_n^*}{1+t_r^*}, \tag{3.26}$$

where $I_n \equiv [(1+t_r)/(1+\alpha t_r)]w(1-u)\overline{L}$ and $I_n^* \equiv [(1+t_r^*)/(1+(1-\alpha)t_r^*)]w^*(1-u^*)\overline{L}^*$. Substituting and rearranging, we obtain from equation (3.26)

$$\frac{w}{w^*} = \left[\frac{\alpha}{1-\alpha}\right]\left[\frac{1+\alpha t_r}{1+(1-\alpha)t_r^*}\right]\left[\frac{(1-u^*)\bar{L}^*}{(1-u)\bar{L}}\right], \tag{3.27}$$

which gives us the double factoral terms of trade. From equation (3.27), the international relative price is given by

$$p_f = \left[\frac{a_x}{a_y^*}\right]\left[\frac{\alpha}{1-\alpha}\right]\left[\frac{1+\alpha t_r}{1+(1-\alpha)t_r^*}\right]\left[\frac{(1-u^*)\bar{L}^*}{(1-u)\bar{L}}\right]. \tag{3.28}$$

Under the assumption that tariff revenues are distributed in a lump-sum manner to both employed and unemployed workers, the NSC in steady state for Home becomes

$$(1-u) = 1 - \frac{b}{g\left[A\left(\frac{p_f}{1+t_r}\right)^{1-\alpha} a_x^{-1} - 1\right] - \rho}. \tag{3.29}$$

Note that because tariff revenues are distributed in a lump-sum manner to all workers regardless of their employment status, they do not directly distort work incentive. Instead what affects incentive is the nominal value of the pay taken as a ratio to the consumer price index, that is, $w/[(p_x^f)^{\alpha}((1+t_r)p_y^f)^{1-\alpha}]$, which, using the demand wage relationship, can be expressed as $[p_f/(1+t_r)]^{1-\alpha}ea_x^{-1}$. A similiar procedure applied to Foreign yields

$$(1-u^*) = 1 - \frac{b}{g[A((1+t_r^*)p_f)^{-\alpha}a_y^{*-1} - 1] - \rho}. \tag{3.30}$$

Let us first consider the effects of a unilateral rise of tariff, say, in Home, that is, we set $t_r > 0$ and $t_r^* = 0$ above. Appendix 3.1 shows that this results in a downward shift of the $(1 \dot{-} u) = 0$ locus and an upward shift of the $(1 \dot{-} u^*) = 0$ locus in Figure 3.3, implying a gradual rise in equilibrium unemployment in both Home and Foreign. What explains the rise of each country's equilibrium unemployment rate? Consider Home, the protecting country. Its wage in terms of good X, the export good, is fixed at $a_x^{-1}e$. The tariff it imposes, however, raises the domestic price of the import good. Consequently, the purchasing power of the pay a worker in Home earns falls thus leading to reduced work incentive. (As the tariff revenue is rebated to all workers regardless of their employment status, the receipt of lump-sum rebates does not directly affect work incentive.) The result is a rise in unemployment in Home. Foreign suffers an adverse terms of trade shock, which makes the product wage earned by its workers buy less in terms of the consumption basket, hence worsening work incentives and raising the path of equilibrium unemployment. The welfare effects on Foreign of a unilateral tariff by Home are, therefore, unambiguously negative. The expected utility of a worker in Foreign, given by $(1-u^*)Ap_f^{-\alpha}e(a_y^*)^{-1}$, clearly

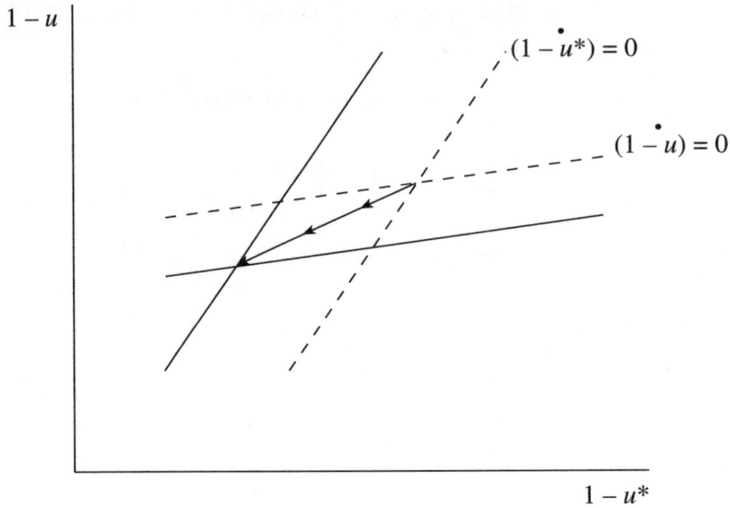

Figure 3.3 Multilateral tariffs

declines not only because the international terms of trade, p_f, turn against it but also because $1-u^*$ rises. The expected utility of a worker in Home, the protecting country, however, may rise despite the upward shift of the equilibrium unemployment path because of the terms of trade gains it enjoys.

Now suppose that Foreign retaliates with an imposition of its own tariffs so t_r^* is also positive. Appendix 3.1 shows that this leads to a further downward shift of the $(1\dot{-}u)=0$ locus and a further upward shift of the $(1\dot{-}u^*)=0$ locus in Figure 3.3. Since Foreign has imposed its own tariffs, its wage in terms of good Y, its export good, is fixed at $a_y^{*-1}e$ but the tariff it imposes raises the domestic price of good X, its import good. The result is that the purchasing power of the pay level of a worker in Foreign similarly declines thus reducing work incentive and raising equilibrium unemployment. The result is that multilateral protection in the global economy results in a southwesterly movement towards even higher equilibrium unemployment in both Home and Foreign compared to a unilateral tariff.

What are the welfare effects of multilateral protection? To answer this question, we note that the expected utility of a worker in Home can be expressed as

$$\left[\frac{(1+t_r)^{\alpha}}{1+\alpha t_r}\right](1-u)Ap_f^{1-\alpha}ea_x^{-1},$$

which is decreasing in t_r for given expected real income inclusive of the tariff rebate while the expected utility of a worker in Foreign can be expressed as

$$\left[\frac{(1+t_r^*)^{1-\alpha}}{1+(1-\alpha)t_r^*}\right](1-u^*)Ap_f^{-\alpha}e(a_y^*)^{-1},$$

which is also decreasing in t_r^* for given expected real income inclusive of tariff rebate. On impact, $1-u$ and $1-u^*$ are unchanged. Whether the expected real incomes inclusive of the tariff rebates go up or down depends on the values of t_r and t_r^* chosen by Home and Foreign, respectively, since the choice determines the international terms of trade. In a convenient case where t_r and t_r^* are chosen to leave p^f unchanged so that there are no terms of trade effects from multilateral protection, expected utilities in both Home and Foreign must fall on impact. In the transition to the new steady state, unemployment rises in both Home and Foreign, which is apt to lower expected utilities along the transition path and in the new steady state as well. A trade war then unambiguously hurts all trading nations.

In the interwar period when unemployment rose sharply in many countries, it is commonly observed that there was a collapse of world trade (see, for example, Capie, 1994). What does our model say about the correlation between the volume of world trade and global unemployment? In this simple two-country world, it is easy to infer that the imposition of the multilateral tariffs leads to a decline in the volume of world trade along with increased joblessness. After some substitutions, the volume of trade, V_T, is easily shown to be given by

$$V_T=\frac{2(1-\alpha)eA\left[\left(\frac{\alpha}{1-\alpha}\right)\left(\frac{1}{a_y^*}\right)\right]^{1-\alpha}[(1-u^*)\bar{L}^*]^{1-\alpha}[(1-u)\bar{L}]^{\alpha}}{a_x^{\alpha}[1+\alpha t_r]^{\alpha}[1+(1-\alpha)t_r^*]^{1-\alpha}}.$$

On impact, we see that protection leads to a decline in the volume of trade. However, in the transition to the new steady state, the volume of trade continues to decline as unemployment rises. Thus the collapse of world trade is positively associated with a rise in equilibrium unemployment in both economies. The welfare cost of protectionism, especially when it leads to a worldwide collapse of trade, therefore, is greater in an endogenous natural rate model than in a conventional trade model with full employment.

In Arthur Lewis' masterful survey of the interwar years (Lewis, 1949), he made a useful characterisation of the United States: 'The problems of the United States were domestic. In 1929 the ratio of imports to national income was only 5 per cent and of exports was only 6 per cent, and while changes in American foreign trade most profoundly affected the rest of the world, they were of little importance to the American economy itself.' (p.

104) Bearing this characterisation in mind, let us consider what is the effect of a Smoot–Hawley tariff imposed by a large, incompletely specialised country in a Ricardian world with many other small, completely specialised trading nations. For simplicity, suppose that all the small countries export the same good, say, good Y. Let the large country impose a unilateral tariff on its import from all the small trading nations. Assuming that the large country remains incompletely specialised under protection, the domestic relative price, $p_f/(1+t_r)$, must continue to be equal to the original autarkic relative price given by a_x/a_y. This implies that the international terms of trade move against all the small trading nations by an amount which depends on the size of the tariff. Since the adverse terms of trade reduce the real purchasing power of workers in the small trading nations, hence reducing the value of holding a job in these countries, the result of protection is to raise the equilibrium rate of unemployment abroad. In the large protecting country, as the domestic relative price is unchanged, there is no effect on the natural rate if we assume that the tariff revenue collected is redistributed to all workers regardless of their employment status, although welfare is increased on account of the terms of trade improvement. In particular, the expected utility of a worker in the large protecting country is given by $[(1+t_r)/(1+\alpha t_r)]A(1-u)(a_x/a_y)^{1-\alpha}ea_x^{-1}$, which is greater than expected utility in the absence of tariff, $A(1-u)(a_x/a_y)^{1-\alpha}ea_x^{-1}$, remembering that $1-u$ is unaffected by protection.

3.3.2 Welfare State

Consider the introduction of unemployment benefits in Home financed by the imposition of payroll taxes. Letting t_a be the proportional payroll tax rate, and $\theta_b \equiv B/w$, where B is the amount of unemployment benefit and w is the labour cost to the firm so θ_b is the replacement ratio, balanced budget implies

$$(1+t_a)^{-1} = \frac{(1-u)}{[1-(1-\theta_b)u]}, \tag{3.31}$$

where we assume that unemployment benefits are also taxed at the rate t_a.[7] The international relative price is given by equation (3.23) but the locus along which $(1 \dot{-} u) = 0$ is now given by[8]

$$(1-u) = 1 - \frac{b}{g\left\{\left[\frac{(1-\theta_b)(1-u)}{1-(1-\theta_b)u}\right]Ap_f^{1-\alpha}a_x^{-1} - 1\right\} - \rho}. \tag{3.32}$$

Equation (3.25) continues to hold. The effect of introducing unemployment benefits financed by payroll taxes is shown in Figure 3.4, where we see

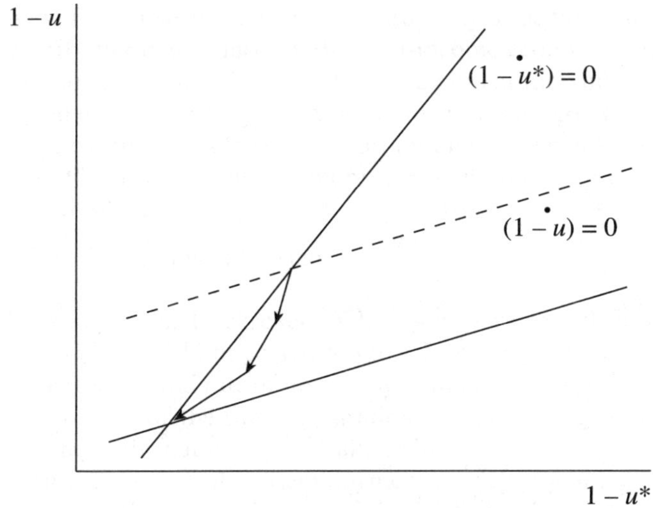

Figure 3.4 Unemployment benefits and payroll taxes

that both $1-u$ and $1-u^*$ decline over time to settle down at a steady state with both economies suffering increased joblessness.

The introduction of unemployment benefits that are financed by payroll taxes in Home produces the expected result of shifting up the whole path of equilibrium unemployment thereby creating disincentive towards work and raising the opportunity cost of labour. That is not all, however. Part of the adjustment to the introduction of the welfare state in Home falls on Foreign, as the latter's terms of trade worsen and consequently the value of holding a job there is reduced as well.

To restore workers' work incentive, the equilibrium rate of unemployment in Foreign has to rise. Thus the path of equilibrium unemployment in Foreign is raised as well.

As part of welfare reform, let us consider a policy of transferring a fraction of current unemployment benefits to firms as employment subsidies. In particular, let $B=(1-s)\theta_b w$ and $S=s\theta_b w$, where S is the amount of employment subsidy given per employed worker. Under a balanced-budget policy, we have the constraint

$$(1+t_a)^{-1}=\frac{(1-u)(1-s\theta_b)}{1-[1-(1-s)\theta_b]u}.$$

The no-shirking constraint in steady state faced in Home is given by

$$(1-u)=1-\frac{b}{g\{\Upsilon A p_f^{1-\alpha} a_x^{-1}-1\}-\rho}, \tag{3.33}$$

where

$$\Upsilon \equiv \frac{[1-\theta_b+2s\theta_b](1-s\theta_b)(1-u)}{1-[1-(1-s)\theta_b]u}.$$

Evaluated around $s=0$, differentiation shows that $\partial\Upsilon/\partial s > 0$ (see Appendix 3.1). Equations (3.23) and (3.25) continue to hold. Since an increase of s raises Υ (starting from an initial value of $s=0$), we see that by transferring a fraction of unemployment benefits to firms as employment subsidies, workers have a greater incentive to exert effort as their fall-back income falls and at the same time firms have a higher inducement to hire as the marginal cost of hiring workers falls. Following from our earlier analysis, such a scheme not only raises the employment rate at Home but also has beneficial effects abroad as the terms of trade effect now works in reverse and workers in Foreign find an increased stake in job-holding.

3.3.3 Productivity Improvement

Productivity improvement in Home represented by a one-time decline in a_x has the effect of shifting the $(1\dot{-}u)=0$ locus upwards and the $(1\dot{-}u^*)=0$ locus downwards (see Appendix 3.1). The new steady-state equilibrium then lies northeast of the original equilibrium. Both countries benefit from Home's productivity improvement with Foreign benefiting through a terms of trade improvement. The productivity improvement in Home more than offsets the terms of trade deterioration so that real incomes rise, and with it, there is an increased inducement to work harder.

3.3.4 Labour Force Size Increase

An extraordinary event took place in recent history with the coming down of the Berlin Wall. If we interpret this event in our model as an enlargement of the labour force of Foreign, a country already integrated into the world economy through trade, is there a prospect for jobs to be created for all the new entrants to Foreign's labour force, and what effect does this have on Home's employment prospects? In Appendix 3.1, we show that an increase in $\overline{L}^*$ shifts up both the $(1\dot{-}u)=0$ and the $(1\dot{-}u^*)=0$ loci. However, it shifts up the $(1\dot{-}U^*)=0$ locus by more. Hence, the new steady state lies to the northwest of the original steady state. Consequently, the increase in Foreign labour force results in increased joblessness there but has salutary effects for Home. Again, the intuition here is that the increase in Foreign labour force results in a terms of trade improvement for Home, so that

Home workers value their jobs more. This results in a decline in unemployment for Home. However, the terms of trade deterioration suffered by the expanding country means that although transitorily employed workers hold on more tightly to their jobs because there is now more competition for jobs, the economy as a whole now faces a worsened trade-off. With the affordable wage that firms can pay reduced in terms of what workers consume, the economy can maintain worker discipline only at a higher rate of unemployment.[9]

3.3.5 Introducing Labour Standards

Let us introduce endogenous labour standards as in Casella (1996) into our model. We examine the amount of labour standard first in autarky. We can think of labour standard here as things like workplace safety and hygiene. Consider Home. The worker's utility function is written, for convenience, as $c_x^{1/2}c_y^{1/2}G^{\gamma};\gamma>0$, where G is a measure of labour standard treated as a public good and consumed only when a worker is employed. Each employed person pays a specific tax, τ, which is endogenously determined at an optimal level, to finance the labour standard. The public good, G, is produced with the two private goods according to the technology $G= X_G^{1/2}Y_G^{1/2}$, where X_G and Y_G are public demands for goods X and Y, respectively. The worker's indirect utility function, conditioned on being employed, can be written as $\{(1/2)[w/(p_x^{1/2}p_y^{1/2})]-\tau\}G^{\gamma}$. The optimal τ is chosen to maximise $\{(1/2)[w/(p_x^{1/2}p_y^{1/2})]-\tau\}G^{\gamma}$ subject to the balanced-budget constraint $G=\tau L$. This yields the optimal choice of τ, namely, $\tau=[\gamma/(1+\gamma)](1/2)[w/(p_x^{1/2}p_y^{1/2})]$. In autarky, $p_x/p_y=a_x/a_y$, and hence $(1/2)[w/(p_x^{1/2}p_y^{1/2})]=(1/2)ea_x^{-\alpha}a_y^{-(1-\alpha)}$. The no-shirking constraint is given by

$$(1\dot{-}u)_t=[ge^{-1}(D[(1-u)\overline{L}]^{\gamma}\{(1/2)ea_x^{-\alpha}a_y^{-(1-\alpha)}\}^{1+\gamma}-e)-\rho]\,[1-(1-u)_t]-b, \tag{3.34}$$

where $D\equiv(1+\gamma)^{-(1+\gamma)}\gamma^{\gamma}$. Notice that when labour standards are high, a job is more valuable; consequently, the incentive wage required to maintain worker discipline at any given level of unemployment is lower, the higher is the labour standard. However, in the general equilibrium, as labour standards are financed by a specific wage tax on the employed workforce, so that $G=\tau(1-u)\overline{L}$, we see here that as $(1-u)$ rises, the demand for labour standard rises leading to the possibility of dynamic instability. We shall impose dynamic stability so that $d(1\dot{-}u)/d(1-u)<0$.

Under free trade, the international relative price is determined according to equation (3.23), with α set equal to 0.5. Using $(1/2)[w/(p_x^{1/2}p_y^{1/2})]= (1/2)p_f^{1/2}ea_x^{-1}$, the condition that $(1\dot{-}u)=0$ yields

$$(1-u)=1-\frac{b}{ge^{-1}[D[(1-u)\overline{L}]^{\gamma}[(1/2)p_f^{1/2}ea_x^{-1}]^{1+\gamma}-e]-\rho}. \quad (3.35)$$

A similiar procedure applied to Foreign yields

$$(1-u^{*})=1-\frac{b}{ge^{-1}[D[(1-u)^{*}\overline{L}^{*}]^{\gamma}[(1/2)p_f^{-(1/2)}ea_y^{*-1}]^{1+\gamma}-e]-\rho}. \quad (3.36)$$

Imposing the restriction that $\gamma<1$, both the $(1 \dot{-} u)=0$ and $(1 \dot{-} u^{*})=0$ loci are positively sloped. If we assume that the latter locus remains steeper, and make the further assumptions that $d(1 \dot{-} u)/d(1-u)<0$ and $d(1 \dot{-} u^{*})/d(1-u^{*})<0$, it is straightforward to construct a diagram like Figure 3.2 and show that the move from autarky to free trade involves a northeasterly movement towards a new steady state with higher employment for both Home and Foreign. We see that higher labour standards evolve as a *consequence* of opening up to free trade. As expected incomes rise, workers value their jobs more and express a greater demand for higher labour standards. The higher labour standards in turn improve worker discipline and expand employment. With the conditions imposed to ensure dynamic stability, the world economy converges to a new steady state with higher aggregate employment and higher labour standards.

Notice that in autarky, the country with the lower absolute labour productivity, and hence the poorer country, would have the lower labour standard. If the more advanced economy were to close its door to trade, it would hinder the less advanced country from evolving a higher demand for labour standards and from improving its labour market conditions. Free trade, therefore, acts to raise the demand for higher labour standards by workers in the poorer countries themselves just as their unemployment rates decline from integration into the world economy.

3.4 GENERALISATIONS

We consider in this section two generalisations: the extension to more than two countries and the generalisation of preferences to the CES utility function.

3.4.1 Size of Country and Distribution of Gains from Trade

One argument that has been advanced by some economists is that trade has had only a small impact on the rise in wage inequality in America and the rise in unemployment in Europe in the past two decades (see, for example,

Lawrence and Slaughter, 1993 and Bhagwati and Dehejia, 1994). On the other hand, a big part of the story behind the rise of East Asia is its dependence on international trade. A useful characterisation of this situation is one in which we can think of the world economy as being comprised of a large country (called OECD) and many small open economies. In this extended framework, we can show that the large country is unaffected by trade but the small economies experience rising real wages and declining unemployment as they move from autarky to free trade.

Suppose that there is one large economy, denoted N, and $N-1$ small countries denoted $N-1$, $N-2$, . . .,2,1 with relative productivities arrayed according to

$$\frac{a_x^1}{a_y^1}<\frac{a_x^2}{a_y^2}<\ldots<\frac{a_x^{N-1}}{a_y^{N-1}}<\frac{a_x^N}{a_y^N}.$$

Preferences and shirking behaviour are identical in all countries. Under steady-state conditions, we can depict a world production possibilities frontier (using $p^f=a_x^N/a_y^N$ in the corresponding equations (3.24) to derive the steady-state level of employment). Analogously, we can depict a relative world supply schedule juxtaposed against a relative world demand schedule. The world equilibrium is determined at point E in Figure 3.5, with the international relative price given by $p_f=a_x^N/a_y^N$. Notice in the figure that country N can be large primarily because its absolute labour productivities

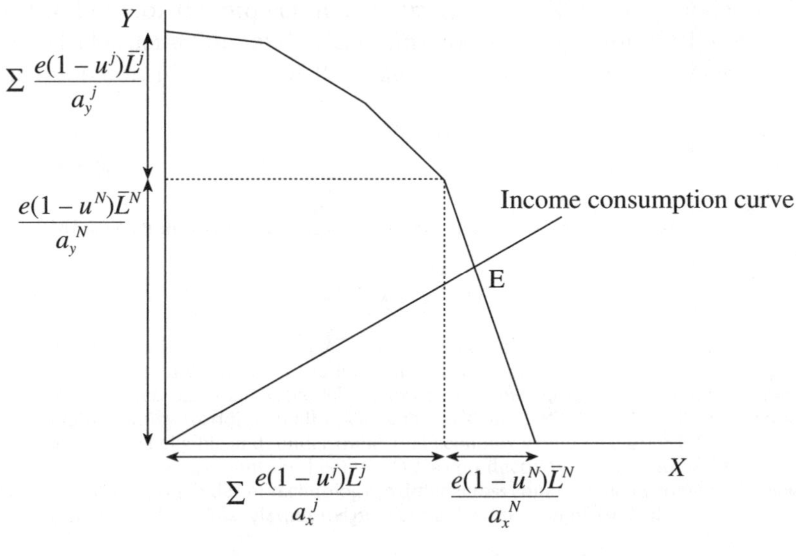

Figure 3.5 World production possibilities frontier

are high. It is the product $e(1/a_x^N)\overline{L}^N$ that affects the horizontal intercept and $e(1/a_y^N)\overline{L}^N$ that affects the vertical intercept. Hence, although India has a larger population than America, it may still be economically small in the sense that its absolute labour productivities are low. It is clear that trade leaves the production possibilities frontier (PPF) for the large economy unchanged. However, for all the other small countries, there is an outward shift of their PPFs (illustrated for country 1 in Figure 3.6). In addition to the traditional gain from trade depicted by the dotted line whose slope is given by p_f, there is a further outward shift of the consumption possibilities line due to the expansion of employment resulting from free trade. Thus all the gains from trade – rising real wages and declining equilibrium unemployment – accrue to small open economies while the large country is unaffected by trade.

The total value of exports of country 1 to country $N-1$ taken as a ratio to the large country N's GDP is given by

$$\frac{1-\alpha\sum_{j=1}^{N-1}(1-u^j)(\overline{L}^j/a_x^j)}{(1-u^N)(\overline{L}^N/a_x^N)}.$$

Krugman (1995) reports that although the share of exports of the Newly Industrialising Countries (NICs) – the supertraders of the postwar era – have grown dramatically in the past quarter of a century, it remains small as a share of OECD spending. For example, in 1990 the share of NICs'

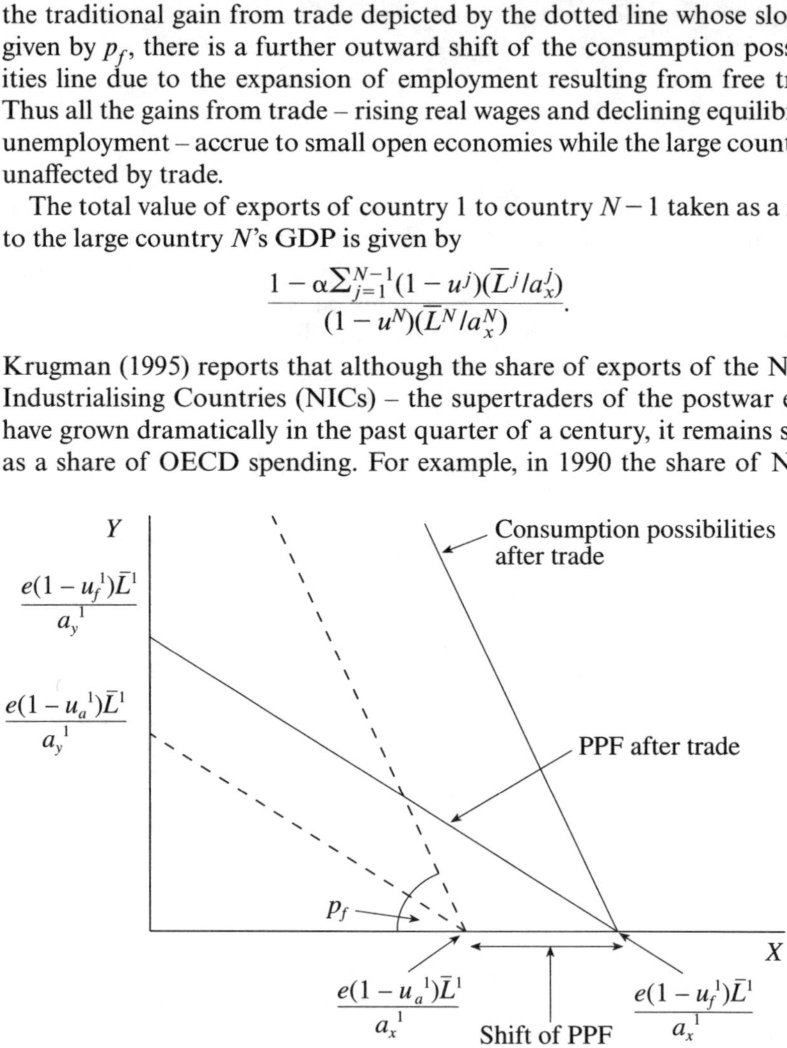

Figure 3.6 Shift of PPF as a result of trade

exports in total GDP of all industrial economies is 1.61 per cent. The relative size of the OECD suggests that it may be able to absorb the exports of newly emerging economies without the need for substantial resource reallocation. Although the OECD may largely be unaffected by trade, the individual emerging economies, being small open economies, could enjoy substantial incentive effects from job-holding by integrating into the global economy.

A worker's welfare can be expressed as his expected utility, which is given by $(1-u)A[w/(p_x^{\alpha}p_y^{1-\alpha})]$. For any country j, the indirect utility from real consumption is $Ap_f^{1-\alpha}e(a_x^j)^{-1}$ under free trade compared to $A(p_a^j)^{1-\alpha}e(a_x^j)^{-1}$ in autarky. Since $p_f > p_a^j$ for $j=1,2,\ldots, N-1$, trade not only raises the real consumption wage but also the equilibrium rate of employment. Moreover, the increase in the real consumption wage and employment rate are greatest for countries whose relative productivities differ most from those of the large country.

Notice that when we incorporate endogenous labour standards into such a world, trade would lead to higher labour standards in all the small countries but there would not be any change in labour standards in the large country. There is some convergence of labour standards to the level set by the large economy, a sort of 'race to the top'.

3.4.2 The Case of CES Utility Function and Immiserising Growth

Let us suppose that the utility function is given by the form $[c_x^{\theta}+c_y^{\theta}]^{1/\theta}$, where $\sigma \equiv (1-\theta)^{-1}$ is the elasticity of substitution in consumption. The indirect utility function is easily shown to be equal to

$$\frac{w}{[p_x^{1-\sigma}+p_y^{1-\sigma}]^{\frac{1}{1-\sigma}}}.$$

If we normalise by setting the price index to unity, that is,

$$[p_x^{1-\sigma}+p_y^{1-\sigma}]^{\frac{1}{1-\sigma}} \equiv 1,$$

we can express p_x and p_y as

$$p_x = \frac{1}{[1+p^{-(1-\sigma)}]^{\frac{1}{1-\sigma}}},$$

$$p_y = \frac{1}{[1+p^{1-\sigma}]^{\frac{1}{1-\sigma}}},$$

where $p \equiv p_x/p_y$. Since Home is a net exporter of good X, the condition

$$w = \frac{ep_x}{a_x} \equiv \frac{e}{a_x[1 + p^{-(1-\sigma)}]^{\frac{1}{1-\sigma}}},$$

holds before and after trade, with the appropriate autarkic and free trade prices substituted for p. Since $p_f > p_a$, the real consumption wage (indirect utility from consumption) is increased whether $\sigma < 1$ or $\sigma > 1$. Hence, again, trade raises the stake in holding a job, and hence lowers the natural rate in general equilibrium.

In Foreign, being a net exporter of good Y, the condition

$$w^* = \frac{ep_y}{a_y^*} \equiv \frac{e}{a_y^*[1 + p^{1-\sigma}]^{\frac{1}{1-\sigma}}},$$

holds before and after trade, with the appropriate autarkic and free trade prices substituted for p. Since $p_f < p_a^*$, the real consumption wage (indirect utility from consumption) is increased whether $\sigma < 1$ or $\sigma > 1$. Hence, again, trade raises the stake in holding a job, and hence lowers the natural rate in general equilibrium.

The general-equilibrium free trade relative price is now determined by the condition

$$p_f = \left\{\left[\frac{a_x^*}{a_y}\right]\left[\frac{(1-u^*)\bar{L}^*}{(1-u)\bar{L}}\right]\right\}^{\frac{1}{\sigma}}.$$

We follow the same procedure as before to solve the problem in general equilibrium. In Appendix 3.1, we show that in the $(1-u^*)$–$(1-u)$ plane, the $(1 \dot{-} u^*) = 0$ locus is positively sloped and steeper than the $(1 \dot{-} u) = 0$ locus. The system once again exhibits dynamic global stability.

The rise of East Asia in the past two decades has been associated with export-led growth. An interesting question to ask is whether this threatens jobs in the West. If we view East Asia as economically small compared to the West as in the model of the last sub-section, then the international terms of trade are pinned down by relative labour productivities of the West, which remain unaffected by East Asian growth. However, if we think of growth occurring in an economically large region of the world, we can analyse the welfare effects in a two-country model with the more general utility function. We now ask how export-led growth, interpreted as a productivity improvement in the export sector of home country, affects jobs and wages domestically and abroad and show that when $\sigma < b_y$, where $b_y \equiv [1 + p^{1-\sigma}]^{-1}$ is the share of total expenditure on good Y, the import good of Home, a productivity improvement in Home can actually lead to rising unemployment and declining real wage domestically. However, Foreign, which exhibits no growth, must benefit from the growth of its trading partner.

When $\sigma < b_y$, both the $(1 \dot{-} u) = 0$ and $(1 \dot{-} u^*) = 0$ loci shift down in response to productivity improvement in Home, namely, a rise in a_x^{-1}. However, as Appendix 3.1 proves, the $(1 \dot{-} u^*) = 0$ locus shifts down by more. Consequently, $1 - u^*$ must expand. However, it is now possible for $1 - u$ to decline (not shown). Thus technical advance in the export sector in one large region of the world can lead to rising domestic unemployment via a sufficiently large terms of trade deterioration but it *must* improve job prospects for the rest of the world. (The immiserisation result depends upon a sufficiently large share of the growing country's consumption expenditure to go to the import good – here a large b_y – and a sufficiently low elasticity of substitution in consumption between the import and export good – here a low σ.)

3.5 ROBUSTNESS OF RESULTS

How robust is the result that under free trade, all nations gain from trade through a rise in real earnings and expansion of employment? In Chapter 4, we show that in a Hecksher–Ohlin model with homogeneous labour and physical capital, trade raises wages and lowers equilibrium unemployment for the relatively labour abundant country but lowers real wages and raises equilibrium unemployment for the relatively labour-scarce country.[10] In contrast to the Heckscher–Ohlin model, the Ricardian model leaves out capital. Empirically, is this a serious omission? If we accept the observation in Krugman (1995, p. 345) that the share of labour in total value added has been remarkably stable over time, it may be that the omission of capital does not weaken the basic message that international trade, through strengthening the work incentive, raises real earnings and expands employment among participating countries. It should be pointed out, however, that in Singapore, the wage share increased from about 39 per cent in 1972 to nearly 44 per cent in 1981 (see Lim, 1998, p. 43), a development that would be consistent with the Stolper–Samuelson mechanism at work, raising factor rewards to labour relative to capital as the country increased exports of relatively labour-intensive goods. From what we have learned from the multi-country model involving a large country (the OECD) and many small countries, it is logically consistent for small open economies to benefit from trade through selling labour-intensive exports to the world market and therefore to see a rise in the wage share à la Stolper–Samuelson, while the countries in the OECD taken as a whole are not much affected by their trade with the small economies.

Nevertheless, if we accept that the Heckscher–Ohlin mechanism is at work in the global economy, we can ask whether there are other forces that under trade will counteract the negative Stolper–Samuelson effects on wages and employment in the labour-scarce country. In Chapter 6 and earlier in Hoon (1994), it is shown that a love for variety provides an additional incentive for workers to hold on more tightly to their jobs in an open economy. Additionally, two other forces are at work in the global economy that may offset the effect arising from different factor proportions and imperfect factor substitutability. Firstly, trade reduces market power, and in particular, reduces the mark-up of price over marginal cost. This is translated into a rise in the real demand wage, and hence acts to stimulate employment among all trading nations. We explore this channel in Chapter 5. Secondly, an increase in the range of intermediate goods made available through trade acts to increase the productivity of labour and can offset the negative effects of factor proportions at work in the relatively capital abundant country. This channel is studied in Matusz (1996) and explored in Chapter 6.

We have seen that when small countries trade with a large country, all the gains go to the small countries but the large country is unaffected by trade. There is hope that as the small economies become richer as a result of trade and grow in economic influence, their factor proportions also converge towards the levels of the large country. As factor proportions converge, the forces that act to raise the real incomes of *all* factors in *all* countries engaged in trade can be expected to become stronger. Then, all workers of the world will have an increased stake in job-holding through economic integration, and consequently, all economies will be able to enjoy increased employment as a result of trade. Garnaut (1996, pp. 108–10), looking at the East Asian growth experience, has shown that each country's export-oriented growth was initially built upon the rapid expansion of relatively labour-intensive exports, especially garments and textiles but over time a wider range of simple products. The export of relatively labour-intensive goods in exchange for goods intensive in the use of capital and raw materials was important to the establishment of growth momentum at first in Japan and Hong Kong, and then successively in Taiwan, South Korea, Singapore and Malaysia, Thailand, China, Indonesia and most recently Vietnam and the Philippines. Garnaut notes that the continued rapid expansion of exports of relatively labour-intensive goods from relative newcomers to the East Asian growth process was accommodated increasingly not from increased total imports of inter-regional markets in advanced countries (although these did grow considerably), but through increased exports to the higher-income East Asian economies whose comparative advantage had shifted away from relatively labour-intensive commodities. Hence there is potential today for the newly emerging low-income economies to undergo the sort of labour market developments through integration into the world economy that the East Asian economies underwent in the sixties and seventies without causing adverse movements in jobs and wages in the high-income countries.

3.6 CONCLUSION

There has been widespread concern, especially in policy circles, that the exports of manufactures from low-wage to high-wage countries have had adverse effects on the latter – driving down the wages of low-end workers and increasing joblessness there (see Commission of the European Communities, 1993). This chapter has been directed at examining this concern. We have done so by developing a general-equilibrium model with a Ricardian structure to analyse the effects of trade when wages and equilibrium unemployment are both endogenous. A basic insight that is obtained from the study is that in an open economy, workers have an increased stake in job-holding, and hence are less likely to shirk; more generally, shirking, absenteeism and quitting should decline when workers are employed in a world economy integrated through international commerce rather than in a splintered world of isolated autarkies. As workers find that their pay can afford them a bigger consumption basket under trade, they value their jobs more. This makes it possible for the general equilibrium of these economies to sustain lower equilibrium rates of unemployment under free trade. This incentive effect, it can be argued, will be of great importance as the former Central and Eastern European countries make their transition to market economies. In order to lower the persistently high structural unemployment of these former socialist economies, the importance of an open trading system cannot be overemphasised.[11]

In this chapter, we have also analysed the effects of a series of economic shocks when joblessness is endogenously determined. In the world developed here, trade wars lead to a reduction in economic welfare as trade volume shrinks and equilibrium unemployment rises for all the countries engaged in economic warfare. Generous unemployment benefits supported by payroll taxes lead to higher unemployment in the home country as a result of the higher marginal cost of hiring and increased fall-back incomes. This has the consequence of exporting a slump to the rest of the world through a deterioration in the latter's terms of trade. Technical improvement in the export sector of home country must benefit its trading partner by raising foreigners' welfare through raising their employment prospects and their real consumption wages although it is possible that the country experiencing the productivity improvement may actually face a rise in unemployment and suffer a decline in real incomes – a case of immiserising growth. An expansion of one country's labour force lowers unemployment in the rest of the world but raises joblessness in the expanding country. Labour standards naturally rise as incomes are raised through trade, and employment prospects improve. In turn, the higher labour standards raise the value of job-holding, further expanding aggregate employment.

One other shock not examined in the formal analysis is the effect of an increase in job separations due to reasons other than shirking in some countries. The recent international financial crisis has led to the closing of many businesses, in part prompted by the required restructuring process in these countries. It is straightforward to show that a rise in the job separation parameter, b, leads to a rise in the wage that firms have to pay to maintain worker discipline at each rate of unemployment. The result is that the path of equilibrium unemployment is shifted up in the affected economies.

NOTES

1. In a modern formulation that builds on microfoundations, menu cost is used to derive nominal price rigidity (see Obstfeld and Rogoff, 1995). In this book, we abstract from money but use a microfoundation-based effort-elicitation labour market model to generate equilibrium unemployment. This chapter builds on Hoon (2000a).
2. The treatment of unemployment in an essentially Keynesian fashion in open-economy macroeconomics and the abstraction from an endogenous theory of long-run unemployment in trade theory goes back a long way. In *Readings in the Theory of International Trade* edited by Ellis and Metzler (1950), under the section heading 'Business Cycles and International Trade', is an article by William Salant entitled 'Foreign trade policy in the business cycle' (Salant, 1941). Its approach is essentially that of Keynesian multiplier theory applied to the open economy. The same approach is adopted in another article reprinted in the volume by Joan Robinson entitled 'Beggar-my-neighbour remedies for unemployment' (Robinson, 1947). In contrast, although the classic article by Wolfgang Stolper and Paul Samuelson entitled 'Protection and real wages' (Stolper and Samuelson, 1941) begins with the statement, 'Second only in political appeal to the argument that tariffs increase employment is the popular notion that the standard of living of the American worker must be protected against the ruinous competition of cheap foreign labour . . .' aggregate employment is assumed constant throughout the analysis.
3. Although I am not aware of any careful empirical study linking the good employment performance of the European economies in the fifties and the sixties to trade, it is noteworthy that the decline of European unemployment in the postwar era occurred during a time of unprecedented growth in world trade and intra-European trade. If we accept the empirical finding of Coe and Helpman (1995) that increased trade integration helps trading nations enjoy R&D spillover effects, and combine that with the fact that the world war caused massive destruction of capital, the sprinting of total factor productivity as the war-torn western economies moved closer to the knowledge frontier defined by the US would lead to large increases in labour demand and downward wage pressures. This would explain the unusually low unemployment rates enjoyed by Western Europe in the late fifties and sixties. With the productivity slowdown beginning in the seventies, and given the rise of the welfare state during the earlier era of high producvity growth, there was no longer a substantial upward pull of the affordable wage that firms could

pay to counteract increased wage pressures as the state provided a comfortable cushion to workers in the event of job loss. The result was increased joblessness.

4. Phelps (1994) is a book-length treatment of this particular approach to the general-equilibrium determination of the natural rate – dubbed the 'modern-equilibrium' approach.
5. Despite various critiques of the model, as Kimball (1994) argues, this model reconciles the finding of low elasticity of labour supply in microeconomic data with the finding of high labour supply elasticity in macroeconomic data. Katz (1986) presents a discussion of the empirical relevance of the whole class of efficiency wage models.
6. We assume that the equilibrium employment rate does not immediately jump to its steady-state level. Intuitively, the reason is that when workers at a firm see the aggregate hiring rate up in a boom, they are induced to slacken in their commitment to job-holding, which raises the cost to the firm of maintaining worker discipline. The firm, therefore, tries to delay hiring additional workers. In a recession, workers hold on to their jobs more tightly so the incentive wage required to maintain worker discipline is reduced. Consequently, the aggregate rate of reduction of employment is moderated.
7. In contrast, if unemployment benefits are not taxed, balanced budget implies $t_d/(1+t_a)=\theta_b u/(1-u)$.
8. If unemployment benefits are not taxed, we obtain

$$(1-u)=1-\frac{b}{g\left\{\left[1-\frac{\theta_b}{1-u}\right]Ap_f^{1-\alpha}a_x^{-1}-1\right\}-\rho}.$$

9. There is another way to understand the results. At the original equilibrium, an increase in the labour force of Foreign leads to an excess supply of labour in Foreign and excess demand for labour in Home, and correspondingly, a trade surplus for Home. This surplus is eliminated by a rise in real wages in Home and attendant decline in unemployment there as well as a decline in real wages in Foreign and an attendant rise in unemployment there.
10. This result was first obtained in my PhD dissertation submitted to Columbia University in 1990 and published in Hoon (1991).
11. Allison and Ringold (1996) report that between 1990 and 1993, following the initial output collapse in Central and Eastern Europe, registered unemployment grew in all countries, exceeding 16 per cent in Bulgaria and Poland and climbing to between 12 per cent and 14 per cent in Croatia, Hungary, Slovakia and Slovenia. Although the reported unemployment rate in the Czech Republic is comparatively low, it has had very high levels of labour force withdrawal – the 'discouraged worker' effect. It is particularly worrying that long-term unemployment makes up a significant share of the total pool of unemployed. In 1995, long-term unemployment exceeded 60 per cent of total unemployed in Bulgaria, and exceeded 40 per cent in all countries, except the Czech Republic, which reached 32 per cent in 1995.

APPENDIX 3.1

1. The slope of the locus of $(1\dot{-}u)=0$ is given by

$$\left.\frac{d(1-u)}{d(1-u^*)}\right|_{(1\dot{-}u)=0}=\frac{\left[\frac{\alpha}{1-\alpha}\right]\left[\frac{a_x}{a_y^*}\right]\left[\frac{\overline{L}^*}{(1-u)\overline{L}}\right]}{B+\left[\frac{\alpha}{1-\alpha}\right]\left[\frac{a_x}{a_y^*}\right]\left[\frac{(1-u^*)\overline{L}^*}{(1-u)^2\overline{L}}\right]},$$

where

$$B \equiv \frac{[g(Aa_x^{-1}p_f^{1-\alpha} - 1) - \rho]^2}{bgAa_x^{-1}(1-\alpha)p_f^{-\alpha}} > 0.$$

On the other hand, the slope of the locus of $(1 \dot{-} u^*) = 0$ is given by

$$\left.\frac{d(1-u)}{d(1-u^*)}\right|_{(1 \dot{-} u^*)=0} = \frac{\left[\frac{\alpha}{1-\alpha}\right]\left[\frac{a_x}{a_y^*}\right]\left[\frac{\bar{L}^*}{(1-u)\bar{L}}\right] + C}{\left[\frac{\alpha}{1-\alpha}\right]\left[\frac{a_x}{a_y^*}\right]\left[\frac{(1-u^*)\bar{L}^*}{(1-u)^2\bar{L}}\right]},$$

where

$$C \equiv \frac{[g(Aa_y^{*-1}p_f^{-\alpha} - 1) - \rho]^2}{bgAa_y^{*-1}\alpha p_f^{-(1+\alpha)}} > 0.$$

2. Around a zero-tariff equilibrium, at any given $1-u^*$, the change in $1-u$ brought about by a change in t_r is given by

$$\left.\frac{d(1-u)}{dt_r}\right|_{(1 \dot{-} u)=0} = \frac{-(1-\alpha)p_f}{B + \left[\frac{\alpha}{1-\alpha}\right]\left[\frac{a_x}{a_y^*}\right]\left[\frac{(1-u^*)\bar{L}^*}{(1-u)^2\bar{L}}\right]} < 0,$$

$$\left.\frac{d(1-u)}{dt_r}\right|_{(1 \dot{-} u^*)=0} = \alpha(1-u) > 0.$$

Similiarly, around a zero-tariff equilibrium, at any given $1-u^*$, the change in $1-u$ brought about by a change in t_r^* is given by

$$\left.\frac{d(1-u)}{dt_r^*}\right|_{(1 \dot{-} u)=0} = \frac{-(1-\alpha)p_f}{B + \left[\frac{\alpha}{1-\alpha}\right]\left[\frac{a_x}{a_y^*}\right]\left[\frac{(1-u^*)\bar{L}^*}{(1-u)^2\bar{L}}\right]} < 0,$$

$$\left.\frac{d(1-u)}{dt_r^*}\right|_{(1 \dot{-} u^*)=0} = \alpha(1-u) > 0.$$

3. Around a zero-benefit equilibrium, at any given $1-u^*$, the change in $1-u$ brought about by a change in θ_b is given by

$$\left.\frac{d(1-u)}{d\theta_b}\right|_{(1 \dot{-} u)=0} = \frac{\frac{-p_f}{(1-\alpha)(1-u)}}{B + \left[\frac{\alpha}{1-\alpha}\right]\left[\frac{a_x}{a_y^*}\right]\left[\frac{(1-u^*)\bar{L}^*}{(1-u)^2\bar{L}}\right]} < 0,$$

both when benefits are taxed as well as when they are tax-exempt.

Evaluated around $s=0$, we have

$$\frac{\partial Y}{\partial s}=\frac{\{\theta_b[1-(1-\theta_b)u](1+\theta_b)+\theta_b(1-\theta_b)u\}(1-u)}{[1-(1-\theta_b)u]^2}>0.$$

4. At any given $1-u^*$, the change in $1-u$ brought about by a change in a_x is given by

$$\left.\frac{d(1-u)}{da_x}\right|_{(1\dot{-}u)=0}=\frac{-\left[\frac{\alpha}{1-\alpha}\right]ea_x^{-1}p_f}{B+\left[\frac{\alpha}{1-\alpha}\right]\left[\frac{a_x}{a_y^*}\right]\left[\frac{(1-u^*)\overline{L}^*}{(1-u)^2\overline{L}}\right]}<0.$$

$$\left.\frac{d(1-u)}{da_x}\right|_{(1\dot{-}u^*)=0}=\frac{e(1-u)}{a_x}>0.$$

5. At any given $1-u^*$, the change in $1-u$ brought about by a change in $\overline{L}^*$ is given by

$$\left.\frac{d(1-u)}{d\overline{L}^*}\right|_{(1\dot{-}u)=0}=\left[\frac{p_f}{(1-u)B+p_f}\right]\left[\frac{(1-u)}{\overline{L}^*}\right]>0,$$

$$\left.\frac{d(1-u)}{d\overline{L}^*}\right|_{(1\dot{-}u^*)=0}=\frac{(1-u)}{\overline{L}^*}>0,$$

so

$$\left.\frac{d(1-u)}{d\overline{L}^*}\right|_{(1\dot{-}u)=0}<\left.\frac{d(1-u)}{d\overline{L}^*}\right|_{(1\dot{-}u^*)=0}.$$

6. With an endogenous labour standard, the slope of the locus of $(1\dot{-}u)=0$ is given by

$$\left.\frac{d(1-u)}{d(1-u^*)}\right|_{(1\dot{-}u)=0}=\frac{\frac{p_f}{1-u^*}}{B'+\frac{p_f}{1-u}\left[1-\frac{2\gamma}{1+\gamma}\right]},$$

where

$$B'\equiv\frac{[ge^{-1}(D[(1-u)\overline{L}]^{\gamma}[(1/2)p_f^{1-\alpha}ea_x^{-1}]^{1+\gamma}-e)-\rho]^2}{bgD[(1-u)\overline{L}]^{\gamma}(1+\gamma)[(1/2)p_f^{1-\alpha}ea_x^{-1}]^{\gamma}0.25a_x^{-1}p_f^{-\alpha}}>0.$$

The slope is unambiguously positive if $0<\gamma<1$.

On the other hand, the slope of the locus of $(1\dot{-}u^*)=0$ is given by

$$\left.\frac{d(1-u)}{d(1-u^*)}\right|_{(1\dot{-}u^*)=0}=\frac{C'+\dfrac{p_f}{1-u^*}\left[1-\dfrac{2\gamma}{1+\gamma}\right]}{\dfrac{p_f}{1-u}},$$

where

$$C'\equiv\frac{[ge^{-1}(D[(1-u^*)\bar{L}^*]^{\gamma}[(1/2)p_f^{-\alpha}ea_y^{*-1}]^{1+\gamma}-e)-\rho]^2}{bgD[(1-u^*)\bar{L}^*]^{\gamma}(1+\gamma)[(1/2)p_f^{-\alpha}ea_y^{*-1}]^{\gamma}0.25a_y^{*-1}p_f^{-(1+\alpha)}}>0.$$

This slope is also unambiguously positive if $0<\gamma<1$.

7. In the general case with CES utility function, the slope of the locus of $(1\dot{-}u)=0$ is given by

$$\left.\frac{d(1-u)}{d(1-u^*)}\right|_{(1\dot{-}u)=0}=\frac{\left[\dfrac{1}{\sigma}\right]\left[\dfrac{a_x}{a_y^*}\right]^{\frac{1}{\sigma}}\left[\dfrac{(1-u^*)^{\frac{1}{\sigma}-1}\bar{L}^{*\frac{1}{\sigma}}}{(1-u)^{\frac{1}{\sigma}}\bar{L}^{\frac{1}{\sigma}}}\right]}{B''+\left[\dfrac{1}{\sigma}\right]\left[\dfrac{a_x}{a_y^*}\right]^{\frac{1}{\sigma}}\left[\dfrac{(1-u^*)^{\frac{1}{\sigma}}\bar{L}^{*\frac{1}{\sigma}}}{(1-u)^{\frac{1}{\sigma}+1}\bar{L}^{\frac{1}{\sigma}}}\right]},$$

where

$$B''\equiv\frac{[g(a_x^{-1}(1+p_f^{-(1-\sigma)})^{\frac{-1}{1-\sigma}}-1)-\rho]^2}{bga_x^{-1}[1+p_f^{-(1-\sigma)}]^{\frac{-(2-\sigma)}{1-\sigma}}p_f^{-(2-\sigma)}}>0.$$

On the other hand, the slope of the locus of $(1\dot{-}u^*)=0$ is given by

$$\left.\frac{d(1-u)}{d(1-u^*)}\right|_{(1\dot{-}u^*)=0}=\frac{\left[\dfrac{1}{\sigma}\right]\left[\dfrac{a_x}{a_y^*}\right]^{\frac{1}{\sigma}}\left[\dfrac{(1-u^*)^{\frac{1}{\sigma}-1}\bar{L}^{*\frac{1}{\sigma}}}{(1-u)^{\frac{1}{\sigma}}\bar{L}^{\frac{1}{\sigma}}}\right]+C''}{\left[\dfrac{1}{\sigma}\right]\left[\dfrac{a_x}{a_y^*}\right]^{\frac{1}{\sigma}}\left[\dfrac{(1-u^*)^{\frac{1}{\sigma}}\bar{L}^{*\frac{1}{\sigma}}}{(1-u)^{\frac{1}{\sigma}+1}\bar{L}^{\frac{1}{\sigma}}}\right]},$$

where

$$C''\equiv\frac{[g(a_y^{*-1}(1+p_f^{1-\sigma})^{\frac{-1}{1-\sigma}}-1)-\rho]^2}{bga_y^{*-1}[1+p_f^{1-\sigma}]^{\frac{-(2-\sigma)}{1-\sigma}}p_f^{-\sigma}}>0.$$

8. In the CES utility function case, at a given $1-u^*$, the change in $1-u$ in response to a change in a_x is given by

$$\left.\frac{d(1-u)}{da_x}\right|_{(1\dot{-}u)=0}=\left[\frac{\left(\dfrac{1}{\sigma}\right)p_f-\left(\dfrac{1}{b_y}\right)p_f}{\left(\dfrac{1}{\sigma}\right)p_f+(1-u)B''}\right]\left[\frac{e(1-u)}{a_x}\right],$$

$$\left.\frac{d(1-u)}{da_x}\right|_{(1 \div u^*)=0} = \frac{e(1-u)}{a_x} > 0.$$

Since for $\sigma < b_y$,

$$0 < \left[\frac{\left(\frac{1}{\sigma}\right)p_f - \left(\frac{1}{b_y}\right)p_f}{\left(\frac{1}{\sigma}\right)p_f + (1-u)B''}\right] < 1,$$

it follows that

$$0 < \left.\frac{d(1-u)}{da_x}\right|_{(1 \div u)=0} < \left.\frac{d(1-u)}{da_x}\right|_{(1 \div u^*)=0}.$$

4. The Heckscher–Ohlin model with an endogenous natural rate

4.1 INTRODUCTION

In Chapter 3, we obtained the result that trade expands equilibrium employment in both countries in a two-country Ricardian world economy. In particular, despite fears that trade between developed and developing nations could lead to job loss in the former, the result applies to trade between a low-wage country (where labour productivity is low) and a high-wage country (where labour productivity is high). When trade leads to complete specialisation, the pay level measured in terms of the export good is unchanged but, as the free trade relative price of the import good must be lower than the autarkic relative price when trade is based upon comparative advantage, the purchasing power of workers' pay is increased as a result of trade. Consequently, holding a job becomes more valuable under trade with the result that equilibrium unemployment falls in both trading economies. It is sometimes felt, however, that the Heckscher–Ohlin model is the natural one to use to examine the effects of the rise of the Newly Industrialising Countries' trade on jobs and wages. In this chapter, we shall develop the Heckscher–Ohlin model with an endogenous natural rate. We will see that in this model, trade raises the real consumption wage and lowers the natural rate of the relatively labour abundant country; on the other hand, trade reduces the real consumption wage and increases the natural rate of the relatively capital abundant country regardless of the weights in the consumption basket.

We will also re-examine some interesting issues in the global economy in the context of the Hecksher–Ohlin model with an endogenous response of the equilibrium rate of unemployment. What is the effect of a major technological catch-up by the East Asian economies on unemployment in Europe and America? With many socialist countries including the People's Republic of China with a population of over a billion people, the former Soviet Union as well as the economies of Eastern Europe integrating into the world trading system, how might it affect the welfare, including job prospects, of the NICs as well as the Western economies? Does protection in America save American jobs and how does it affect East Asia?

In this chapter, we abstract from labour–market dynamics and cast the Shapiro–Stiglitz steady-state formalisation of workers' behaviour in a Heckscher–Ohlin framework. Section 4.2 develops the basic model and studies the welfare effects of free trade. Section 4.3 studies a few economic shocks in the basic model. Section 4.4 concludes.

4.2 THE BASIC MODEL

4.2.1 Worker's Decision

We first develop the autarkic equilibrium before characterising the free trade equilibrium. There are $\overline{L}$ number of workers in the closed economy with each worker being risk neutral and having the instantaneous utility function, $c_x^{\alpha}c_y^{1-\alpha}-e$, $0<\alpha<1$. Here, c_x and c_y are the individual consumption levels of two competitive goods, X and Y, respectively, and e is the effort level. Again, we assume that e can take only two values, zero if no effort is supplied (when the worker shirks) and a positive constant, otherwise. The worker is indifferent between working in either sector so that, in equilibrium, wage levels will be equalised across sectors. In addition, we assume that the worker has ownership of another factor, capital, which provides him with a source of non-wage income. Each worker maximises the expected present discounted value of lifetime utility, V, with a subjective discount rate equal to ρ.

We first consider the decision problem of a worker whether or not to shirk when he is employed. Let V_{es}, V_{en} denote the expected present value of utility in the case when he shirks and when he does not. Let V_u be the expected present value of utility if unemployed. We want to derive the condition under which V_{en} will exceed V_{es} so that it will be optimal for the worker not to shirk. By solving a simple dynamic programming problem, we can show that V_{es} and V_{en} satisfy the following equations:

$$\rho V_{es}=c_x^{\alpha}c_y^{1-\alpha}+(b+g)(V_u-V_{es}), \tag{4.1}$$

$$\rho V_{en}=c_x^{\alpha}c_y^{1-\alpha}-e+b(V_u-V_{en}). \tag{4.2}$$

Now the worker solves a period by period problem: Maximise $c_x^{\alpha}c_y^{1-\alpha}-e$ subject to $p_xc_x+p_yc_y=w+r\overline{k}$, where it is implicitly assumed that the worker is unable to borrow or lend. Here, p_x is the price of good X, p_y is the price of good Y, w is the wage level, r is the rental rate, and $\overline{k}$ is the quantity of capital owned by the worker, assuming that capital is divided equally among all workers. Solving the worker's period optimisation problem, we derive the indirect utility function $\alpha^{\alpha}(1-\alpha)^{1-\alpha}[w+r\bar{k}]p_x^{-\alpha}p_y^{-(1-\alpha)}-e$ for the non-shirker and $\alpha^{\alpha}(1-\alpha)^{1-\alpha}[w+r\bar{k}]p_x^{-\alpha}p_y^{-(1-\alpha)}$ for the shirker.

Setting $A\equiv\alpha^{\alpha}(1-\alpha)^{1-\alpha}$, and substituting the indirect utilities of the shirker and non-shirker into equations (4.1) and (4.2), we obtain

$$\rho V_{es}=\frac{A(w+r\bar{k})}{p_x^{\alpha}p_y^{1-\alpha}}+(b+g)(V_u-V_{es}), \tag{4.3}$$

$$\rho V_{en}=\frac{A(w+r\bar{k})}{p_x^{\alpha}p_y^{1-\alpha}}-e+b(V_u-V_{en}). \tag{4.4}$$

In order for it not to be worthwhile for the worker to shirk, it is necessary that $V_{es}\leq V_{en}$. From equations (4.3) and (4.4), this condition can be stated as

$$\frac{A(w+r\bar{k})}{p_x^{\alpha}p_y^{1-\alpha}}\geq\rho V_u+\frac{(b+g+\rho)e}{g}. \tag{4.5}$$

The firm, by raising the wage level, raises the worker's indirect utility and provides him an incentive not to shirk. There is, however, no reason for the firm to pay more than necessary to prevent shirking. Thus, equation (4.5) holds with equality, and no worker shirks.

The expected present discounted value of utility for an unemployed worker must obey the asset equation:

$$\rho V_u=\frac{Ar\bar{k}}{p_x^{\alpha}p_y^{1-\alpha}}+a(V_{en}-V_u), \tag{4.6}$$

where a is the accession rate, the rate at which the unemployed gain employment. Notice from equation (4.6) that the worker continues to own income from rents even though he is unemployed, giving rise in this case to the indirect utility function $Ar\bar{k}/(p_x^{\alpha}p_y^{1-\alpha})$. Using equation (4.5) with the equality sign and equation (4.6), we obtain

$$\frac{Aw}{p_x^{\alpha}p_y^{1-\alpha}}=\frac{(a+b+\rho)e}{g}+e, \tag{4.7}$$

where w is the optimal supply wage. In steady state, the accession rate can be expressed as

$$a=\frac{bL}{\bar{L}-L}=\frac{b(1-u)}{u}, \tag{4.8}$$

where $\bar{L}$ is the size of the labour force, L is the number of employed workers, and $1-u\equiv L/\bar{L}$ is the rate of employment. Substituting equation (4.8) into equation (4.7), we finally obtain our aggregate no-shirking constraint (NSC):

$$\frac{Aw^s}{p_x^{\alpha}p_y^{1-\alpha}} = \left\{1 + \frac{\rho}{g} + \frac{b}{g[1-(1-u)]}\right\}e, \tag{4.9}$$

where the superscript s emphasises that this is the supply wage.

The NSC says that the lower the rate of unemployment, and thus the shorter the expected time spent in unemployment if fired, the more tempting it is to shirk. To avoid this, firms must offer a higher wage level. The supply wage, that is, the minimum wage that the firm has to offer to induce non-shirking behaviour by hired employees, therefore rises as the unemployment rate declines. Notice that the aggregate no-shirking constraint does not depend upon the rental rate. This results from the assumption of homothetic tastes as well as the assumption that workers obtain their rental incomes from renting their capital to the firms whether they are employed or not.

4.2.2 Production Side and Autarkic Equilibrium

Turning now to the production side of the model, we let the production functions be given by $Z_x = F_x(K_x, e\Lambda L_x)$ and $Z_y = F_y(K_y, e\Lambda L_y)$, where the production functions exhibit constant returns to scale. Letting $f_x(\tilde{k}_x) = F_x(\tilde{k}_x, 1)$ and $f_y(\tilde{k}_y) = F_y(\tilde{k}_y, 1)$ with the properties: $f_i'(\tilde{k}_i) > 0, f_i''(\tilde{k}_i) < 0, i = x, y$, we can write $z_x = (1-u)e\Lambda l_x f_x(\tilde{k}_x)$, and $z_y = (1-u)e\Lambda\, l_y f_y(\tilde{k}_y)$, where $z_x = Z_x/\overline{L}$ is the per capita output of sector X, Λ being a measure of Harrod-neutral productivity level, and $z_y = Z_y/\overline{L}$ is the per capita output of sector Y. Here, $l_x = L_x/L$ and $l_y = L_y/L$ are the shares of employed labour force allocated to sectors X and Y, respectively; and $\tilde{k}_x = K_x/(e\Lambda L_x)$ and $\tilde{k}_y = K_y/(e\Lambda\, L_y)$ are the sectoral capital–effective labour ratios, respectively. (We use a tilde to represent a variable expressed in effective units.)

In using a measure of the Harrod-neutral productivity level, we are following the lead of Leontief ([1954] 1968, pp. 523–4), who argues that one should interpret the factor proportions model explaining America's position in international trade as involving workers of different abilities:

> Let us, however, reject the simple but tenuous postulate of comparative technological parity and make the plausible alternative assumption that in any combination with a given quantity of capital, one man year of American labor is equivalent to, say, three man years of foreign labor. Then, in comparing the relative amounts of capital and labor possessed by the United States and the rest of the world – a comparison used for the explanation of their respective specialization in capital or labor intensive industries respectively – the total number of American workers must be multiplied by three, which would increase our 1947 labor force from 65 million to three times that number, i.e., 195 million of 'equivalent' foreign man years. Spread thrice as thinly as the unadjusted figures suggest the American capital supply per 'equivalent worker' turns out to be comparatively smaller, rather than larger, than that of many other countries.

He goes on to say, 'This, I submit, is the analytical explanation of the results of our empirical findings. In terms of the relative production possibilities here and abroad, the United States is rich in man power and poor in capital. This country resorts to foreign trade to save its capital and to dispose of its relative surplus labor' (p. 524).

The demand for capital and labour by each firm gives rise to equations (4.10) and (4.11):

$$w=p_x e\Lambda[f_x(\tilde{k}_x)-\tilde{k}_x f'_x(\tilde{k}_x)]=p_y e\Lambda[f_y(\tilde{k}_y)-\tilde{k}_y f'_y(\tilde{k}_y)], \tag{4.10}$$

$$r=p_x f'_x(\tilde{k}_x)=p_y f'_y(\tilde{k}_y). \tag{4.11}$$

Equation (4.10) tells us that labour is allocated to each sector in such a way that demand wages are equalised across the two sectors. Similiarly, rental rates are also equalised across the two sectors. It is useful to derive a few relationships from equations (4.10) and (4.11). Dividing equation (4.10) by equation (4.11), we show that

$$\tilde{k}_x=\tilde{k}_x(\tilde{\omega});\ \tilde{k}'_x(\tilde{\omega})>0, \tag{4.12}$$

$$\tilde{k}_y=\tilde{k}_y(\tilde{\omega});\ \tilde{k}'_y(\tilde{\omega})>0, \tag{4.13}$$

where $\tilde{\omega}=w/(e\Lambda r)$ is the effective wage–rental ratio. In other words, the sectoral capital–effective labour ratios are increasing functions of the effective wage–rental ratio. From equation (4.10), we can also show that $\tilde{\omega}=\tilde{\omega}(p)$, where $p\equiv p_x/p_y$. To determine the sign of the relationship between p and $\tilde{\omega}$, we note, using equations (4.10) and (4.11), that

$$\frac{d\tilde{\omega}}{dp}\frac{p}{\tilde{\omega}}=\frac{(\tilde{\omega}+\tilde{k}_y)+(\tilde{\omega}+\tilde{k}_x)}{\tilde{\omega}(\tilde{k}_y-\tilde{k}_x)}. \tag{4.14}$$

Without any loss of generality, we assume that sector X is relatively labour-intensive implying that $\tilde{k}_x<\tilde{k}_y$ for all effective wage–rental ratios. It follows that an increase in p raises $\tilde{\omega}$.

To link the effective wage–rental ratio to the wage, substitute equation (4.12) into equation (4.10) to obtain

$$w^d=p^{1-\alpha}e\Lambda[f_x(\tilde{k}_x(\tilde{\omega}))-\tilde{k}_x(\tilde{\omega})f'_x(\tilde{k}_x(\tilde{\omega}))], \tag{4.15}$$

where we use the normalisation $p_x^{\alpha}p_y^{1-\alpha}\equiv 1$ to obtain $p_x=p^{1-\alpha}$. The use of the superscript d emphasises that this is the demand–wage relation. From equation (4.15), we obtain a relationship between the demand wage and the relative price as well as the technology parameter:

$$\frac{\partial w^d}{\partial p} = -p^{1-\alpha} e\Lambda \tilde{k}_x f_x'' \tilde{k}_x' \tilde{\omega} + (1-\alpha) p^{-\alpha} e\Lambda [f_x - \tilde{k}_x f_x'], \tag{4.16}$$

$$\frac{\partial w^d}{\partial \Lambda} = e p^{1-\alpha} [f_x - \tilde{k}_x f_x']. \tag{4.17}$$

We, therefore, obtain a relationship linking the demand wage to the goods relative price and the technology parameter, which we can express as $w^d = e\Lambda\psi(p)$ such that $\psi'(p) > 0$.

To close the model, we need the condition that the total sectoral labour allocation be equal to the aggregate employment as well as the condition that capital be fully employed. We choose to express these conditions as

$$l_x + l_y = 1, \tag{4.18}$$

$$e(1-u)[l_x \tilde{k}_x + l_y \tilde{k}_y] = \frac{\bar{k}}{\Lambda}. \tag{4.19}$$

Equating the demand wage given by equation (4.15) to the supply wage given by equation (4.9), and taking note of the normalisation $p_x^{\alpha} p_y^{1-\alpha} \equiv 1$, we obtain:

$$A\Lambda\psi(p) = \left\{1 + \frac{\rho}{g} + \frac{b}{g[1-(1-u)]}\right\}. \tag{4.20}$$

Equation (4.20) can be described as the labour-market equilibrium locus, where the demand wage has been equated to the supply wage, and gives a positive relationship between the current rate of employment, $1-u$, and the relative price of the relatively labour-intensive good, p. The higher the rate of employment is, the less costly it is to be fired, and thus the greater is the incentive to shirk. To induce non-shirking behaviour, firms need to offer a higher wage level. With an unchanging technology parameter, it is profitable to offer a higher wage level only if firms face a higher relative price for the relatively labour-intensive good. We note that the third term in the bracket of the expression on the right-hand side of equation (4.20) is the sum of the accession rate and exogenous separation rate divided by the probability of being caught shirking. When $1-u=1$, that is, when there is full employment, the accession rate is infinitely large, and we require an infinitely high wage to induce non-shirking behaviour. Given an unchanging technology, firms can afford to pay such an infinitely high wage only if the relative price for the relatively labour-intensive good is infinitely high. The labour–market equilibrium locus relating the relative price, p, to the rate of employment, $1-u$, will be a positively-sloped schedule in the employment rate–relative price plane shown in Figure 4.1. An increase in Λ will shift rightwards the locus, that is, to raise the employment rate for any p. We

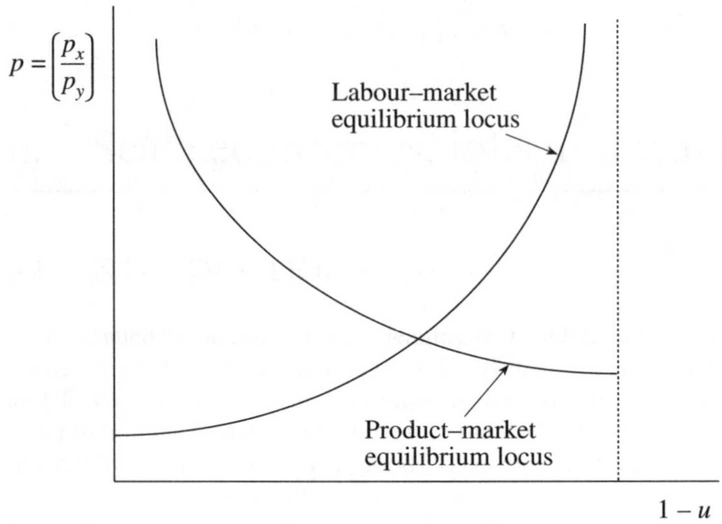

Figure 4.1 Labour– and product–market equilibrium

summarise this relationship as $1-u=\phi(p;\,\Lambda)$; $\phi_p>0$, $\phi_\Lambda>0$, where $\phi_p \equiv \partial\phi/\partial p$, etc.

We want to derive the relative per capita supplies of goods X and Y as well. Making use of equations (4.18) and (4.19), we can write the production functions as

$$z_x = \left[\frac{e\Lambda(1-u)\tilde{k}_y - \bar{k}}{\tilde{k}_y - \tilde{k}_x}\right] f_x(\tilde{k}_x),$$

$$z_y = \left[\frac{\bar{k} - e\Lambda(1-u)\tilde{k}_x}{\tilde{k}_y - \tilde{k}_x}\right] f_y(\tilde{k}_y),$$

where z_x, z_y are the per capita output levels of goods X and Y, respectively. We obtain, after dividing,

$$\frac{z_x}{z_y} = \frac{e\Lambda(1-u)\zeta_y - (\bar{k}/f_y)}{(\bar{k}/f_x) - e\Lambda(1-u)\zeta_x}, \tag{4.21}$$

where we define $\zeta_i \equiv \tilde{k}_i / f_i(\tilde{k}_i)$; $i=x,y$ as the inverse of the average physical productivity of capital in sector i. Under the assumptions made earlier that $f_i'>0, f_i''<0$, we have $\zeta_i'(\tilde{k}_i)>0$. From equation (4.21), we obtain the following derivatives: $\partial(z_x/z_y)/\partial p>0$ and $\partial(z_x/z_y)/\partial(1-u)>0$. The output relationships can be summarised in reduced form as follows:

$$z_x = z_x(p,\, 1-u;\, \bar{k}, \Lambda);\ \frac{\partial z_x}{\partial p} > 0,\ \frac{\partial z_x}{\partial(1-u)} > 0,$$

$$\frac{\partial z_x}{\partial \bar{k}} < 0,\ \frac{\partial z_x}{\partial \Lambda} > 0; \tag{4.22}$$

$$z_y = z_y(p,\, 1-u;\, \bar{k}, \Lambda);\ \frac{\partial z_y}{\partial p} < 0,\ \frac{\partial z_x}{\partial(1-u)} < 0,$$

$$\frac{\partial z_x}{\partial \bar{k}} > 0,\ \frac{\partial z_x}{\partial \Lambda} < 0. \tag{4.23}$$

To determine the relative price of good X in autarky, we need to clear the domestic goods markets. Now the individual demand functions are given by $c_x = \alpha[w + r\bar{k}]p_x^{-1}$ and $c_y = (1-\alpha)[w + \bar{k}]p_y^{-1}$ for those workers who are employed, and $c_x = \alpha r\bar{k}p_x^{-1}$ and $c_y = (1-\alpha)r\bar{k}_y p_y^{-1}$ for those who are unemployed. Aggregating across all individuals, the per capita aggregate demand functions C_x and C_y are given by $C_x = \alpha[(1-u)w + r\bar{k}]p_x^{-1}$ and $C_y = (1-\alpha)[(1-u)w + r\bar{k}]p_y^{-1}$, respectively. Dividing, we obtain

$$\frac{C_x}{C_y} = \left[\frac{\alpha}{1-\alpha}\right]p^{-1} \tag{4.24}$$

so that relative per capita aggregate demands are independent of incomes. (This is the result of homothetic tastes that we are adopting here.)

The requirement for the goods markets to clear gives us the condition:

$$p = \frac{\alpha}{1-\alpha}\left[\frac{z_y}{z_x}\right], \tag{4.25}$$

which can be interpreted as the product–market equilibrium condition. In the employment rate–relative price plane in Figure 4.1, this schedule is downward-sloping since differentiating equation (4.25) yields

$$\frac{dp}{d(1-u)} = \frac{\left[\dfrac{\alpha}{1-\alpha}\right]\dfrac{\partial(z_y/z_x)}{\partial(1-u)}}{1 - \left[\dfrac{\alpha}{1-\alpha}\right]\dfrac{\partial(z_y/z_x)}{\partial p}} < 0. \tag{4.26}$$

Joint equilibrium in the labour and product markets yields the equilibrium values of p and $1-u$.

4.2.3 The Free Trade Equilibrium

In the spirit of the Heckscher–Ohlin theory, we first assume that Home and Foreign are identical in all respects except for relative factor endowments so initially let us set $\Lambda = \Lambda^*$. The relative factor endowment is defined in terms of the ratio of capital stock to the total number of 'raw' or productivity-unadjusted workers including both the employed as well as unemployed workers, that is, the ratio of capital to the total labour force. We make the following assumption: Home is relatively labour abundant whereas Foreign is relatively labour scarce. Thus,

$$\bar{k}^* > \bar{k}, \tag{4.27}$$

where $\bar{k}$ is the amount of capital per unit of labour force in Home. (An asterisk is used to denote a Foreign variable.)

To depict the free trade equilibrium (compared to the autarkic equilibrium) of the two economies, it is useful to develop a back-to-back diagram characterising the labour–market equilibrium locus in one quadrant, and the determination of the product market-clearing relative price in the other. To determine the autarkic equilibrium relative price and the corresponding equilibrium employment rate in this new diagram, we can substitute the reduced form relationship $1 - u = \phi(p; \Lambda)$ into equation (4.21) to give us

$$\frac{z_x}{z_y} = \frac{e\Lambda\phi(p; \Lambda)\zeta_y - (\bar{k}/f_y)}{(\bar{k}/f_x) - e\Lambda\phi(p; \Lambda)\zeta_x}, \tag{4.28}$$

where we make explicit the dependence of $1 - u$ on p through the reduced-form relationship. Expression (4.28) can, in turn, be substituted into the goods market–clearing relationship (4.25) to give us

$$p = \frac{\alpha}{1-\alpha}\left[\frac{(\bar{k}/f_x) - e\Lambda\phi(p; \Lambda)\zeta_x}{e\Lambda\phi(p; \Lambda)\zeta_y - (\bar{k}/f_y)}\right]. \tag{4.29}$$

It is straightforward to check that the right-hand side term in equation (4.29) decreases in p and is described by RR in Figure 4.2. The autarkic rate of equilibrium employment is denoted as $1 - u_a$.

In Foreign, the reduced-form equation characterising the labour market equilibrium is given by $1 - u^* = \phi(p^*; \Lambda)$. Substituting this expression into Foreign's autarkic goods market-clearing condition, and noting that only relative factor endowments differ between the two economies, we obtain

$$p^* = \frac{\alpha}{1-\alpha}\left[\frac{(\bar{k}^*/f_x) - e\Lambda\phi(p^*; \Lambda)\zeta_x}{e\Lambda\phi(p^*; \Lambda)\zeta_y - (\bar{k}^*/f_y)}\right]. \tag{4.30}$$

With $\bar{k}^* > \bar{k}$, the right-hand side term described by RR^* lies above RR. The implied higher relative price p^* means that, in autarky, Foreign enjoys a higher equilibrium rate of employment (denoted by $1 - u_a^*$ in Figure 4.2), and correspondingly, higher real consumption wages.

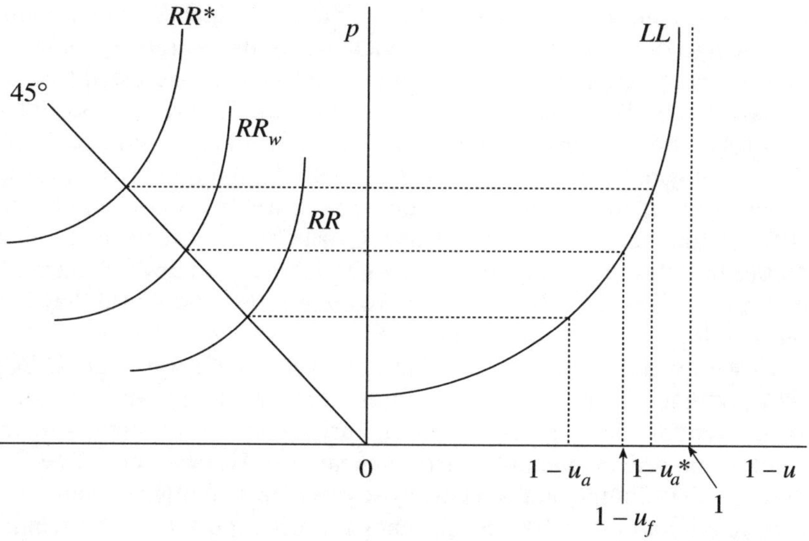

Figure 4.2 Equilibrium in autarky and under trade

Assuming identical and homothetic tastes, the world market-clearing condition under free trade is given by

$$p=\frac{\alpha}{1-\alpha}\left[\frac{s_L z_y+(1-s_L)z_y^*}{s_L z_x+(1-s_L)z_x^*}\right], \qquad (4.31)$$

where we substitute the appropriate reduced-form expressions $1-u=\phi(p;\Lambda)$ and $1-u^*=\phi(p;\Lambda)$, noting that under free trade, $p=p^*$. Here, $s_L=\overline{L}/(\overline{L}+\overline{L}^*)$, that is, s_L is Home's share of the global workforce.[1] The free trade equilibrium relative price lies between the two autarkic relative prices. We let RR_w in Figure 4.2 represent the right-hand side expression of the global market-clearing condition (4.31). As is evident from Figure 4.2, the equilibrium rate of employment under free trade denoted by $1-u_f$ is higher (compared to autarky) for Home but lower for Foreign. Hence we obtain the result that free trade lowers the natural rate of the relatively labour abundant country and raises it in the relatively capital abundant country.

Thus far, we have assumed that technology is identical in both countries. However, Leontief (1954), as we have alluded to before, argued that we should depart from the assumption of 'comparative technological parity' and take account of the differences in labour quality across countries. If we allow for Harrod-neutral productivity differences across countries, a country may be relatively labour scarce in the sense that capital per unit of raw labour (sum of employed and unemployed) is higher in that country but because its productivity level is much higher, its capital per augmented worker, that is, capital taken as a ratio to productivity-adjusted labour, is actually lower. That country, under free trade, would end up exporting the relatively labour-intensive good and experience an expansion of equilibrium employment under free trade. Leontief (1954) found in his study that America exported the relatively labour-intensive good in 1947 and Baldwin (1971) found that in 1962, this was still true of the American economy. Notice that this result implies that insofar as trade had any influence at all on US relative price in the decade or two after the Second World War, it was salutary for American jobs and wages.

To see this formally, suppose that $\Lambda^* > \Lambda$ in such a way that $(\bar{k}^*/\Lambda^*) < (\bar{k}/\Lambda)$. In that case, Foreign, representing America, has a lower autarkic relative price for the relatively labour-intensive good and a higher autarkic equilibrium rate of unemployment compared to Home. Under free trade, Foreign, the country that is relatively scarce in *raw* labour but abundant in productivity-adjusted labour, becomes the net-exporter of the relatively labour-intensive good, and its equilibrium employment expands as a result of trade.

4.2.4 Welfare Measure

The welfare of a representative worker can be represented by his expected indirect utility, $v(p_x, p_y, I)$, where I is the expected income of a worker. Here, v depends on the probability of the worker being employed and is given by $A[(1-u)w + r\bar{k}]p_x^{-\alpha}p_y^{-(1-\alpha)}$ where $I \equiv (1-u)w + r\bar{k}$. We measure the worker's welfare change by dU, where

$$dU \equiv \frac{dv}{(\partial v/\partial I)} = \left[\frac{\partial v/\partial p_x}{\partial v/\partial I}\right]dp_x + \left[\frac{\partial v/\partial p_y}{\partial v/\partial I}\right]dp_y + dI.$$

Next, we use the fact that $I \equiv (1-u)w + r\bar{k} = p_x z_x + p_y z_y$, and Roy's identities $-(\partial v/\partial p_x)/(\partial v/\partial I) = c_x$ and so on to obtain

$$dU = (1-\alpha)p^{-\alpha}(z_x - c_x)dp + \alpha\, p^{-(1+\alpha)}(c_y - z_y)dp + [p^{1-\alpha}dz_x + p^{-\alpha}dz_y], \tag{4.32}$$

recalling that $p_x^{\alpha}p_y^{1-\alpha} \equiv 1$. The first two terms of equation (4.32) give us the usual gains from the terms of trade improvement while the third term indicates the shift in the production possibilities curve resulting from the various shocks we study below. With the wage level equalised across all industries, we have well-behaved transformation curves. The latter, however, shift endogenously in response to variations in p through the effect of p on $1-u$.

In Figure 4.3, we illustrate, for a small open economy that exports the relatively labour-intensive good, the effect of free trade. In addition to the traditional gains from trade, notice that there is an outward shift of the production possibilities curve that occurs as a result of trade. For such a country, which, as we have argued characterises the situation of the East Asian economies of Hong Kong, Singapore, South Korea and Taiwan in the sixties and early seventies, the opportunity to trade raises the relative price of the labour-intensive good. Consequently, the real wage, measured in terms of either the import or export good, rises, leading workers to value their jobs more and thus expanding equilibrium employment.

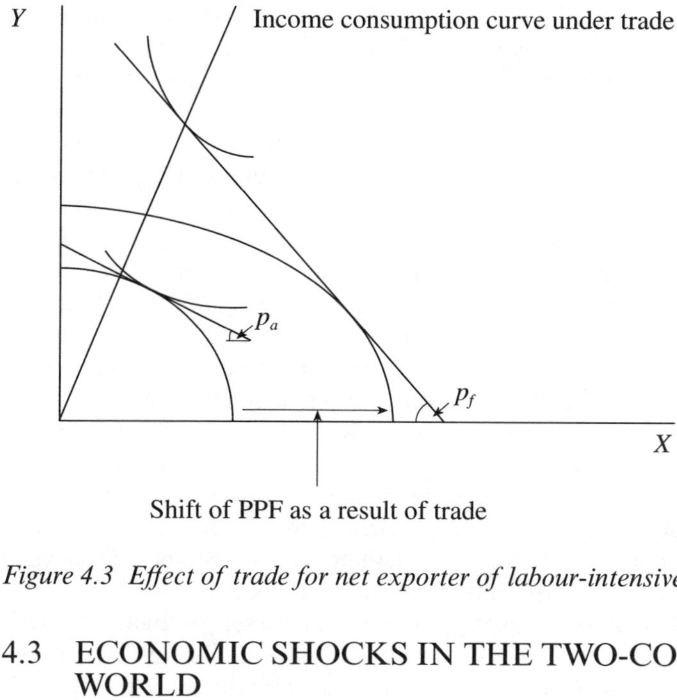

Figure 4.3 Effect of trade for net exporter of labour-intensive good

4.3 ECONOMIC SHOCKS IN THE TWO-COUNTRY WORLD

We apply the two-country model developed in the last section to the examination of the effects of economic shocks on the behaviour of the natural rates of unemployment and wages in the two countries. We ask how a technological catch-up in Home affects Foreign, how the integration of the former socialist economies affect Home and Foreign, and how protection in Foreign affects Home.

4.3.1 Harrod-neutral Technical Progress in Home

We now examine the effect of a technological catch-up taking the form of a level increase in the Harrod-neutral technical progress parameter across all industries in the relatively labour abundant country we identify as Home. We show that this unambiguously raises the equilibrium rate of unemployment of its trading partner.

Suppose that there is a positive Harrod-neutral technological shock across all industries in Home, that is, a rise in the parameter Λ. (In the survey of empirical work by Leamer and Levinsohn (1995), it is argued that when workers are more productive in one sector, they tend to be more productive across all sectors.) Competitive equilibrium requires that at any given relative goods price, the demand wage level that firms find it profitable to offer, should rise. The higher wage is consistent with a decline in the equilibrium rate of unemployment in Home at the original price vector. We refer to this as the 'primary effect' of the shock. At the given world terms of trade, there must, in fact, be a contraction in the world supply of good *Y* and an increase in the supply of good *X*. The increase in the world relative supply of good *X* drives down the relative price of good *X*, *p*. Appendix 4.1 shows the relevant derivative.

In terms of Figure 4.2, there is a downward shift in the RR_w schedule corresponding to a downward shift of *RR* and a downward shift of *LL* representing Home, implying a lower *p* in the new trading equilibrium. From the expressions, $1-u^*=\phi^*(p;\Lambda^*)$; $\phi^*_p>0$ and $1-u=\phi(p;\Lambda)$; $\phi_p>0$, $\phi_\Lambda>0$, we see that the equilibrium rate of unemployment in Foreign rises and Foreign real consumption wage declines although the effect in Home is ambiguous. This is because the increase in relative supply of good *X* in the world brings about a relative price change that tends to offset somewhat the expansionary impact of the positive technological shock taking place in Home. We term this the 'secondary effect'. In Foreign, there is a pure terms of trade effect, which depresses the wage level there via the Stolper–Samuelson channel, and results in a rise in the natural rate. Thus, a positive Harrod-neutral technological shock in Home that raises worker productivity across all sectors in the economy leads to a rise in Foreign's equilibrium unemployment despite a terms of trade improvement. The intuition for this result is that the rise in the Harrod-neutral measure of productivity amounts to an increase in the supply of productivity-adjusted labour supply. By Rybczynski theorem, this results in an excess supply of the relatively labour-intensive good, which depresses its international relative price. If Foreign is incompletely specialised in production, so that the Stolper–Samuelson channel is at work, this reduces the real value of wage earnings there, and raises the natural rate.

Let us now briefly consider what happens when relative factor endowments are sufficiently different that the capital abundant country is completely specialised in the production of the relatively capital-intensive good, good *Y*. The shock still leads to an improvement in Foreign's terms of trade. However, with Foreign producing only a single good, the decline in the world relative price of the relatively labour-intensive good does not produce a Stolper–Samuelson effect. Instead, the terms of trade improvement leads Foreign's workers to value their jobs more, and hence the natural rate is reduced. To see this formally, note that the no-shirking constraint in Foreign, under free trade, can be written as

$$A\left(\frac{w^*}{p_y}\right)^s\left(\frac{p_x}{p_y}\right)^{-\alpha} = \left\{1 + \frac{\rho}{g} + \frac{b}{g[1-(1-u^*)]}\right\}e,$$

while the demand wage is given by

$$\left(\frac{w^*}{p_y}\right)^d = \frac{\partial F_y(\bar{k}^*, e\Lambda^*(1-u^*))}{\partial(1-u^*)}.$$

In a diagram (not shown) with $1-u^*$ on the x-axis and w^*/p_y on the y-axis, the no-shirking constraint has the usual positive slope for a given relative price, $p \equiv p_x/p_y$, while the demand wage schedule is negatively sloped on account of diminishing returns to labour. A decline in p, which is a terms of trade improvement for Foreign, leads to a rightward shift of the wage curve. Consequently, the natural rate of unemployment declines in response to the shock emanating from Home. Thus the earlier result we obtained in the Ricardian model that an export-led growth in one country *must* benefit its trading partners is restored if Foreign is completely specialised in the production of the relatively capital-intensive good.

The welfare of the representative Foreign worker can be expressed as

$$dU^* = -(1-\alpha)p^{-\alpha}(c_x^* - z_x^*)dp - \alpha p^{-(1+\alpha)}(z_y^* - c_y^*)dp + [p^{1-\alpha}dz_x^* + p^{-\alpha}dz_y^*], \tag{4.33}$$

noting that under free trade, $p^* = p$. The first two terms are positive but the third term is negative if Foreign is incompletely specialised since the induced rise in equilibrium unemployment shifts in the Foreign transformation curve. However, all three terms will be positive if Foreign is completely specialised in the production of the relatively capital-intensive good.

4.3.2 Integration of Socialist Economies into World Market

Collins and Rodrik (1991, p. 68), in their statistical estimation, argue that the Eastern European economies and the countries of the former Soviet

Union are likely to be net exporters of agricultural goods and light manufactures and hence will compete with the middle-income developing economies, particularly the East Asian industrialising economies and the more industrialised Latin American countries. They argue that with the collapse of trade in the former Council for Mutual Economic Assistance (CMEA) markets, the former socialist economies will redirect their trade to the West, especially the European Union. The predicted reorientation of trade since 1989 has been confirmed (see Cooper and János Gács [1997]). We now show that when a third country that is the most labour abundant in the world economy joins the trading system, it raises the rates of unemployment in all the less labour abundant countries.

Suppose that the block of current and former socialist economies joins the world trading system. It can be seen that being the most labour abundant economy, it becomes the world net supplier of the relatively labour-intensive good. Continuing to assume identical and homothetic tastes in all countries, the world terms of trade are now determined by

$$p = \frac{\alpha \sum_j s_L^j z_y^j}{(1-\alpha) \sum_j s_L^j z_x^j}, \tag{4.34}$$

where s_L^j is country j's share of the world effective labour force. The new market-clearing p must be lower than that prevailing before the integration of the socialist economies into the world trading system. In terms of Figure 4.2, we would be able to draw a new RR_w schedule corresponding to the right-hand side of equation (4.34), which lies below the original RR_w.

Foreign, being the most capital abundant country, continues to be the world's net exporter of the relatively capital-intensive good, and enjoys a terms of trade improvement but suffers a rise in the natural rate and a decline in wage levels. In terms of equation (4.33), the first two terms are positive but the third bracketed term is negative. For Home, there are two possible equilibria. In one equilibrium, it remains a net exporter of the relatively labour-intensive good and hence suffers both a terms of trade deterioration as well as a rise in equilibrium unemployment. In terms of equation (4.32), all three terms are negative. On the other hand, it may be driven to be a net exporter of the relatively capital-intensive good while suffering a rise in unemployment.

To put the results of this sub-section in perspective, it needs to be pointed out that the influence on the world terms of trade resulting from the integration of the former socialist economies into the world economy depends upon its relative size, and that depends not on the relative size of its labour force in raw labour units but in productivity-adjusted units. Given that these former socialist economies are likely to be far behind the technological frontier determined by the high-income economies, it is plausible that they are economically small. Then their integration into the world economy based upon exporting relatively labour-intensive goods will lift up their real wage earnings and lower equilibrium unemployment without any discernible effect on the relatively more capital abundant countries.

4.3.3 Protection in Foreign

We study in the Heckscher–Ohlin framework the effects of unilateral protection in the labour-scarce country. Imposing a unilateral tariff, we show, raises the natural rate of unemployment in the labour abundant country. In the absence of the Metzler paradox, the protecting country experiences a decline in the natural rate of unemployment.

In the context of full-employment models, there is little validity in the argument that protection saves jobs. In the model examined here, where the natural rate of unemployment is no longer a constant but an endogenous variable that depends on the supply and demand conditions in the world economy, we see a channel through which protection can affect the world market-clearing relative goods price, which, in turn, can shift conditions to favour the demand for workers in the protecting country. Referring to our two-country model, we let Foreign, the capital abundant country, impose a tariff on good X, starting from an initial free trade situation, so that now $p^*_x = (1+\tau)p_x$, where τ is the *ad valorem* tariff rate. At the given world terms of trade, a rise in the domestic relative price of the relatively labour-intensive good drives up the wage level in Foreign thus stimulating employment. Also, z^*_x/z^*_y rises while c^*_x/c^*_y declines. An import tariff imposed in Foreign, therefore, leads to a decline in the world relative demand for good X and an increase in the world relative supply of good X. Accordingly, we experience a decline in the world relative price of good X. In Home, the effect is to cause a rise in the natural rate of unemployment; in Foreign, however, in the absence of the Metzler paradox, the domestic relative price has shifted so as to raise the wage levels. Foreign wages rise, as Stolper–Samuelson showed in 1941, reflecting an increase in the demand for labour but now there is also a decline in the natural rate of unemployment. Appendix 4.1 calculates the change in p.

The change in welfare of a representative worker in Foreign under protection is given by

$$dU^* = -(c^*_x - z^*_x)d[(1+\tau)p^{1-\alpha}] + (z^*_y - c^*_y)dp^{-\alpha} + [(1+\tau)p^{1-\alpha}dz^*_x + p^{-\alpha}dz^*_y] + d(\tau p^{1-\alpha}m^*_x), \qquad (4.35)$$

where $m_x^* \equiv c_x^* - z_x^*$ is Foreign's per capita import of good X and $I^* \equiv p_x^* z_x^* + p_y^* z_y^* + \tau p_x^* m_x^*$. (We also use the following relationships: $p^\alpha p_y^{1-\alpha} \equiv 1$, $p_y^* = p_y$ and $p_x^* = (1+\tau)p_x$.) The first term gives us (absent the Metzler paradox) the loss to consumers from paying a higher price for imports although the world relative price for imports is now lower; the second term gives the gains from terms of trade improvement; the third bracketed term gives us the outward shift of the transformation schedule resulting from a lower natural rate of unemployment, while the fourth term gives us the increase in tariff revenue. The third term captures the effect of the employment creating role of protecting a labour-intensive import-competing sector. The tariff imposed raises the real wage of workers, and shifts outwards the economy-wide demand for labour, which juxtaposed against the wage curve, implies a decline in equilibrium unemployment. This channel is absent in the traditional full-employment model.

4.4 CONCLUSION

In this chapter, we have incorporated a theory of the efficiency-wage labour market into an otherwise traditional Heckscher–Ohlin trade model. The result is that we have a tractable model with which to analyse the impact on equilibrium unemployment of free trade and economic shocks in a two-country world economy. In such a world economy, where informational imperfections characterise national labour markets, an incentive constraint taking the form of the no-shirking condition has to be satisfied. The equilibrium unemployment in each economy has to endogenously adjust in response to shocks to the global general-equilibrium system.

The reader would have recognised that the influence of trade on the real consumption wages of workers is crucial for predicting how trade affects the natural rate. In the Ricardian model studied in Chapter 3, the real export wage is unaffected by trade. However, when all countries become completely specialised in production under trade, the purchasing power of workers' pay is elevated by trade in all participating economies. Consequently, the no-shirking condition is satisfied at a lower equilibrium rate of unemployment in all trading nations. The Heckscher–Ohlin model delivers a different result. In this model, trade raises the relative price of the labour-intensive good in the labour abundant country but lowers it in the labour scarce country.[2] The Stolper–Samuelson linkage between the relative goods price and real factor rewards leads to the result that trade increases the real consumption wage of workers in the labour abundant country but reduces it in the labour scarce country regardless of the consumption pattern of workers. Consequently, the no-shirking condition is satisfied at a lower natural rate in the labour abundant country but at a higher natural rate in the labour scarce country.

There are two other channels, however, that are at work when nations trade, both being operative in an imperfectly competitive environment, which can lead *all* trading nations to experience a decline in the natural rate. In Chapter 5, we show that trade increases the degree of product-market competition in the sense of lowering the price-marginal cost mark-up. When this feature is incorporated into a factor proportions model, we show that despite the Stolper–Samuelson mechanism, the real consumption wage of workers in the labour scarce country could still rise due to the fact that trade enlarges the size of the market and so reduces the price-marginal cost mark-up. We show that this is translated into a rise of the real demand wage at a given relative goods price. Then in Chapter 6, we show, in a model where workers have a love for variety and there are scale effects, that trade leads to an increased range of differentiated intermediate products and differentiated consumer products. Via this channel, the increased market size that results from trade can lead to an increase in the measure of real consumption wage and so reduce the natural rate despite an adverse shift in the relative goods price. Trade in intermediate inputs also raises the marginal productivity of labour through an increase in diversity effect and works to offset the adverse relative goods price effect in the capital abundant country. Put another way, the recognition of the importance of intra-industry trade in the total volume of world trade suggests that the adverse shift in wage levels due to the Stolper–Samuelson channel could be offset by these other mechanisms that work to raise real wages in an enlarged market. It is noteworthy that over the period 1965–90, intra-industry trade grew as a share of the total trade of the four Newly Industrialising Countries, Hong Kong, Singapore, South Korea and Taiwan, which made up more than 50 per cent of total manufactured exports of all developing countries by the end of the eighties. For example, by 1990, intra-industry trade constituted over 40 per cent of Singapore's trade with the European Union. The corresponding figures for Hong Kong, South Korea and Taiwan were 37.9 per cent, 27.9 per cent and 30.1 per cent, respectively (see Chow and Kellman, 1993).

In this chapter, a number of positive predictions of the model have also been derived along with a characterisation of overall welfare effects in a two-country world. We showed that a technological catch-up taking the form of a level increase in the measure of Harrod-neutral technical progress across all industries in Home, the labour abundant country, unambiguously raises Foreign's equilibrium unemployment rate. In the traditional full-employment Heckscher–Ohlin trade model, this shock must unambiguously favour Foreign through the latter's improvement in its terms of trade. In our model with an endogenous natural rate, however, this welfare gain must be weighed against the welfare loss resulting from higher unemployment. This result also contrasts with that obtained in Chapter 3, where it was shown that technical advance in the export sector of Home must lower the natural rate of Foreign. The reason is that in the Ricardian model, the wage of the Foreign worker in terms of its own export good is a constant. Consequently, the technical advance in Home leads to a terms of trade improvement for Foreign, and that leads to a rise in real purchasing power of Foreign's workers and a decline in Foreign's natural rate. In the Heckscher–Ohlin model with an endogenous natural rate, the across-the-board technical advance also leads to a terms of trade improvement for Foreign. However, as the relative price movement takes the form of a cheapening of the relatively labour-intensive good, the Stolper–Samuelson relationship implies that the real returns to labour must decline in Foreign, which weakens work incentives, and so leads to a rise of the natural rate. However, we showed that if production is completely specialised in the two-country Heckscher–Ohlin model so that Foreign produces only the capital-intensive good, the terms of trade improvement that it enjoys as a result of the level increase in the measure of Harrod-neutral technical progress overseas must lead to a lower natural rate as predicted by the Ricardian model.

The integration of the block of socialist economies based upon exports of the labour-intensive good into the world market creates jobs for these former socialist economies but worsens job prospects for the less labour abundant countries. It is the relative abundance of labour in the block of former socialist economies, which implies that they become net-exporters of the relatively labour-intensive good, that is crucial for employment expansion under free trade. If Home remains a net exporter of the relatively labour-intensive good, it faces both a rise in unemployment as well as a terms of trade deterioration. Foreign, being the most capital abundant country, experiences a terms of trade improvement, though the decline in the relative price of the labour-intensive good leads to a fall in workers' real wage and hence a rise in the natural rate. Notice, however, that if the most capital abundant country is completely specialised in the production of the capital-intensive good, the integration of the most labour abundant country into the world trading system must lead to a decline in the natural rate in both the most labour abundant as well as the most capital abundant countries. Also, if the former socialist economies are economically small because they remain far behind the world technological frontier, their ability to export the relatively labour-intensive good will lift their real wage earnings and lower their natural rate without any discernible effects on their trading partners.

Finally, in the Heckscher–Ohlin model, unilateral protection of the relatively labour-intensive import-competing sector in Foreign lowers Foreign's natural unemployment rate but raises Home's natural unemployment rate. In contrast, we showed that in the Ricardian model of Chapter 3, although the imposition of unilateral tariffs brings about a terms of trade improvement in the protecting country, it nevertheless raises the protecting country's natural rate of unemployment. The difference in the results relies upon the fact that in the Ricardian model, the wage in terms of the export good is constant in the Ricardian model. By assuming that the tariff revenue is redistributed to all workers regardless of their employment status, the tariff rebates do not distort the incentive to shirk. As the constant real export wage translates into a lower wage in terms of the whole consumption basket, work incentives are weakened and so the protecting country experiences a rise in the natural rate. In contrast, in the Heckscher–Ohlin model, protection of the labour-intensive import-competing sector raises the relative price of the relatively labour-intensive good and, via the Stolper–Samuelson effect, works to make workers value their jobs more and so reduce the natural rate. If Foreign is completely specialised in the production of the relatively capital-intensive good, however, the Stolper–Samuelson effect will not be operative. If tariff revenues are distributed in a lump-sum manner to both employed and unemployed workers, the higher domestic relative price of the import good translates into a leftward shift of the wage curve in the employment rate–real product wage plane along an invariant demand-wage schedule. Then protection will also raise the natural rate of the protecting country as in the Ricardian model. In both the Heckscher–Ohlin and Ricardian models, protection by Foreign leads unambiguously to a rise of the natural rate in its trading partner.

NOTES

1. More generally, we can express the relevant share as

$$s_L = \frac{\Lambda \overline{L}}{\Lambda \overline{L} + \Lambda^* \overline{L}^*},$$

which reduces to $s_L = \overline{L}/(\overline{L} + \overline{L}^*)$ when technology is identical across countries. The influence of a country on the international terms of trade is large when its effective labour force size, that is, the labour force size adjusted for productivity, is large. In a multi-country world, a small open economy's share of the global effective workforce would be negligible and, under trade, that economy would be a price taker.

2. If we take into account the Leontief (1954) productivity adjustment and allow for the Harrod-neutral index of technology to differ across countries, it is a comparison between $\overline{k}/\Lambda$ and $\overline{k}^*/\Lambda^*$ that is relevant for predicting the direction of trade flows.

APPENDIX 4.1

1. The effect of a change in Λ on p is given by

$$\frac{dp}{d\Lambda}=\frac{\alpha}{1-\alpha}\left\{\frac{s_L[(\partial z_y/\partial(1-u))\phi_\Lambda+\partial z_y/\partial\Lambda]}{s_L z_x+(1-s_L)z_x^*}-\frac{[s_L z_y+(1-s_L)z_y^*]s_L[(\partial z_x/\partial(1-u))\phi_\Lambda+\partial z_x/\partial\Lambda]}{[s_L z_x+(1-s_L)z_x^*]^2}\right\}\frac{1}{\Delta},$$

where

$$\Delta\equiv 1-\frac{\alpha}{1-\alpha}\left\{\frac{s_L[\partial z_y/\partial p+(\partial z_y/\partial(1-u))\phi_p]}{[s_L z_x+(1-s_L)z_x^*]}+\frac{(1-s_L)[\partial z_y^*/\partial p+(\partial z_y^*/\partial(1-u^*))\phi_p^*]}{[s_L z_x+(1-s_L)z_x^*]}-\frac{[s_L z_y+(1-s_L)z_y^*]s_L[\partial z_x/\partial p+(\partial z_x/\partial(1-u))\phi_p]}{[s_L z_x+(1-s_L)z_x^*]^2}-\frac{[s_L z_y+(1-s_L)z_y^*](1-s_L)[\partial z_x^*/\partial p+(\partial z_x^*/\partial(1-u^*))\phi_p{}^*]}{[s_L z_x+(1-s_L)z_x^*]^2}\right\}.$$

The denominator, Δ, is positive but the numerator is negative.

2. The response of p to a rise in τ in Foreign is given by

$$\frac{dp}{d\tau}=\frac{\alpha}{1-\alpha}\left\{\frac{(1-s_L)[(\partial z_y^*/\partial(1-u^*))\phi_{p*}^*+\partial z_y^*/\partial p^*]p}{s_L z_x+(1-s_L)z_x^*}-\frac{[s_L z_y+(1-s_L)z_y^*](1-s_L)[(\partial z_x^*/\partial(1-u^*))\phi_{p*}^*+\partial z_x^*/\partial p^*]p}{[s_L z_x+(1-s_L)z_x^*]^2}\right\}\frac{1}{\Delta}-\left[\frac{(1-s_L)c_y^*}{s_L c_y+(1-s_L)c_y^*}\right]\frac{p}{\Delta},$$

where we evaluate the derivative at an initial free trade equilibrium with $\tau=0$, and we note that $p^*=(1+\tau)p$. The first term in the derivative gives the effect of the tariff in expanding the world relative supply of good X while the second term gives the effect of the tariff in contracting the world relative demand for good X at the original price vector. The total effect of the tariff is to cause a deterioration in the terms of trade as well as a rise in the equilibrium unemployment rate for Home.

5. International product–market competition, jobs and wages

5.1 INTRODUCTION

Is trade good for jobs?[1] Surprisingly, this is not a question that the bulk of trade theory is well poised to answer. The reason, as we have argued, is that conventional trade models – whether of the perfectly competitive or imperfectly competitive type – assume at the outset that full employment prevails. More accurately, the economy is assumed to be at the natural rate of unemployment – one that is treated for practical purposes as a constant and *invariant* to the international economic environment as well as economic policy. Yet this assumption of an exogenously determined equilibrium rate of unemployment seems at odds with the persistent rise of unemployment in many of the OECD countries in the past two and a half decades, especially in Western Europe, and the steady decline of unemployment in East Asia over the past quarter-century.

The persistent increase in the average jobless rate in the medium to long run has prompted various economists to develop theories of the endogenous movements of the equilibrium rate of unemployment. Layard, Nickell and Jackman (1991) develop a bargaining framework to explain the factors determining the natural rate of unemployment in Western Europe while Lindbeck and Snower (1988) develop an insider–outsider approach to the determination of the equilibrium unemployment rate. In Hoon and Phelps (1992), we apply an efficiency-wage story of labour turnover to provide a macroeconomic account of the shocks that can impinge on the natural rate. In broad terms, the view that has emerged is one that can be represented in a Marshallian employment rate–real wage diagram where two curves intersect to give the general-equilibrium determination of the natural rate of unemployment – an upward-sloping wage curve and a non-positively-sloped demand wage curve. Product–market developments and such shocks as higher payroll taxes to finance generous unemployment benefits can be analysed within this framework.

In this chapter, we adopt an endogenous natural rate framework to analyse the effects of international trade. We focus on one key aspect of trade that has been given prominence in the international trade literature of the eighties – the role of international trade in increasing the degree of product–market competition. As economies open up to international trade, there are pressures for the price–marginal cost mark-ups to decline. (See Markusen (1981) for an early theoretical analysis, Phelps (1991) for the effects of a unified European market in a customer markets model, and Levinsohn (1993) for an empirical test using Turkish industry-level data.) In a set-up where workers are prone to shirk on the job, and where monitoring workers' efforts is costly and imperfect, we study how the price–marginal cost mark-up adjusts to international competition and what that implies for the natural rate of unemployment and wage earnings for trading nations. This research can be thought of as a response to the challenge given by Professor Alan Blinder to international trade economists in his Richard T. Ely lecture to develop trade models that deal explicitly with unemployment (see Blinder, 1988).

The chapter is organised as follows. In Section 5.2, we develop the basic model with homogeneous labour as the single factor of production. Section 5.3 extends the model to include capital and thus introduces a role for different factor proportions to influence trade patterns while section 5.4 concludes.

5.2 THE BASIC MODEL

To capture the influence of trade on the price–marginal cost mark-up and the effect on the natural rate of unemployment without the complication brought about by different factor proportions, we develop in this section a model with homogeneous labour and two sectors – a constant-returns-to-scale competitive sector and an increasing-returns oligopolistic sector. As in Markusen (1981), firms in the non-competitive sector choose quantities in a Cournot–Nash fashion and, under international trade, sell in an integrated world market.

5.2.1 Autarkic Equilibrium

The competitive good, good Y, is produced using a Ricardian technology so we write $Y = a_y^{-1} e L_y$, where a_y is the labour input per unit of output coefficient and L_y gives the amount of labour employed in the competitive sector. Here, e is the effort level of an employed worker and takes the value of zero when the worker shirks and is a positive constant otherwise. In the equilibrium scenario that we will focus on, firms pay the incentive wage to induce non-shirking behaviour so that no worker shirks, though involuntary equilibrium unemployment results. Letting p_y be the price of good Y, perfect competition gives the price equal to unit cost condition, $p_y = we^{-1}a_y$. Hence,

$$w = \frac{ep_y}{a_y}. \tag{5.1}$$

Workers are assumed to possess identical Cobb–Douglas utility functions, denoted $c_x^{\alpha}c_y^{1-\alpha}$, $0<\alpha<1$, where c_x and c_y are the individual levels of consumption of the non-competitive good X and competitive good Y, respectively. With preferences assumed to be homothetic, we can derive a map of community indifference curves. Denoting the community income as I, utility maximisation subject to I yields the following aggregate demand functions for the non-competitive and competitive goods, respectively:

$$C_x = \frac{\alpha I}{p_x}, \tag{5.2}$$

$$C_y = \frac{(1-\alpha)I}{p_y}. \tag{5.3}$$

Firm i in the oligopolistic sector faces the following problem: Maximise

$$p_x\beta e[l_{xi} - f] - wl_{xi}$$

subject to

$$\sum_{i=1}^{n}\beta e[l_{xi} - f] = \frac{\alpha I}{p_x},$$

where $x_i = \beta e[l_{xi} - f]$. Here, x_i is the output of firm i, $e\beta$ is the marginal physical productivity of labour, l_{xi} is the number of employed workers at firm i, f is the fixed cost incurred in setting up the firm in labour units, and w is the wage. The total output of the non-competitive good is $\sum_{i=1}^{n} x_i$, and firm i behaves in a Cournot–Nash fashion, treating its rivals' outputs as given. The number of firms, n, is endogenously determined by the free entry and exit condition and we assume that it always exceeds one. Integer problems are ignored.

Choosing the optimal number of workers to hire (or equivalently the optimal level of output to produce), treating its rivals' outputs as given, we obtain the following first-order condition:

$$p_x\left[1 - \frac{s_i}{\epsilon_x}\right]e\beta = w, \tag{5.4}$$

where s_i is the share of firm i in total industry output, and ϵ_x is the elasticity of market demand for the non-competitive good X. The left-hand side of equation (5.4) gives the marginal revenue product perceived by firm *i* of employing an additional worker while the right-hand side gives the marginal factor cost of hiring an additional worker. In a symmetric equilibrium, we write

$$p_x\left[1-\frac{1}{n}\right]e\beta = w, \tag{5.5}$$

since $s_i = n^{-1}$ and we use the fact that with a Cobb–Douglas utility function, the elasticity of demand, ϵ_x, is one. Noting that $w[e\beta]^{-1}$ gives the marginal cost of producing an additional unit of output, the price–marginal cost mark-up is given by

$$\frac{\text{Price}}{\text{Marginal Cost}} = \left[1-\frac{1}{n}\right]^{-1}. \tag{5.6}$$

In addition to choosing the optimal number of workers to hire, all firms in this economy have to tackle the problem of shirking by their employed workforce. We assume that firms use wages as an incentive device to induce their workers not to shirk. As in Shapiro and Stiglitz (1984), we model shirking as a zero-one decision. In general equilibrium, the wage level is driven up far enough so that each employed worker does not shirk. However, with the wage level driven up above the market-clearing level, equilibrium unemployment results. To derive the incentive-wage condition, we turn to an analysis of the worker's decision whether or not to shirk. Following the procedure in Chapter 4, we obtain our aggregate no-shirking constraint (NSC) or incentive-wage condition:

$$\frac{Aw}{p_x^{\alpha}p_y^{1-\alpha}} = \left\{1+\frac{\rho}{g}+\frac{b}{g[1-(1-u)]}\right\}e, \tag{5.7}$$

where $A \equiv \alpha^{\alpha}(1-\alpha)^{1-\alpha}$; ρ is the subjective discount rate; b is the separation rate (due to exogenous reasons other than shirking) and is the same for all firms; and g is the probability of being caught if shirking (also exogenous). The NSC says that the lower the rate of unemployment, and thus the shorter the expected time spent in unemployment if fired, the more tempting it is to shirk. To avoid this, firms must offer a higher wage level. The incentive wage, that is, the minimum wage the firm has to offer to induce non-shirking behaviour by its employed workforce, therefore, rises as the unemployment rate declines.

Turning to the free entry and exit condition, we obtain

$$p_x\left[1-\frac{f}{l_x}\right]e\beta = w. \tag{5.8}$$

Equating equation (5.8) to equation (5.5), we obtain

$$l_x = nf, \tag{5.9}$$

which implies that

$$x = \beta e[n-1]f. \tag{5.10}$$

Next, the condition that the value of spending on good *Y* be equal to the value of production of good *Y* can be written as

$$p_y\left[\frac{eL_y}{a_y}\right] = (1-\alpha)(1-u)w\overline{L},$$

where $\overline{L}$ is the labour force size. Using equation (5.1), this simplifies to

$$L_y = (1-\alpha)(1-u)\overline{L}. \tag{5.11}$$

The adding-up constraint that the sum of labour allocation across the two sectors be equal to the number of employed workers can be expressed as

$$nl_x + L_y = (1-u)\overline{L}.$$

Using equations (5.9) and (5.11), this condition reduces to

$$n = \sqrt{\frac{\alpha[1-u]\overline{L}}{f}}. \tag{5.12}$$

We graph the relationship between the number of oligopolistic firms, n, and the employment rate, $1-u$, as *NN* in Figure 5.1.

Next, equating equations (5.1) and (5.5), we obtain an expression for the relative price, $p \equiv p_x/p_y$:

$$p = \frac{1}{\beta a_y[1-n^{-1}]}. \tag{5.13}$$

Noting that with the normalisation, $p_x^{\alpha}p_y^{1-\alpha} \equiv 1$, we can write $p_x = p^{1-\alpha}$, and we can use equation (5.13) in equation (5.5) to obtain an expression for the wage:

$$w = e\beta^{\alpha}a_y^{-(1-\alpha)}\left[1-\frac{1}{n}\right]^{\alpha}. \tag{5.14}$$

Using equation (5.13) in equation (5.7), we obtain another relationship that gives the n that is required at each $1-u$ to induce non-shirking behaviour:

$$A\beta^{\alpha}a_y^{-(1-\alpha)}\left[1-\frac{1}{n}\right]^{\alpha} = 1 + \frac{\rho}{g} + \frac{b}{g[1-(1-u)]}. \tag{5.15}$$

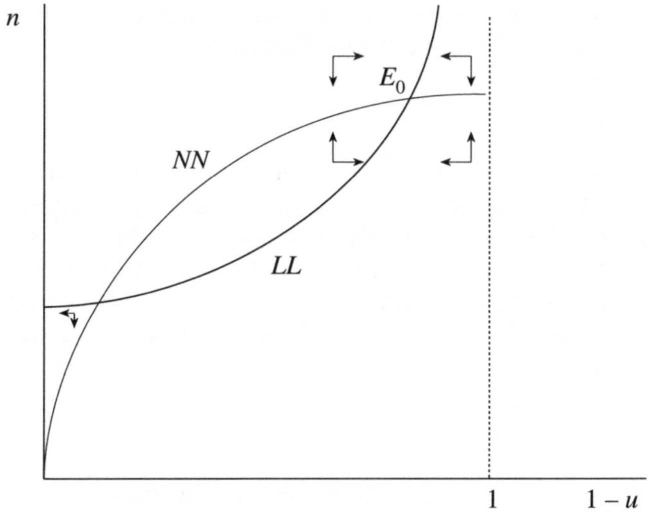

Figure 5.1 Equilibrium in a closed economy

This relationship is depicted as *LL* in Figure 5.1.

Looking at Figure 5.1, we notice that there are two intersections. It can be argued, however, that the intersection corresponding to the lower employment rate is unstable. Recall that at each level of $1-u$, the corresponding n that lies on the *NN* schedule corresponds to zero profit. By raising n above the zero-profit level, the profitability of producing good X declines (to a negative value), prompting the exit of firms from the industry. This is indicated by the arrows pointing in a downward direction above the *NN* schedule. Conversely, below the *NN* schedule, firms in the oligopolistic industry are making supernormal profits, prompting the entry of new firms into the industry. The arrows below the *NN* schedule accordingly point upwards. Turning to the *LL* schedule, recall that at each level of $1-u$, a point on the schedule gives the number of firms that is required to produce an incentive-compatible wage. At any point above the *LL* schedule, the value of n gives rise to a wage that is higher than the minimum level that is required to induce non-shirking behaviour. With the wage premium paid to workers increased, workers now value their jobs more at each rate of unemployment. Firms are therefore encouraged to raise their pace of hiring without inducing more shirking. Consequently, above the *LL* schedule, we draw arrows pointing in a rightward direction. On the other hand, at any point below the *LL* schedule, the value of n is below the level required to induce non-shirking behaviour. As employers find more rampant shirking, they cut back on their pace of hiring. Accordingly, below the *LL* schedule, we draw arrows pointing in a leftward direction.

5.2.2 Free Trade Equilibrium

Consider a world economy in which there are *N* countries, each with identical tastes and technology with only the size of the domestic labour force possibly differing. Each oligopolistic firm faces an integrated world market for its output, so arbitrage ensures that the prices of goods are equated globally. Since every country faces the same relative price, *p*, and each firm faces rivals both domestically and in the rest of the world, the firm-level employment is now given by

$$l_x = n_w f, \tag{5.16}$$

where $n_w = \sum_{j=1}^{N} n_j$. The incentive-wage condition in each country is given by

$$A\beta^{\alpha} a_y^{-(1-\alpha)} \left[1 - \frac{1}{n_w}\right]^{\alpha} = 1 + \frac{\rho}{g} + \frac{b}{g[1-(1-u)]}, \tag{5.17}$$

noting that since wage levels are equated under free trade, the equilibrium employment rate is also equalised across countries. The condition that the global demand for good *Y* is equal to its global supply gives rise to

$$\sum_{j=1}^{N} L_{yj} = (1-\alpha)(1-u) \sum_{j=1}^{N} \overline{L}_j. \tag{5.18}$$

Using the individual countries' adding-up constraints and equation (5.18), we obtain

$$n_w = \sqrt{\frac{\alpha[1-u]\sum_{j=1}^{N} \overline{L}_j}{f}}. \tag{5.19}$$

Figure 5.2 depicts the global conditions represented by equations (5.17) and (5.19). Notice that the *LL* schedule remains unchanged in Figures 5.1 and 5.2. There is, however, an upward shift of the *NN* schedule (to *NN'*) as the home country opens up to international trade. An illustrative transition path is shown in Figure 5.2, showing the movement from an autarkic to a free trade position. Thus, we obtain the following result: When a country opens up to international trade with other nations, every country enjoys a decline in the equilibrium rate of unemployment as the price-marginal cost mark-up declines. Under trade, each economy faces a larger number of firms in the integrated world market than the number it faces in autarky. The real consumption wage also rises in every country.

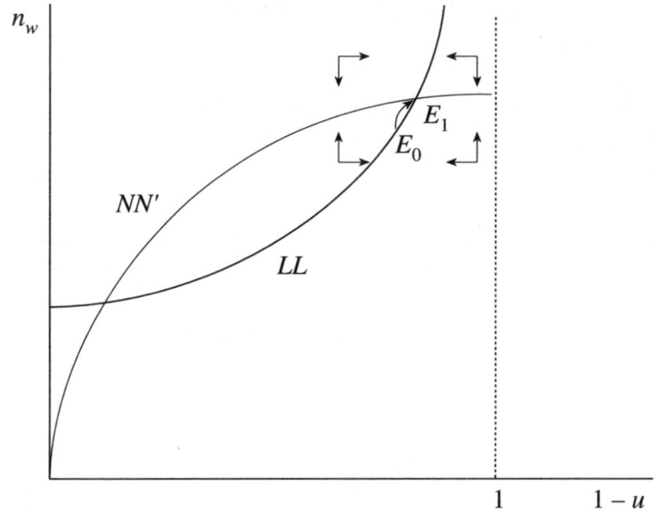

Figure 5.2 Effects of trade

The essential mechanism that is at work here is the pressure that international trade places on product-market competition. As the price-marginal cost mark-up declines (see equation (5.6)), firms pay a higher wage in terms of the good that workers produce. This creates an incentive effect as workers find the cost of being caught shirking is increased. In general equilibrium, each economy, under free trade, is capable of supporting a lower natural rate of unemployment without inducing more shirking or, more generally, without weakening job attachments. It is clear that the smaller the country in question is relative to the size of the global labour force – a city-state such as Singapore, for example – the larger are its gains from trade since the greater is the incentive effect of trade. The expected utility of a worker is given by $(1-u)Aw$, using the normalisation $p_x^{\alpha} p_y^{1-\alpha} \equiv 1$, which can be expressed as $(1-u)Ae\beta^{\alpha}a_y^{-(1-\alpha)}[1-n^{-1}]$. Since free trade raises both $1-u$ and n, the welfare of each worker is improved as a result of trade.

We also obtain the following result: Although every firm expands its size, the total number of firms in each economy under trade might actually increase because each country's natural rate of unemployment declines under trade. The number of firms in economy j is given by $n_j = [(1-u_j)\alpha\bar{L}]/l_{xj}$, with $l_{xj} = n_w f$. Since $1-u_j$ rises along with the increase in l_{xj}, it is possible that n_j also rises.

5.3 INTRODUCING DIFFERENT FACTOR PROPORTIONS

We consider a departure from the basic model in this section by analysing the effects of trade when factor proportions also play a role. To do so, we set up a minimal model with two factors of production – capital and labour.

We suppose that producing good Y, the competitive good, requires both capital and labour. We let its production function be given by $Y=(eL_y)^{\eta}K_y^{1-\eta}$, $0<\eta<1$, where L_y is employment of labour in sector Y and K_y is capital allocated to sector Y. Competitive behaviour implies

$$w=\eta e^{\eta}p_y k_y^{1-\eta}, \tag{5.20}$$

$$r=(1-\eta)e^{\eta}p_y k_y^{-\eta}, \tag{5.21}$$

where $k_y \equiv K_y/L_y$ and r is the rental rate. From equations (5.20) and (5.21), we obtain

$$k_y=\left[\frac{1-\eta}{\eta}\right]\left[\frac{w}{r}\right]. \tag{5.22}$$

In the non-competitive sector, we assume that capital is the fixed factor, and so the fixed cost of setting up a firm is rf_k. The optimal choice of employment gives rise to

$$w=p_x\left[1-\frac{1}{n}\right]e\beta. \tag{5.23}$$

Free entry and exit now imply $p_x x-[wx/e\beta]=rf_k$. Using equation (5.23), the zero-profit condition gives

$$x=e\beta[n-1]\left[\frac{r}{w}\right]f_k. \tag{5.24}$$

Noting that $l_x=x/(e\beta)$, we also have

$$l_x=[n-1]\left[\frac{r}{w}\right]f_k. \tag{5.25}$$

Capital intensity in the non-competitive sector is given by

$$k_x \equiv \frac{f_k}{l_x}=\left[\frac{1}{n-1}\right]\left[\frac{w}{r}\right]. \tag{5.26}$$

Equating equations (5.20) and (5.23), we obtain

$$p \equiv \frac{p_x}{p_y} = \left[1 - \frac{1}{n}\right]^{-1}\left[\frac{\eta}{\beta}\right]e^{-(1-\eta)}k_y^{1-\eta}. \tag{5.27}$$

Noting that with our normalisation, $p_x^{\alpha}p_y^{1-\alpha} \equiv 1$, we can write $p_y = p^{-\alpha}$, and using equations (5.22) and (5.27), we obtain

$$w = \eta\left[1 - \frac{1}{n}\right]^{\alpha}\left[\frac{\eta}{\beta}\right]^{-\alpha}\left[\frac{1-\eta}{\eta}\right]^{(1-\alpha)(1-\eta)}\left[\frac{w}{r}\right]^{(1-\alpha)(1-\eta)}e^{\eta+\alpha(1-\eta)}. \tag{5.28}$$

Under the assumption that rental income is divided equally among all workers (employed and unemployed), equation (5.7) continues to hold. Using equation (5.28) in equation (5.7), we obtain

$$\eta A\left[1 - \frac{1}{n}\right]^{\alpha}\left[\frac{\eta}{\beta}\right]^{-\alpha}\left[\frac{1-\eta}{\eta}\right]^{(1-\alpha)(1-\eta)}\left[\frac{w}{r}\right]^{(1-\alpha)(1-\eta)} =$$

$$\left\{1 + \frac{\rho}{g} + \frac{b}{g[1-(1-u)]}\right\}e^{(1-\eta)(1-\alpha)}. \tag{5.29}$$

The adding-up constraints are given by

$$(1-u)\overline{L} = nl_x + L_y, \tag{5.30}$$

$$\overline{K} = nf_k + K_y. \tag{5.31}$$

Using equations (5.30) and (5.31) along with (5.22) and (5.26) gives an expression for n in terms of w/r:

$$n = \frac{\overline{L}\left[\left(\frac{\overline{K}}{\overline{L}}\right) - \left(\frac{1-\eta}{\eta}\right)(1-u)\left(\frac{w}{r}\right)\right]}{\left[1 - \frac{(n-1)(1-\eta)}{\eta}\right]f_k}. \tag{5.32}$$

Finally, using the condition that the total demand for good Y is equal to the supply of good Y, we obtain, after some tedious steps,

$$\frac{w}{r} = \left\{\frac{(1-\alpha)\eta + \alpha\left[1 - \frac{1}{n}\right]}{(1-\alpha)(1-\eta) + \frac{\alpha}{n}}\right\}\left[\frac{\overline{K}}{(1-u)\overline{L}}\right]. \tag{5.33}$$

From equation (5.33), notice that the product $(1-u)(w/r)$ is a function of n, given $\overline{K}/\overline{L}$ and the other parameters. Using $(1-u)(w/r)$ in equation (5.32), we have an equation in the one unknown n. Substituting the solution of n into equation (5.29), we obtain an upward-sloping schedule in Figure 5.3, giving the w/r required to satisfy the incentive-wage constraint at each $1 - u$. We depict this schedule as LL in Figure 5.3. Further substituting the solution of n into equation (5.33), we derive a hyperbola denoted GG in Figure 5.3. The intersection gives us the equilibrium rate of employment.

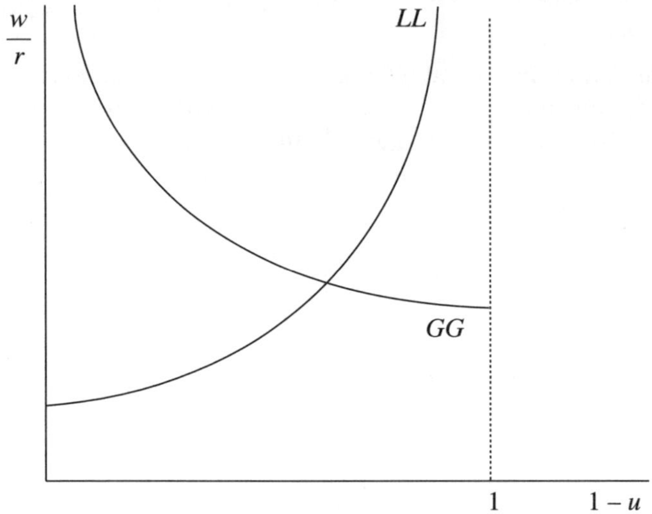

Figure 5.3 Model with capital and labour

It is now straightforward to analyse the effects of trade. For simplicity, let us first consider trade among nations exhibiting identical factor proportions. Notice from Figure 5.3 that an increase in n shifts the hyperbola upwards and the no-shirking constraint downwards. Consequently, whenever an economy faces a larger number of firms in an integrated world market than under autarky, trade itself leads to a decline in the natural rate of unemployment. Thus we obtain the following result: in a trading world in which all countries exhibit identical factor proportions, free trade leads to a decline in the natural rate of unemployment for all countries if the number of firms in the integrated world market is larger than the number of firms each country faces in autarky.

To see how the number of firms in an integrated world economy is determined, it is useful to study the effects of an increase in the size of the labour force. If the non-competitive sector is relatively capital-intensive, the numerator and denominator of equation (5.32) are both positive. Notice that an increase in n raises the product $(1 - u)(w/r)$ and so reduces the numerator of the right-hand side of equation (5.32) but also reduces the denominator of the right-hand side of equation (5.32). Hence it is ambiguous whether an increase in n raises or lowers the value of the right-hand side of equation (5.32). If the non-competitive sector is relatively labour-intensive, a similiar ambiguity arises. To understand why the ambiguity arises, note that we can express n as

$$n = \frac{\overline{L}[(1-u) - (L_y/\overline{L})]}{l_x}.$$

An increase in n affects the three terms, $1-u$, $L_y/\overline{L}$ and l_x. Firstly, $1-u$ increases in response to the increase in n. Next, via a Rybczynski effect, the rise in $1-u$ induces a more than proportionate increase in $L_y/\overline{L}$ if the non-competitive sector is relatively more capital-intensive but a decline in $L_y/\overline{L}$ if the non-competitive sector is relatively labour-intensive. From equation (5.25), we also see that an increase in n, *ceteris paribus*, raises l_x. Moreover, the change in w/r brought about by the rise in n has an indirect effect on $L_y/\overline{L}$ and l_x.

If we impose the restriction that the right-hand side of equation (5.32) is either negatively sloped or, if it is positively sloped, that it is flatter than a forty-five degree line in Figures 5.4(a) and 5.4(b), an increase in $\overline{L}$ unambiguously leads to an increase in n. Since trade here, in effect, works like an increase in the size of the labour force, the result is that every trading nation in such a world experiences a decline in the natural rate of unemployment.

Next, suppose that there are two countries, Home and Foreign, that open up to trade with one another. We denote a Foreign variable with an asterisk. Suppose that Foreign is relatively capital abundant in the sense that $\overline{K}^*/\overline{L}^* > \overline{K}/\overline{L}$. Specifically, we let $\overline{L} = (2-\gamma)\,\overline{L}^*$ and $\overline{K} = \gamma\overline{K}^*$, where $0<\gamma<1$. With identical tastes and technology, we have an equalisation of wages and unemployment rates under free trade. Consequently, the free trade wage–rental ratio is given by

$$\left(\frac{w}{r}\right)_{FT} = \left\{\frac{(1-\alpha)\eta + \alpha\left[1 - \dfrac{1}{n_w}\right]}{(1-\alpha)(1-\eta) + \dfrac{\alpha}{n_w}}\right\}\left[\frac{1+\gamma}{3-\gamma}\right]\left[\frac{\overline{K}^*}{(1-u)\overline{L}^*}\right], \tag{5.34}$$

recalling that the equilibrium unemployment rates are equalised under free trade. The incentive-wage condition under free trade in both countries is given by

$$\eta A\left[1 - \frac{1}{n_w}\right]^{\alpha}\left[\frac{\eta}{\beta}\right]^{-\alpha}\left[\frac{1-\eta}{\eta}\right]^{(1-\alpha)(1-\eta)}\left[\frac{w}{r}\right]_{FT}^{(1-\alpha)(1-\eta)} =$$

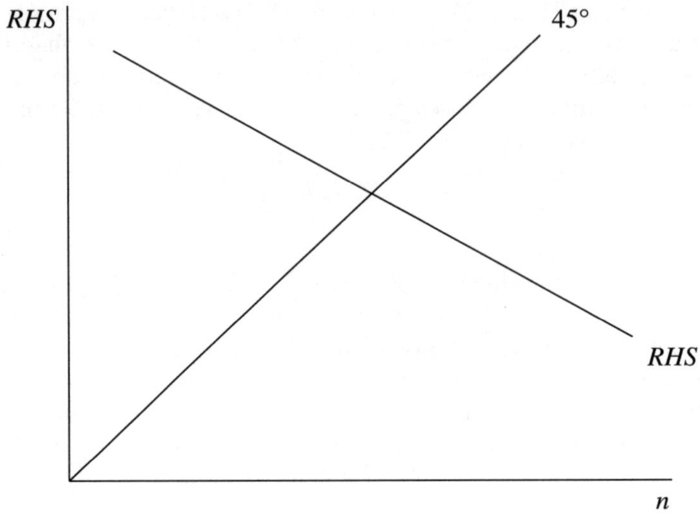

Figure 5.4(a) Downward-sloping RHS

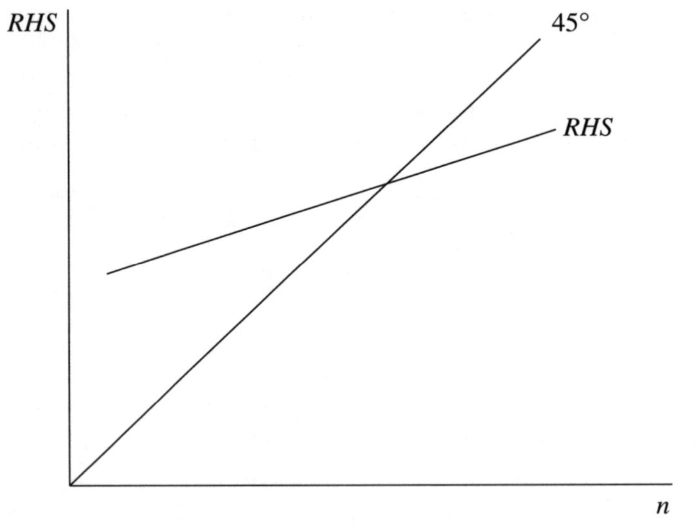

Figure 5.4(b) Upward-sloping RHS

$$\left\{1 + \frac{\rho}{g} + \frac{b}{g[1 - (1 - u)_{FT}]}\right\} e^{(1-\eta)(1-\alpha)}. \quad (5.35)$$

Finally, the number of firms under free trade is given by

$$n_w = \frac{(3 - \gamma)\,\overline{L}^*\left[\left(\frac{1 + \gamma}{3 - \gamma}\right)(\overline{K}^*/\overline{L}^*) - \left(\frac{1 - \eta}{\eta}\right)(1 - u)_{FT}\left(\frac{w}{r}\right)_{FT}\right]}{\left[1 - \frac{(n_w - 1)(1 - \eta)}{\eta}\right] f_k}. \quad (5.36)$$

What is the effect of trade? We see that if the number of firms in the integrated world market is larger than the number prevailing in autarky in each economy, Home's unemployment rate unambiguously declines. This is because both the increased degree of product–market competition as well as the relative abundance of labour work to lift up the real earnings of workers in Home under trade and hence induces greater work effort. On the other hand, the unemployment rate in Foreign can either decline or rise. This is because there are two opposing forces at work. The increased product-market competition raises real wage earnings but the relative abundance of capital works to depress real wage earnings. Only if the first channel dominates, will Foreign also experience a decline in unemployment under trade. Thus we obtain the following result: Under free trade, the relatively labour abundant country experiences a decline in the natural rate of unemployment. On the other hand, the natural rate of unemployment in the relatively capital abundant country can either decline or rise.

This result stands in contrast to the result we obtained in Chapter 4 and Hoon (1991). There, in a two-country Heckscher–Ohlin model, we showed that trade between a relatively capital abundant country with a labour abundant country *necessarily* leads to a decline in the natural rate of unemployment in the labour abundant country but a rise in the natural rate of unemployment in the capital abundant country. Here, we show that when trade reduces the price–marginal cost mark-up, it is possible that both countries experience a decline in the natural rate of unemployment despite differences in factor proportions.

5.4 CONCLUDING REMARKS

Econometric studies by Levinsohn (1993) and Harrison (1994) based upon firm-level data demonstrate that international trade increases product–market competition in the sense that the price–marginal cost mark-ups have declined as a result. In this chapter, we have extended this insight to the general equilibrium and demonstrated that the result of increased product–market competition is to lead to a rise in workers' real consumption wages and consequently a decline in the amount of joblessness. Under the condition that trade results in an increase in the number of firms competing in an integrated world market compared to the autarkic number of firms in each trading nation, all countries experience a decline in the natural rate of unemployment if factor proportions do not differ. When factor proportions differ, the relatively labour abundant country must experience a decline in the natural rate both on account of increased product–market competition as well as on account of a relative factor abundance that favours a rise in the wage–rental ratio under trade. Although the relatively capital abundant country faces an unfavourable movement of the wage–rental ratio on account of its relative capital abundance, the increased product–market competition offsets the adverse effect so that both countries can experience a decline in the natural rate despite differences in the factor proportions.

The latter result is of some practical importance in the light of the integration of many developing countries and former socialist economies into the world trading system. As the developed countries tend to be relatively more capital abundant, an analysis based on a perfectly competitive Heckscher–Ohlin world as in Hoon (1991) implies that trade with the relatively labour-abundant developing countries would raise the amount of joblessness in the developed world. The contribution of this chapter is to show that in an imperfectly competitive world, where firms have some degree of market power, trade works through another channel – by raising the degree of product–market competition – to decrease the amount of joblessness in all trading countries. Empirically, Helpman and Krugman (1989) make the point that more than half of world trade is in manufactured goods, where markets are often oligopolistic rather than competitive. Rodrik (1988), on the other hand, has argued that scale economies and product–market imperfections tend to be pervasive in developing countries. This additional channel suggests that further liberalisation of trade among developed countries themselves can help to promote a more competitive international integrated market, which helps the developed countries absorb the shock of importing the goods from the developing world that are exported based on differences in factor proportions.

There is also a fiscal channel through which trade can work to further contract the equilibrium unemployment rate that can be noted. Since payroll taxes are typically imposed to finance unemployment benefits in many of the OECD countries, we see that trade, through reducing the number of unemployed, allows the payroll tax rate to be reduced. At each wage that the firm can afford to pay, the reduced payroll tax rate translates into a higher take-home pay. With the take-home pay increased relative to the unemployment benefits, workers are induced to value their jobs more and to shirk less. Consequently, equilibrium employment is expanded through this channel as well.

NOTES

1. This chapter draws on Hoon (2000b).

6. Scale economies, jobs and wages

6.1 INTRODUCTION

As we argued earlier, one channel leading to a decline in the volume of joblessness in the East Asian economies of Hong Kong, Singapore, South Korea and Taiwan in the sixties and seventies as they launched their industrialisation programme based upon selling into the world market was the ability to sell relatively labour-intensive goods. The increased demand for labour-intensive goods translated into a higher wage that firms could afford to pay. Juxtaposed against the wage curve, this implies a decline in the natural rate. Apart from this channel, one benefit of economic integration must surely be the availability both of the wide range of consumer products as well as intermediate inputs through trade. As we pointed out before, intra-industry trade has become an increasing share of total East Asian trade flows.

This chapter focuses on the role played by intra-industry trade in shaping jobs and wages. It illustrates that when internal scale economies determine international specialisation, and factor proportions do not differ, all countries participating in international trade gain from participating in the global economy. Gains from trade arise from a wider variety of consumption goods being made available to workers (see Hoon, 1994) and from a wider range of inputs being made available in production (see Matusz, 1996). The availability of the wider range of inputs raises the marginal productivity of labour used in production while the wider range of consumption goods satisfies a need for variety in consumption. The former channel raises the firms' demand wage while the latter leads to a lowering of the incentive wage necessary to elicit optimal effort. Both channels lead to a lowering of the natural rate in all trading countries. Even when factor proportions differ, it is possible for trade to decrease the natural rate in both the labour abundant as well as the labour scarce countries because the enlarged market size due to trade counteracts the adverse effect of the relative price shift on real wages in the labour scarce country.

The chapter is organised as follows. In Section 6.2, we develop a pure intra-industry trade model with intermediate inputs and love for variety. Section 6.3 introduces differing factor proportions while Section 6.4 concludes.

6.2 MODEL WITH INTERMEDIATE INPUTS AND LOVE FOR VARIETY

6.2.1 Worker's Decision

We assume there are N completely identical economies initially in autarky. There are $\overline{L}$ number of workers in each economy with every worker being risk neutral and having the utility function $c_y^{1-\alpha}[\int_0^{n_x} c_{xj}^{\theta} dj]^{\alpha/\theta} - e$, $0 \leq \theta \leq 1$, where e is the exogenously specified positive level of effort exerted (when the worker does not shirk), c_y is the consumption of a homogeneous final good, c_{xj} is the consumption of the j-th differentiated consumption good, and n_x is the number of differentiated consumption goods. With symmetry, we can write the utility function as $n_x^{\alpha/\theta} c_y^{1-\alpha} c_x^{\alpha}$. We note that each differentiated consumption good will be consumed in the same quantity, c_x. The elasticity of substitution between any two differentiated consumption goods is given by $(1-\theta)^{-1}$, and is greater than unity by our assumption that θ lies between zero and one. The requirement for an elasticity of substitution larger than one is needed in order to make sense of monopolistic competition since each individual differentiated good firm must face an elasticity of demand greater than one. The utility function also captures clearly the notion that variety is valued *per se*. Suppose that n_x varieties of the differentiated product are available to consumers, and they are equally priced at p_x, using the homogeneous good as the numeraire. Then whatever the spending level, E, it is optimal to purchase all varieties in equal quantities. With α being the share of total expenditure devoted to the differentiated products, the utility level achieved from a total expenditure level E is $An_x^{\alpha(1-\theta)/\theta} E^{1-\alpha}[E/p_x]^{\alpha}$ where $A \equiv \alpha^{\alpha}(1-\alpha)^{1-\alpha}$. Hence, for a given level of spending and a given price for the available varieties, welfare increases as the number of varieties becomes larger. This is the sense in which variety is valued *per se*.

Solving a worker's decision problem regarding whether or not to shirk, and focusing on the steady state, it is straightforward to obtain the requirement that

$$An_x^{\frac{\alpha(1-\theta)}{\theta}} p_x^{-\alpha} w = \frac{(a+b+\rho)e}{g} + e, \tag{6.1}$$

where good Y, the competitive final good is chosen as the numeraire. Here, a is the job acquisition rate, b is the exogenously given probability of job separation for reasons other than shirking, g is the exogenously given probability of being caught if shirking, and ρ is the rate of time discount. In a steady state, the flow into employment is equal to the flow out of employment. Thus, we have

$$a = \frac{bL}{\bar{L} - L}. \tag{6.2}$$

Substituting equation (6.2) into equation (6.1), we obtain our aggregate no-shirking constraint (NSC):

$$An_x^{\frac{\alpha(1-\theta)}{\theta}} p_x^{-\alpha} w = \left[1 + \frac{b+\rho}{g} + \frac{b(1-u)}{gu}\right]e, \tag{6.3}$$

where $1-u$ is the employment rate. The NSC says that the lower the rate of unemployment, and thus the shorter the expected time spent in unemployment if fired, the less costly it is to be fired and the more tempting it is to shirk. To avoid this, firms must pay a higher real wage. Another very interesting result from equation (6.3) is that the larger the number of differentiated consumption products available in the economy, the lower the real wage that has to be offered by the firm to induce non-shirking behaviour for a given level of employment. The worker has a love for variety but he can afford to buy the whole range of differentiated products available for consumption only when he is employed. (We assume that there are no unemployment benefits. However, even if there are unemployment benefits and they are only a fraction of the wage, workers will value their jobs more when the number of product varieties increases.) When the economy has a wider range of differentiated products available in the market, the opportunity cost to the worker of losing his job is higher, and thus the less incentive there is to shirk. Accordingly, at a given rate of employment, the lower is the real wage that has to be offered by the firm to induce non-shirking behaviour.

6.2.2 Production Side

We suppose that the single homogeneous consumption good is assembled from differentiated intermediate inputs or 'producer services'. Competitive firms produce the single homogeneous good according to a technology given by

$$Y = \left[\int_0^{n_m} m_j^{\mu} dj\right]^{\frac{1}{\mu}}, \; 0 \leq \mu \leq 1, \tag{6.4}$$

where m_j denotes the input of intermediate good or service j into the manufacture of the final homogeneous good. Notice that for a given number of differentiated inputs, the technology exhibits constant returns to scale. That is, if a firm manufacturing the homogeneous final good were to increase its use of every available input in the same proportion, then output would increase proportionately. With perfect competition in the supply of the homogeneous final good, the unit cost of production is equal to the price (being unity since we take the homogeneous final good as numeraire), that is,

$$1 = \left[\int_0^{n_m} p_{mj}^{\frac{-\mu}{1-\mu}} dj \right]^{\frac{-(1-\mu)}{\mu}}. \tag{6.5}$$

Using Shephard's lemma, the derived demand for input i by a firm selling Y units of the homogeneous final good is given by

$$m_i = \frac{p_{mi}^{\frac{-1}{1-\mu}} Y}{\left[\int_0^{n_m} p_{mj}^{\frac{-\mu}{1-\mu}} dj \right]^{\frac{-(1-\mu)}{\mu}}}. \tag{6.6}$$

Turning to the problem faced by an intermediate input firm, the supplier of input i maximises profits given by

$$p_{mi} m_i - w[f_m + (e\beta_m)^{-1} m_i],$$

where we assume that to produce a differentiated input of the amount m_i requires a labour input of $f_m + (e\beta_m)^{-1} m_i$. Here, f_m is the fixed cost in labour units and can be interpreted as the usual product development cost, and $e\beta_m$ is the marginal product of labour in the intermediate input sector. Also, p_{mi} is the intermediate input price in terms of the homogeneous final good and w is the real wage in terms of the same numeraire. The first-order condition from solving the differentiated input firm's maximisation problem is

$$w = \mu p_m e\beta_m, \tag{6.7}$$

where the elasticity of demand for the input is given by $(1-\mu)^{-1}$. (We leave out the subscript i as we assume symmetry.) With free entry and exit of firms in the differentiated intermediate input sector, excess profits will be competed away, implying a price equal to average cost, that is,

$$p_m = \left[\frac{f_m}{m} + \frac{1}{e\beta_m} \right] w. \tag{6.8}$$

Using this equation with the differentiated input firm's first-order condition, we obtain

$$m = \frac{\mu e\beta_m f_m}{(1-\mu)}. \tag{6.9}$$

Note that the assumption of a CES production function results in the equilibrium size of each differentiated input firm being a constant.

Correspondingly, the employed size of the labour force at each firm is a constant, given by

$$l_m = \frac{f_m}{1-\mu}. \tag{6.10}$$

Next, turning to the problem faced by a firm selling a differentiated consumption good, the supplier of variety i maximises profits given by

$$p_{xi}x_i - w[f_x + (e\beta_x)^{-1}x_i],$$

where we assume that to produce a differentiated product of the amount x_i requires a labour input of $f_x + (e\beta_x)^{-1}x_i$. Here, f_x is the fixed cost in labour units and can be interpreted as the usual product development cost, and $e\beta_x$ is the marginal product of labour in the differentiated product sector. Also, p_{xi} is the differentiated product price in terms of the homogeneous final good and w is the real wage in terms of the same numeraire. The first-order condition from solving the differentiated product firm's maximisation problem is

$$w = \theta p_x e\beta_x, \tag{6.11}$$

where the elasticity of demand for the differentiated product is given by $(1-\theta)^{-1}$. (We leave out the subscript i as we assume symmetry.) With free entry and exit of firms in the differentiated product sector, excess profits will be competed away, implying a price equal to average cost, that is,

$$p_x = \left[\frac{f_x}{x} + \frac{1}{e\beta_x}\right]w. \tag{6.12}$$

Using this equation with the differentiated product firm's first-order condition, we obtain

$$x = \frac{\theta e\beta_x f_x}{(1-\theta)}. \tag{6.13}$$

Note that the assumption of a CES utility function results in the equilibrium size of each differentiated product firm being a constant. Correspondingly, the employed size of the labour force at each firm is a constant, given by

$$l_x = \frac{f_x}{1-\theta}. \tag{6.14}$$

6.2.3 General Equilibrium

In the general equilibrium, we require that the goods markets clear. We can express this using the relationship that the marginal rate of substitution in consumption is equal to the relative price and setting total demands for final goods to total supplies. Thus,

$$p_x = \left[\frac{\alpha}{1-\alpha}\right]\left[\frac{n_m^{\frac{1}{\mu}} m}{n_x x}\right]. \tag{6.15}$$

From the condition that the price of the homogeneous final good is equal to the unit cost, we have (assuming symmetry), that

$$p_m = n_m^{\frac{(1-\mu)}{\mu}}. \tag{6.16}$$

Using equation (6.16) in equation (6.7), we obtain

$$w = \mu e \beta_m n_m^{\frac{(1-\mu)}{\mu}}, \tag{6.17}$$

which shows that the real wage in terms of the homogeneous final good is increasing in the number of varieties of intermediate inputs.

Using equation (6.17) in equation (6.11), we obtain

$$p_x = \left[\frac{\mu}{\theta}\right]\left[\frac{\beta_m}{\beta_x}\right] n_m^{\frac{(1-\mu)}{\mu}}. \tag{6.18}$$

Noting the equilibrium values of m and x given by equations (6.9) and (6.13), respectively, and using equation (6.18), we have

$$n_x = \left[\frac{\alpha}{1-\alpha}\right]\left[\frac{1-\theta}{1-\mu}\right]\left[\frac{f_m}{f_x}\right] n_m. \tag{6.19}$$

This gives us a linear relationship between n_x and n_m. We plot the relationship as a positively-sloped schedule in Figure 6.1.

The other general equilibrium condition requires that the total demand for labour in the aggregate equals the equilibrium supply of labour. This can be expressed as

$$n_m l_m + n_x l_x = (1-u)\bar{L}. \tag{6.20}$$

Using the expressions for the constant sizes of the differentiated input and differentiated product, respectively, we obtain

$$\left[\frac{f_m}{1-\mu}\right] n_m + \left[\frac{f_x}{1-\theta}\right] n_x = (1-u)\bar{L}. \tag{6.21}$$

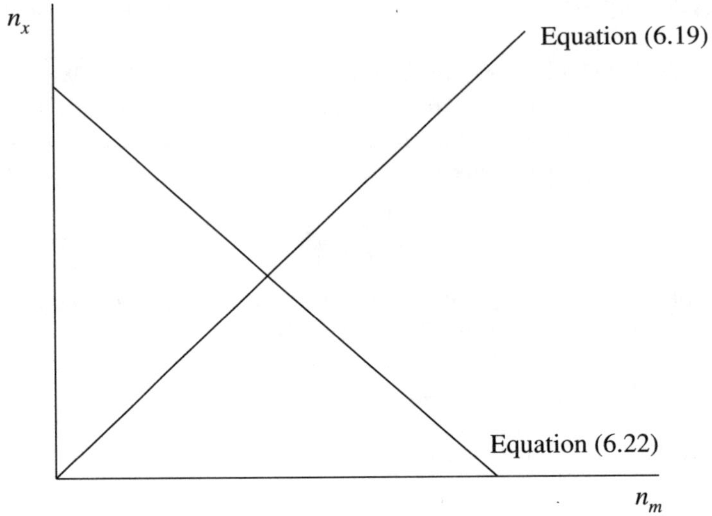

Figure 6.1 Equilibrium in full-information model

To understand what this relationship says, it helps to ask what the condition will be in a full information model. In that case, we would set the right-hand side of the relationship simply to $\overline{L}$, that is,

$$\left[\frac{f_m}{1-\mu}\right]n_m + \left[\frac{f_x}{1-\theta}\right]n_x = \overline{L}. \tag{6.22}$$

In that case, the schedule in Figure 6.1 would simply be linear and negatively sloped. The relationship says that with a fixed labour force, an increase in the number of intermediate good firms (each with a constant employed labour force) must result in a decrease in the number of differentiated product firms (each also with a constant employed labour force).

What is the effect of international trade in the full information model? In this model, as in Krugman (1979), we can think of international trade simply as an enlargement of the labour force. In this world economy of N number of identical economies, the right-hand side of equation (6.22) above is increased to $N\overline{L}$. Consequently, we see that the equilibrium values of n_m and n_x both rise. Recalling the expression for the equilibrium real wage in equation (6.17), we see that w is increased. Since $w/p_x = \theta\beta_x$, a constant, it follows also that the real consumption wage is raised. Consumer welfare is raised both on account of the higher real wage as well as a wider variety of differentiated products. The worker's consumer welfare would be given by $An_x^{\alpha(1-\theta)/\theta}e[\mu\beta_m]^{1-\alpha}n_m^{(1-\alpha)(1-\mu)/\mu}[\theta\beta_x]^{\alpha}$.

The crucial new aspect of the efficiency-wage perspective is that workers respond to the new incentives afforded by trade. In particular, as equation (6.3) shows, the higher real consumption wage and the wider variety of consumption goods available make workers value their jobs more and hence lead to a lower natural rate of unemployment. Formally, equating the demand wage to the supply wage, the labour–market equilibrium locus is represented by the following equation:

$$An_x^{\alpha(1-\theta)/\theta}[\mu\beta_m]^{1-\alpha}n_m^{(1-\alpha)(1-\mu)/\mu}[\theta\ \beta_x]^{\alpha}=\left[1+\frac{b+\rho}{g}+\frac{b(1-u)}{gu}\right]. \quad (6.23)$$

From equation (6.23), we can write $1-u=\Psi(n_x, n_m)$; $\Psi_1>0$; $\Psi_2>0$. Using this in equation (6.21), which gives the labour constraint, we have a second equation in terms of n_m and n_x. Since an increase in n_m raises the real wage and stimulates equilibrium employment, it is potentially possible that the labour constraint schedule is positively sloped in a diagram like Figure 6.1. However, so long as it is not as steep as the positively-sloped linear relationship given by equation (6.19), trade must lead to a decline in the natural rate. The welfare of a worker can be expressed as his expected utility, which depends on the probability of gaining employment. This is given by $(1-u)An_x^{\alpha(1-\theta)/\theta}e[\mu\beta_m]^{1-\alpha}n_m^{(1-\alpha)(1-\mu)/\mu}[\theta\beta_x]^{\alpha}$. Free trade not only expands the range of varieties available for consumption and raises the real wage but also lowers the equilibrium rates of unemployment in all participating economies.

6.3 INTRODUCING CAPITAL

To simplify the analysis, we now abstract from an intermediate input sector. We suppose that producing good Y, the competitive good, requires both capital and labour. We let its production function be given by $Y=(eL_y)^{\eta}K_y^{1-\eta}$, $0<\eta<1$, where L_y is employment of labour in sector Y and K_y is capital allocated to sector Y. Competitive behaviour implies

$$w=\eta e^{\eta}p_y k_y^{1-\eta}, \quad (6.24)$$

$$r=(1-\eta)e^{\eta}p_y k_y^{-\eta}, \quad (6.25)$$

where $k_y\equiv K_y/L_y$ and r is the rental rate. From equations (6.24) and (6.25), we obtain

$$k_y=\left[\frac{1-\eta}{\eta}\right]\left[\frac{w}{r}\right]. \quad (6.26)$$

In the monopolistically competitive sector which produces the horizontally differentiated consumption good, we assume that capital is the fixed factor, and so the fixed cost of setting up a firm is rf_k. The optimal choice of employment gives rise to

$$w = p_x \theta \, e\beta_x. \tag{6.27}$$

Free entry and exit now imply $p_x x - [wx/e\beta_x] = rf_k$. Using equation (6.27), the zero-profit condition gives

$$x = e\beta_x \left[\frac{\theta}{1-\theta}\right]\left[\frac{r}{w}\right] f_k. \tag{6.28}$$

Noting that $l_x = x/(e\beta_x)$, we also have

$$l_x = \left[\frac{\theta}{1-\theta}\right]\left[\frac{r}{w}\right] f_k. \tag{6.29}$$

Capital intensity in the monopolistically competitive sector is given by

$$k_x \equiv \frac{f_k}{l_x} = \left[\frac{1-\theta}{\theta}\right]\left[\frac{w}{r}\right]. \tag{6.30}$$

Equating equations (6.24) and (6.27), we obtain

$$p \equiv \frac{p_x}{p_y} = \left[\frac{1}{\theta}\right]\left[\frac{\eta}{\beta_x}\right] e^{-(1-\eta)} k_y^{1-\eta}. \tag{6.31}$$

Now, using the normalisation, $p_x^{\alpha} p_y^{1-\alpha} \equiv 1$, we can write $p_x = p^{1-\alpha}$, and using equations (6.26) and (6.31), we obtain

$$w = n_x^{\alpha\left(\frac{1-\theta}{\theta}\right)} \eta A \theta^{\alpha} \left[\frac{\eta}{\beta_x}\right]^{-\alpha} \left[\frac{1-\eta}{\eta}\right]^{(1-\alpha)(1-\eta)} \left[\frac{w}{r}\right]^{(1-\alpha)(1-\eta)} e^{\eta + \alpha(1-\eta)}. \tag{6.32}$$

Under the assumption that rental income is divided equally among all workers (employed and unemployed), the labour–market equilibrium locus is characterised by

$$n_x^{\alpha\left(\frac{1-\theta}{\theta}\right)} \eta A \theta^{\alpha} \left[\frac{\eta}{\beta_x}\right]^{-\alpha} \left[\frac{1-\eta}{\eta}\right]^{(1-\alpha)(1-\eta)} \left[\frac{w}{r}\right]^{(1-\alpha)(1-\eta)} =$$

$$\left\{1 + \frac{\rho}{g} + \frac{b}{g[1-(1-u)]}\right\} e^{(1-\eta)(1-\alpha)}. \tag{6.33}$$

The adding-up constraints are given by

$$(1-u)\bar{L} = n_x l_x + L_y, \tag{6.34}$$

$$\bar{K} = n_x f_k + K_y. \tag{6.35}$$

Using equations (6.34) and (6.35) along with equations (6.26) and (6.30) gives an expression for n_x in terms of w/r:

$$n_x = \frac{\bar{L}\left[\left(\frac{\bar{K}}{\bar{L}}\right) - \left(\frac{1-\eta}{\eta}\right)(1-u)\left(\frac{w}{r}\right)\right]}{\left[1 - \left(\frac{\theta}{1-\theta}\right)\frac{(1-\eta)}{\eta}\right]f_k}. \tag{6.36}$$

Finally, using the condition that the total demand for good Y is equal to the supply of good Y, we obtain, after some tedious steps,

$$\frac{w}{r} = \left\{\frac{(1-\alpha)\eta + \alpha\theta}{(1-\alpha)(1-\eta) + \alpha(1-\theta)}\right\}\left[\frac{\bar{K}}{(1-u)\bar{L}}\right]. \tag{6.37}$$

From equation (6.37), notice that the product $(1-u)(w/r)$ is a function of $\bar{K}/\bar{L}$ and the other parameters. Using $(1-u)(w/r)$ in equation (6.36), we have an equation in the one unknown n_x. Substituting the solution of n_x into equation (6.33), we obtain an upward-sloping schedule in Figure 6.2, giving the w/r required to satisfy the incentive-wage constraint at each $1-u$. We depict this schedule as LL in Figure 6.2. From equation (6.37), we derive a hyperbola denoted GG in Figure 6.2. The intersection gives us the equilibrium rate of employment.

It is now straightforward to analyse the effects of trade. For simplicity,

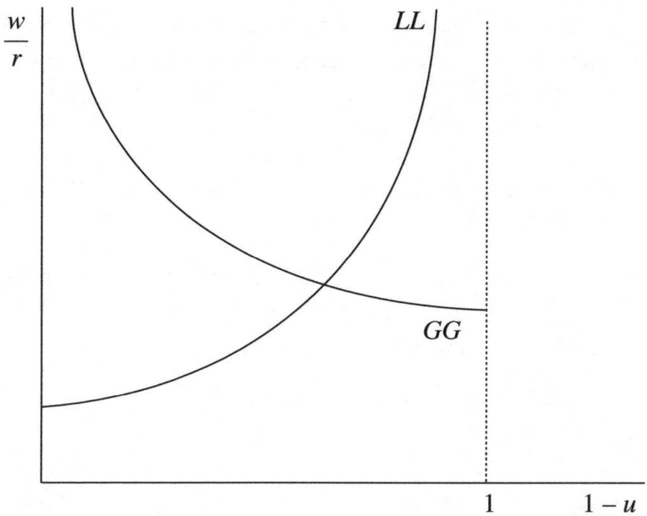

Figure 6.2 Equilibrium with capital and labour

let us first consider trade among nations exhibiting identical factor proportions. Notice from Figure 6.2 that an increase in n_x does not affect the hyperbola but shifts the no-shirking constraint downwards. Consequently, whenever an economy faces a larger number of firms in an integrated world market than under autarky, trade itself leads to a decline in the natural rate of unemployment. We obtain the following result: In a trading world in which all countries exhibit identical factor proportions, free trade leads to a decline in the natural rate of unemployment for all countries if the number of firms in the integrated world market is larger than the number of firms each country faces in autarky.

Can we say unambiguously that under free trade workers indeed face a larger number of differentiated products? The answer is yes. To see how the number of firms in an integrated world economy is determined, it is useful to study the effects of an increase in the size of the labour force. If the monopolistically competitive sector is relatively capital-intensive, the numerator and denominator of equation (6.36) are both positive. (In the reverse factor intensity case, both the numerator and denominator of equation (6.36) are negative.) Notice that an increase in n_x does not affect the product $(1-u)(w/r)$ and so, as we can observe from equation (6.36), an increase in $\overline{L}$ unambiguously raises n_x. Since trade here, in effect, works like an increase in the size of the labour force, the result is that under trade each worker faces a wider variety of consumption goods and consequently every trading nation in such a world experiences a decline in the natural rate of unemployment.

Next, suppose that there are two countries, Home and Foreign, that open up to trade with one another. We denote a Foreign variable with an asterisk. Suppose that Foreign is relatively capital abundant in the sense that $\overline{K}^*/\overline{L}^* > \overline{K}/\overline{L}$. Specifically, we let $\overline{L}=(2-\gamma)\,\overline{L}^*$ and $\overline{K}=\gamma\overline{K}^*$, where $0<\gamma<1$. With identical tastes and technology, we once again have an equalisation of wages and unemployment rates under free trade. Consequently, the free trade wage–rental ratio is given by

$$\left(\frac{w}{r}\right)_{FT}=\left\{\frac{(1-\alpha)\eta+\alpha\theta}{(1-\alpha)(1-\eta)+\alpha(1-\theta)}\right\}\left[\frac{1+\gamma}{3-\gamma}\right]\left[\frac{\overline{K}^*}{(1-u)_{FT}\overline{L}^*}\right]. \tag{6.38}$$

The incentive-wage condition under free trade is given by

$$n_w^{\alpha\left(\frac{1-\theta}{\theta}\right)}\eta A\theta^{\alpha}\left[\frac{\eta}{\beta_x}\right]^{-\alpha}\left[\frac{1-\eta}{\eta}\right]^{(1-\alpha)(1-\eta)}\left[\frac{w}{r}\right]_{FT}^{(1-\alpha)(1-\eta)}=$$

$$\left\{1+\frac{\rho}{g}+\frac{b}{g[1-(1-u)_{FT}]}\right\}e^{(1-\eta)(1-\alpha)}. \tag{6.39}$$

Finally, the number of firms under free trade is given by

$$n_w = \frac{(3-\gamma)\,\overline{L}^*\left[\left(\frac{1+\gamma}{3-\gamma}\right)(\overline{K}^*/\overline{L}^*) - \left(\frac{1-\eta}{\eta}\right)(1-u)_{FT}\left(\frac{w}{r}\right)_{FT}\right]}{\left[1-\left(\frac{\theta}{1-\theta}\right)\frac{(1-\eta)}{\eta}\right]f_k}. \quad (6.40)$$

What is the effect of trade? We see that if the number of firms in the integrated world market is larger than the number prevailing in autarky in each economy, Home's unemployment rate unambiguously declines. This is because both the increased range of products available under trade as well as the relative abundance of labour work to lift up the utility value of real earnings of workers in Home and hence induces greater work effort. On the other hand, the unemployment rate in Foreign can either decline or rise. This is because there are two opposing forces at work. The increased range of product varieties stimulates work effort but the relative abundance of capital works to depress real wage earnings. Only if the first channel dominates will Foreign also experience a decline in unemployment under trade. We obtain the following result: Under free trade, the relatively labour abundant country experiences a decline in the natural rate of unemployment. On the other hand, the natural rate of unemployment in the relatively capital abundant country can either decline or rise.

Again, this result stands in contrast to the result obtained in Hoon (1991) and Chapter 4. There, in a Heckscher–Ohlin model, trade between a relatively capital abundant country with a labour abundant country *necessarily* leads to a decline in the natural rate of unemployment in the labour abundant country but a rise in the natural rate of unemployment in the labour scarce country. Here, we show that when trade increases product diversity, it is possible that *both* countries experience a decline in the natural rate of unemployment despite differences in factor proportions.

6.4 CONCLUSION

This chapter has applied the modern theory of the natural rate of unemployment to the study of the impact of international trade on unemployment. We obtained the result that free trade in a world of pure intra-industry trade reduces the equilibrium rate of unemployment for each of the participating economies. The model focuses on the role of love for variety and increased specialisation of intermediate products to generate the result that free trade expands the employment rate. The central idea is that when workers have a love for variety and when production relies on intermediates produced under monopolistic competition, the availability of a wider range of differentiated consumer and producer goods through international trade raises the opportunity cost of shirking since an unemployed worker suffers a loss in his purchasing power. Even when factor proportions differ, it is possible that the increase in market size due to trade raises the real earnings of workers and lowers the natural rate in all trading nations. The benefits of trade highlighted here – where both worker-consumers and firms enjoy product diversity by buying from the world market – are especially large for small countries, such as the East Asian economies. From this point of view, one factor acting to reduce the amount of joblessness in these economies when they chose to launch into an export-oriented industrialisation strategy in the sixties is that the ability of workers to buy products from the whole world with their pay made holding on to a job more worthwhile, hence lowering wage pressure. Simultaneously, the firms operating in these economies could benefit from an international division of labour in the use of intermediate inputs, which acted to raise labour demand. Consequently, the natural rate fell in these economies.

The analysis here may also throw light on the fact that the Western European economies saw historically low unemployment rates in the two decades or so after the Second World War as the world economy returned to more unhindered trade that it knew before the interwar period. On top of this, important steps were taken to liberalise trade among the European economies themselves in the formation of the European Community in 1957. As is well-known, the bulk of trade among the European economies was based upon product differentiation and scale economies, and not comparative advantage. Based upon the framework developed in this chapter, such trade must reduce the amount of joblessness of all the trading nations. There may also have been a more dynamic aspect to the favourable influence of trade on joblessness based upon the empirical findings of Coe, Helpman and co-authors (see Coe and Helpman, 1995; Coe, Helpman and Hoffmaister, 1997; and Bayoumi, Coe and Helpman, 1996) that there are important international R&D spillover effects. According to this hypothesis, increased trade linkages enabled individual European economies to benefit from R&D undertaken by their trading partners. Most importantly, trade with the US – the leader defining the knowledge frontier – in the early postwar years enabled the European economies to experience rapid total factor productivity growth as they moved closer to the knowledge frontier. The rapid productivity growth encouraged firms to raise hiring and so shift out labour demand, while the sprint of total factor productivity relative to the non-human wealth level of workers, substantially diminished as a result of the war, led to a reduction of wage pressures. Consequently, unemployment in Europe fell to unusually low numbers.

7. Trade, high-wage jobs and the wage gap

7.1 INTRODUCTION

After the collapse of world trade during the interwar years, the two decades that followed have been characterised by growing international integration. This is especially true for the Western European economies. Ben-David (1993), in particular, has argued that income convergence there has been facilitated by the high degree of trade integration among the industrialised countries. One aspect of the trade pattern among these economies that has been highlighted is the dominance of intra-industry trade. For example, Krugman (1995, p. 340) cites the following figures for the trade of European Union countries: Taken individually, the average trade share is 28.0 per cent in 1990. However, more than 60 per cent of their merchandise trade is with each other. If the European Union is taken as a unit, its merchandise trade with the external world is only 9 per cent of GDP. (Katz and Summers (1989) have also stressed the importance of intra-industry trade in the US trade flows.)

Following the work of Doeringer and Piore (1971), there is also a large empirical literature that documents the presence of inter-industry wage differentials that are stable over time and across space. In particular, apparently identical workers earn higher wages in the primary sector than in the secondary sector, making a distinction between good and bad jobs analytically meaningful. Kenneth Judd, in the general discussion of Katz and Summers (1989) published in the Brookings papers, has noted that the primary sector is monopolistically competitive, being characterised by high price–cost ratios but zero excess profits.

In this chapter, we draw together these empirical facts to show that integration among industrial economies leads to the expansion of good jobs in all participating countries. In addition, we show that intra-industry trade also leads to a narrowing of the wage gap. The combination of an expansion of good jobs along with a narrowing wage gap is a property not found in the literature. For example, in the oft-cited paper of Bulow and Summers (1986), which generates an endogenous wage gap via a shirking story, international trade leads either to an expansion of good jobs along with a rising wage gap or a decline in the number of good jobs along with a declining wage gap depending upon whether the trading country ends up as a net exporter or net importer of the high-wage good.[1] When trade leads, say, to more high-wage jobs, the cost to a worker of dismissal from being caught shirking is reduced thus necessitating a higher wage gap to enforce worker discipline. We show that in an intra-industry trade model, trade raises the stake in holding a good job due to a love for variety effect. This makes possible an expansion of employment in the primary sector together with a reduced wage gap. We show also that when trade reduces the price–marginal cost mark-up, an expansion of primary sector jobs can take place along with a reduced wage gap. Our results within an imperfectly competitive framework, therefore, turn on its head the popular supposition that globalisation widens the wage gap.

The chapter is organised as follows. In Section 7.2, we develop a model where scale economies give rise to specialisation in the production of a range of differentiated consumer goods. We then explore a model of international product–market competition in Section 7.3. Finally, in Section 7.4, we develop a two-sector *competitive* model with a dual labour market structure, where trade expands the number of good jobs in the economy that ends up as the net exporter of the primary sector good while widening the wage gap, and contracts the primary sector while narrowing the wage gap in the economy that ends up as the net importer of the primary sector good. A striking result we obtain here is that differences in absolute productivities across countries can form the basis for international trade. Moreover, contrary to popular fears that trade by the advanced country with developing economies will cause it to lose good jobs, the competitive model predicts that under free trade the advanced country ends up being the net exporter of the primary sector good and so increases the number of good jobs under trade.

7.2 MODEL EXHIBITING PRODUCT DIVERSITY

There are two sectors in this economy initially under autarky: a monopolistically competitive primary sector, called sector X, which produces a differentiated range of products that enter workers' utility functions, and a secondary sector, which produces a competitive good, called sector Y. The consumer's utility function is given by $n_x^{\alpha/\theta} c_y^{1-\alpha} c_x^{\alpha}$, $0<\alpha, \theta<1$, under symmetry. Here, n_x is the number of differentiated products, and c_i; $i=x,y$ is consumption of good i. The elasticity of substitution between any two differentiated products is equal to $(1-\theta)^{-1}$. Choosing the competitive good

Y as numeraire so $p_y \equiv 1$, the indirect utility function for a worker with a job in the primary sector and therefore earning w_x is $An_x^{\alpha(1-\theta)/\theta} p_x^{-\alpha} w_x$, where $A \equiv \alpha^{\alpha}(1-\alpha)^{1-\alpha}$. We just replace w_x by w_y to obtain the indirect utility function of a worker employed in the secondary sector.

Jobs in the primary sector are of a responsible nature that require monitoring (which are imperfect) whereas no supervision problem arises in a job in the secondary sector. The problem solved by a worker employed in the primary sector leads to the asset equation,

$$\rho V_{xn} = An_x^{\alpha(1-\theta)/\theta} p_x^{-\alpha} w_x - e + b(V_y - V_{xn}), \tag{7.1}$$

where V_{xn} is the expected lifetime discounted utility if the worker employed in the primary sector does not shirk, and V_y is the expected lifetime discounted utility if he works in the secondary sector. Here, ρ is the discount rate, e is the effort level, which takes the value of zero if the worker shirks and is a positive constant otherwise, and b is probability of job loss due to exogenous reasons other than for being caught shirking. If the worker shirks, his expected lifetime discounted utility follows

$$\rho V_{xs} = An_x^{\alpha(1-\theta)/\theta} p_x^{-\alpha} w_x + (b+g)(V_y - V_{xs}), \tag{7.2}$$

where g is the probability of being caught if shirking. For a worker not to shirk, we require that $V_{xn} \geq V_{xs}$, so that

$$An_x^{\alpha(1-\theta)/\theta} p_x^{-\alpha} w_x \geq \rho V_y + \frac{(\rho + b + g)e}{g}. \tag{7.3}$$

The value V_y follows the following asset equation, assuming that the worker achieves the indirect utility $An_x^{\alpha(1-\theta)/\theta} p_x^{-\alpha} w_y$ if employed in the secondary sector, and zero utility if unemployed:

$$\rho V_y = \left[\frac{L_y}{\bar{L} - L_x}\right] [An_x^{\alpha(1-\theta)/\theta} p_x^{-\alpha} w_y - e] + a(V_{xn} - V_y), \tag{7.4}$$

where we assume that any worker who leaves the primary sector has the probability $L_y/(\bar{L} - L_x)$ of employment in the secondary sector. Here, $\bar{L}$ is the size of the fixed labour force and L_i; $i = x,y$ denotes total employment in sector i. The alternative is to be unemployed. (We assume that there are no unemployment benefits.)

Given that $V_{xn} = V_{xs}$ holds in equilibrium, and solving, using the resulting expresssion for V_y and substituting for a, the rate of obtaining a job in the primary sector, with the formula, $bL_x = a(\bar{L} - L_x)$, we arrive at the no-shirking-constraint (NSC):

$$An_x^{\alpha(1-\theta)/\theta}p_x^{-\alpha}w_x = \left[\frac{L_y}{\bar{L}-L_x}\right](An_x^{\alpha(1-\theta)/\theta}p_x^{-\alpha}w_y - e)$$

$$+e+\left[\frac{b\bar{L}}{\bar{L}-L_x}+\rho\right]\frac{e}{g}. \quad (7.5)$$

A wage differential is required in order to discipline workers. If we focus on an equilibrium where the secondary sector wage, w_y, leaves the worker's indirect utility above the effort level, e, equation (7.5) simplifies to

$$An_x^{\alpha(1-\theta)/\theta}p_x^{-\alpha}w_x = An_x^{\alpha(1-\theta)/\theta}p_x^{-\alpha}w_y + \left[\frac{b\bar{L}}{\bar{L}-L_x}+\rho\right]\frac{e}{g}. \quad (7.6)$$

Writing the production function in the secondary sector as $Y = a_y^{-1}eL_y$, competition gives

$$w_y = \frac{e}{a_y}, \quad (7.7)$$

where we recall that good Y is chosen as the numeraire and a_y is the unit input coefficient in the production of good Y. This condition pins down the secondary sector wage in terms of the numeraire. Next, monopolistic competition implies

$$w_x = \theta p_x e \beta_x, \quad (7.8)$$

where p_x is the relative price of the differentiated good and $e\beta_x$ is the marginal productivity of labour in the primary sector. Rewriting equation (7.8), we have

$$p_x = \frac{w_x}{\theta e \beta_x}. \quad (7.9)$$

Free entry and exit gives

$$x = \frac{\theta e \beta_x f_x}{1-\theta}, \quad (7.10)$$

where x is the size of output of the typical differentiated firm and f_x is the fixed cost in labour unit. The size of the workforce employed at each differentiated product firm is, therefore,

$$l_x = \frac{f_x}{1-\theta}. \quad (7.11)$$

Letting n_x denote the number of differentiated product firms, note that $L_x = n_x l_x$. The adding up constraint is that

$$\frac{L_x}{\overline{L}} + \frac{L_y}{\overline{L}} = 1. \tag{7.12}$$

The market clearing of the secondary sector yields

$$ea_y^{-1}L_y = (1-\alpha)[w_x L_x + w_y L_y]. \tag{7.13}$$

Using the adding-up constraint, equation (7.12), and noting that $w_y = ea_y^{-1}$, we have

$$ea_y^{-1}\frac{L_y}{\overline{L}} = (1-\alpha)\left[w_x - \left(w_x - \frac{e}{a_y}\right)\frac{L_y}{\overline{L}}\right]. \tag{7.14}$$

Differentiating equation (7.14), we have

$$\frac{dw_x}{d(L_y/\overline{L})} = \frac{ea_y^{-1} + (1-\alpha)\left(w_x - \dfrac{e}{a_y}\right)}{(1-\alpha)[1-(L_y/\overline{L})]}, \tag{7.15}$$

which is positive. In Figure 7.1, this goods market–clearing condition is depicted as *GG*.

Turning to the incentive-wage condition, we rewrite equation (7.6) as

$$\frac{A[w_x - w_y]}{p_x^{\alpha}} n_x^{\frac{\alpha(1-\theta)}{\theta}} = \frac{e}{g}\left[\frac{b}{(L_y/\overline{L})} + \rho\right]. \tag{7.16}$$

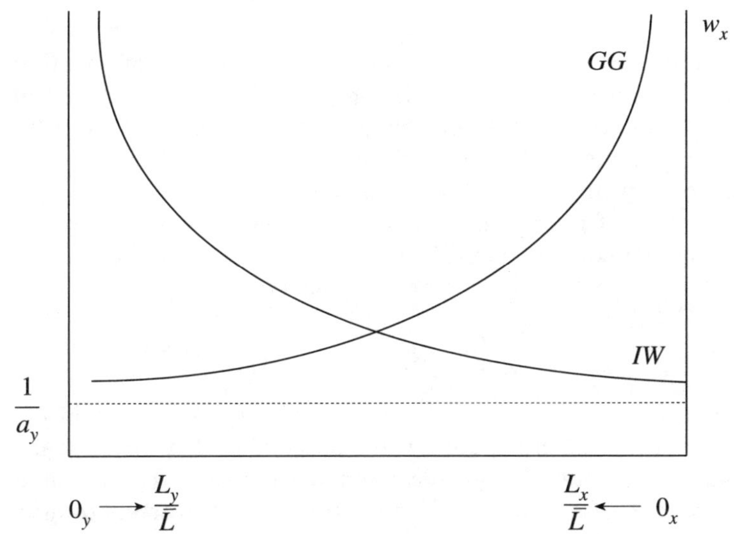

Figure 7.1 Equilibrium in dual labour market

Noting that $p_x = (\theta\, e\beta_x)^{-1} w_x$ and $w_y = e a_y^{-1}$, equation (7.16) can further be rewritten as

$$A[\theta e\beta_x]^{\alpha}\left[w_x^{1-\alpha} - \frac{e}{w_x^{\alpha} a_y}\right] n_x^{\frac{\alpha(1-\theta)}{\theta}} = \frac{e}{g}\left[\frac{b}{(L_y/\overline{L})} + \rho\right]. \qquad (7.17)$$

Given n_x, the incentive-wage condition gives a relation between w_x and $L_y/\overline{L}$. It is clear that w_x rises as $L_y/\overline{L}$ declines, which is the key condition for disciplining workers in the primary sector. As $L_y/\overline{L}$ declines (and so $L_x/\overline{L}$ increases), there is a greater abundance of good jobs in the economy, making it less costly to be dismissed if caught shirking. To maintain worker discipline, it is then necessary to raise the incentive wage, w_x. Thus, for any given level of n_x, we obtain a schedule giving the incentive wage at each $L_y/\overline{L}$ denoted as *IW* in Figure 7.1.

Using equations (7.14) and (7.17), depicted by the *GG* and *IW* schedules in Figure 7.1, respectively, we note that an increase in n_x shifts the *IW* schedule down along the *GG* schedule. By varying n_x, we obtain an inverse relationship between $L_y/\overline{L}$ and n_x, which we represent as $L_y/\overline{L} = \Psi(n_x)$, $\Psi' < 0$. Using this condition in

$$n_x = \frac{(1-\theta)[1-(L_y/\overline{L})]\overline{L}}{f_x}, \qquad (7.18)$$

we obtain

$$n_x = \frac{(1-\theta)[1-\Psi(n_x)]\overline{L}}{f_x}, \qquad (7.19)$$

an equation in the unknown n_x. We express the left-hand side of equation (7.19) as the forty-five degree line in Figure 7.2. The right-hand side of equation (7.19) is a positively-sloped schedule (represented by *RR*). If we make the assumption that $-[(1-\theta)/f_x]\Psi'(n_x) < 1$, a condition that is satisfied for a sufficiently large θ, we obtain a unique intersection.[2]

What is the effect of international trade? To obtain the answer, suppose that there is another country that is identical in all respects to the country considered above. Equation (7.17) is now replaced by

$$A[\theta e\beta_x]^{\alpha}\left[w_x^{1-\alpha} - \frac{e}{w_x^{\alpha} a_y}\right][n_x + n_x^{*}]^{\frac{\alpha(1-\theta)}{\theta}} = \frac{e}{g}\left[\frac{b}{(L_y/\overline{L})} + \rho\right], \qquad (7.20)$$

where n_x^{*} denotes the number of differentiated products produced in the foreign country. In terms of Figure 7.1, the effect of trade is to cause the *IW* schedule to shift down along the given *GG* schedule. The essential mechanism at work here is that the love for variety leads workers to hold on more tightly to their high-wage jobs at each level of $L_y/\overline{L}$ under trade; this allows a reduction of the incentive wage needed to enforce worker discipline. Equation (7.19) is also replaced by

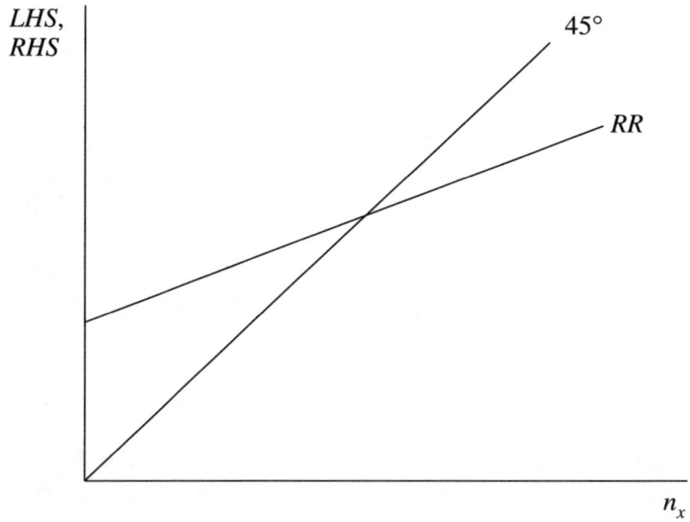

Figure 7.2 Determination of n_x

$$n_x = \frac{(1-\theta)[1-\Psi(n_x+n_x^*)]\overline{L}}{f_x}, \tag{7.21}$$

implying that the *RR* schedule shifts up along the forty-five degree line. Hence international trade leads to an expansion of high-wage-premium jobs and decline in w_x.

What is the effect of trade on real consumption wages? To obtain an answer, we define the consumer price index as

$$\left[\frac{\left(\int_0^{n_x} p_{xj}^{\frac{-\theta}{1-\theta}} dj\right)^{\frac{-(1-\theta)}{\theta}}}{\alpha}\right]^{\alpha}\left[\frac{p_y}{1-\alpha}\right]^{1-\alpha}.$$

Under symmetry, and using equation (7.9) as well as the normalisation $p_y \equiv 1$, the real consumption wage under trade is $A(n_x+n_x^*)^{\alpha(1-\theta)/\theta}[\theta e\beta_x]^{\alpha} w_x^{1-\alpha}$ for a high-wage worker and $A(n_x+n_x^*)^{\alpha(1-\theta)/\theta}[\theta e\beta_x]^{\alpha} w_x^{-\alpha} a_y^{-1}$ for a low-wage worker. The ratio between the high wage and the low wage given by $w_x a_y$ is reduced since w_x was shown to fall. Notice that the narrowing of the wage gap is associated with an unambiguous rise in the real consumption wage of the low-wage worker; it is also possible that the real consumption wage of the high-wage worker is on balance increased as a result of trade. (Although w_x is reduced, this is counterbalanced by the rise in the number of varieties available for consumption under free trade.)

7.3 MODEL OF INTERNATIONAL PRODUCT COMPETITION

In parallel with the model of Section 7.2, suppose that the competitive sector is a secondary sector, which offers low-wage jobs, whereas the non-competitive sector is the primary sector, where jobs offer a high-wage premium. Firms in the non-competitive sector behave in a Cournot–Nash fashion.

Choosing good Y as numeraire, we set $p_y \equiv 1$. For a non-shirking worker employed in the non-competitive sector, the following asset equation is satisfied:

$$\rho V_{xn} = Ap_x^{-\alpha} w_x - e + b[V_y - V_{xn}], \tag{7.22}$$

where V_y is the present discounted value of utility derived from holding a job in sector Y. If the worker in sector X shirks, his asset equation satisfies:

$$\rho V_{xs} = Ap_x^{-\alpha} w_x + (b+g)[V_y - V_{xs}]. \tag{7.23}$$

Non-shirking behaviour requires that $V_{xn} \geq V_{xs}$, which implies

$$Ap_x^{-\alpha} w_x \geq \rho V_y + \frac{(\rho + b + g)e}{g}. \tag{7.24}$$

Assuming that the secondary sector job pays a wage high enough to leave a worker employed there with an indirect utility above his disutility from exerting effort, a worker will either be employed in the primary sector or the secondary sector. The value V_y must obey the following asset equation:

$$\rho V_y = Ap_x^{-\alpha} w_y - e + a[V_{xn} - V_y], \tag{7.25}$$

where a is the rate of accessing a primary sector job. Given that in equilibrium, $V_{xn} = V_{xs}$, and solving, using the resulting expression for V_y and substituting for a with the formula, $bL_x = a[\overline{L} - L_x]$, we arrive at the no-shirking constraint:

$$Ap_x^{-\alpha}[w_x - w_y] = \left[\frac{b\overline{L}}{\overline{L} - L_x} + \rho\right]\frac{e}{g}. \tag{7.26}$$

We see from equation (7.26) that a wage premium is required in order to discipline workers. *Ceteris paribus*, the greater the number of primary sector jobs available, the bigger must be the size of the wage premium.

Solving the model is now straightforward. With $p_y \equiv 1$, $w_y = a_y^{-1}e$. Profit maximisation in the non-competitive sector yields $w_x = p_x[1 - n_x^{-1}]e\beta_x$

while free entry and exit yield the zero-profit condition: $w_x = p_x[1-(f_x/l_x)]e\beta_x$. Here, f_x is the fixed cost incurred in setting up the firm in labour units, l_x is the number of employed workers at a typical non-competitive firm and $e\beta_x$ is the marginal physical productivity of labour. Together, these two conditions imply $l_x = n_x f_x$, and hence $x = [n_x - 1] f_x e\beta_x$, where x is the output of the typical non-competitive firm. Noting that $L_x \equiv n_x l_x$, the adding-up constraint is given by $L_x + L_y = \bar{L}$. Dividing throughout by $\bar{L}$, the adding-up constraint can be expressed as:

$$\frac{L_x}{\bar{L}} + \frac{L_y}{\bar{L}} = 1. \tag{7.27}$$

Finally, the clearing of the market for good Y yields

$$\frac{L_y}{\bar{L}} = \frac{1-\alpha}{(1-\alpha) + \left(\dfrac{e\alpha}{a_y w_x}\right)}, \tag{7.28}$$

which yields the analogous schedule *GG* in Figure 7.1.

Using the expression $p_x = w_x[1-n_x^{-1}]^{-1}[e\beta_x]^{-1}$ and equation (7.27) in (7.26), we can write the no-shirking constraint as

$$A[e\beta_x]^\alpha\left[w_x^{1-\alpha} - \frac{e}{w_x^\alpha a_y}\right]\left[1 - \frac{1}{n_x}\right]^\alpha = \left[\frac{b}{(L_y/\bar{L})} + \rho\right]\frac{e}{g}. \tag{7.29}$$

Equation (7.29) gives the analogous *IW* schedule in Figure 7.1. Notice that an increase in n_x shifts the *IW* schedule downwards in Figure 7.1 along an unshifted *GG* schedule. Hence, an increase in n_x lowers $L_y/\bar{L}$, that is, we can write $L_y/\bar{L} = \Psi(n_x)$, $\Psi'(n_x) < 0$. The basic mechanism at work here is that an increase in the number of firms reduces the price–marginal cost mark-up so that at given w_x, the price p_x falls. With the consumption set of a worker employed in the primary sector expanded, each worker values his primary sector job more. Consequently, non-shirking behaviour is satisfied despite an increased availablity of primary sector jobs.

Using the relationship $L_y/\bar{L} = \Psi(n_x)$ in equation (7.27), and noting that $L_x = nl_x$, we have one equation in the unknown n_x:

$$n_x = \frac{\bar{L}[1-\Psi(n_x)]}{l_x}, \tag{7.30}$$

where $l_x = n_x f_x$. To understand the effects of trade, it is again useful to analyse the consequences of increasing the size of the labour force. Looking at the right-hand side of equation (7.30), we see that an increase in $\bar{L}$, taken by itself, increases n_x. The increase in n_x, however, brings about a decline in $L_y/\bar{L}$ and an expansion of l_x. The right-hand side of equation

(7.30) can again be depicted either as a downward-sloping schedule in a diagram like Figure 7.2 or an upward-sloping schedule. If upward-sloping, we impose the restriction that it be less steep than a forty-five degree line. Then, free trade, which acts like an increase in $\overline{L}$, leads to an increase in n_x and consequently to an expansion of primary sector jobs. Thus we obtain the following result: when countries trade in a Cournot–Nash imperfectly competitive model with labour as the single factor of production, there is an increase in the number of high-wage premium jobs in all the trading countries as the price–marginal cost mark-up is reduced.

7.4 MODEL WITH TWO COMPETITIVE SECTORS

Suppose that both the primary and secondary sectors produce homogeneous goods under constant returns to scale. Let $X = a_x^{-1}eL_x$ and $Y = a_y^{-1}eL_y$. With firms behaving competitively, we have

$$w_x = \frac{ep}{a_x}, \tag{7.31}$$

$$w_y = \frac{e}{a_y}, \tag{7.32}$$

where we choose good Y as numeraire. Here, $p \equiv p_x/p_y$, and we set $p_y \equiv 1$. The incentive-wage condition can be written as

$$\frac{A}{p^{\alpha}}[w_x - w_y] = \frac{e}{g}\left[\frac{b\overline{L}}{L_y} + \rho\right]. \tag{7.33}$$

Using the conditions $w_y = ea_y^{-1}$ and $p = w_x a_x / e$, equation (7.33) can be rewritten as

$$\frac{e^{\alpha}A}{a_x^{\alpha}}\left[w_x^{1-\alpha} - \frac{e}{a_y w_x^{\alpha}}\right] = \frac{e}{g}\left[\frac{b\overline{L}}{L_y} + \rho\right]. \tag{7.34}$$

In Figure 7.3, this condition is represented as a downward-sloping *IW* schedule.

The adding-up constraint is given by

$$L_x + L_y = \overline{L}. \tag{7.35}$$

Using equations (7.32) and (7.35) in the condition that good Y market clears, namely,

$$a_y^{-1}eL_y = (1-\alpha)[w_y L_y + w_x L_x], \tag{7.36}$$

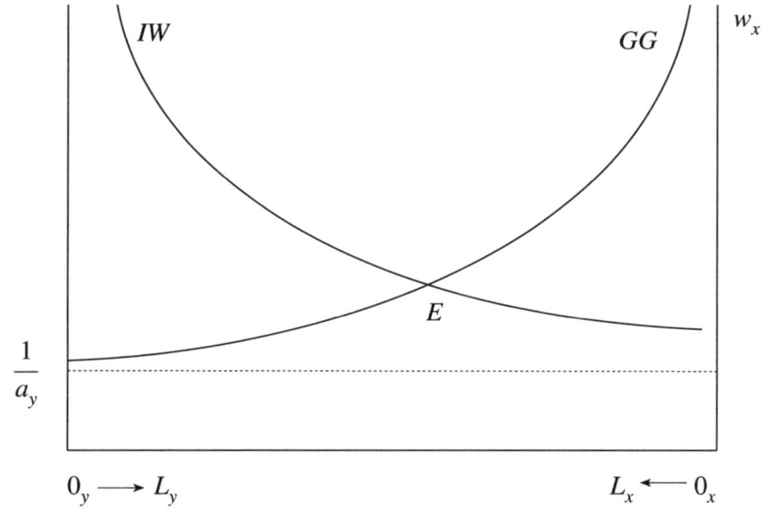

Figure 7.3 Equilibrium with two competitive sectors

gives

$$a_y^{-1}eL_y = (1-\alpha)\left[w_x\bar{L} - \left(w_x - \frac{e}{a_y}\right)L_y\right]. \tag{7.37}$$

This condition is represented by the *GG* schedule in Figure 7.3. The unique equilibrium is given at point *E*. With w_x determined, we also pin down the equilibrium relative good price, *p*.

In Figure 7.4, we depict the equilibrium in the transformation curve plane. The slope of the transformation curve is given by a_x/a_y, but the relative price is given by $p=[w_x/w_y][a_x/a_y]$. Since w_x/w_y exceeds one, the relative price is higher than the slope of the transformation curve.

Suppose that under free trade, Home remains incompletely specialised but becomes a net importer of the primary sector good. The country faces a given foreign offer curve. To determine the free trade equilibrium relative price, let us construct Home's offer curve. To do that, note that the relative price must be given by $p=w_x a_x e^{-1}$, and $w_y = ea_y^{-1}$. We depict the incentive–wage curve in Figure 7.5. Notice that at any given *p*, we pin down w_x, and consequently L_x (or alternatively, L_y, given $\bar{L}$.) The wage w_x^0 is drawn to correspond to the autarkic *p*, say, p^0. The labour allocation at point E_0 corresponds to the output mix at point E_0 in Figure 7.6. At $p^1 < p^0$, $w_x^1 < w_x^0$, and so less *X* is produced (point E_1 in Figure 7.6). The income consumption curve also moves in a clockwise direction giving us the trade triangle. This trade triangle is transferred to Figure 7.7. Following the same

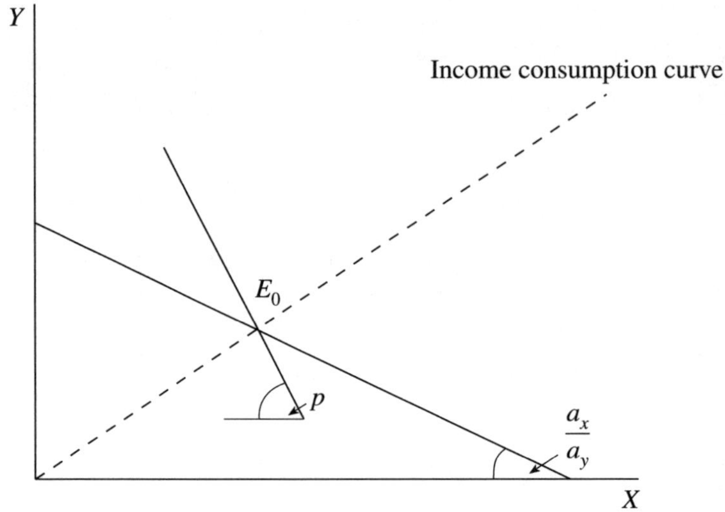

Figure 7.4 Equilibrium in PPF diagram in autarky

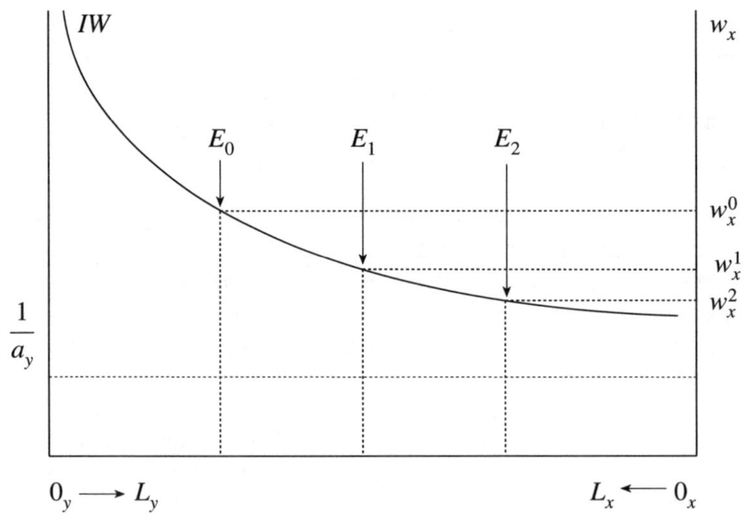

Figure 7.5 Home's incentive-wage curve

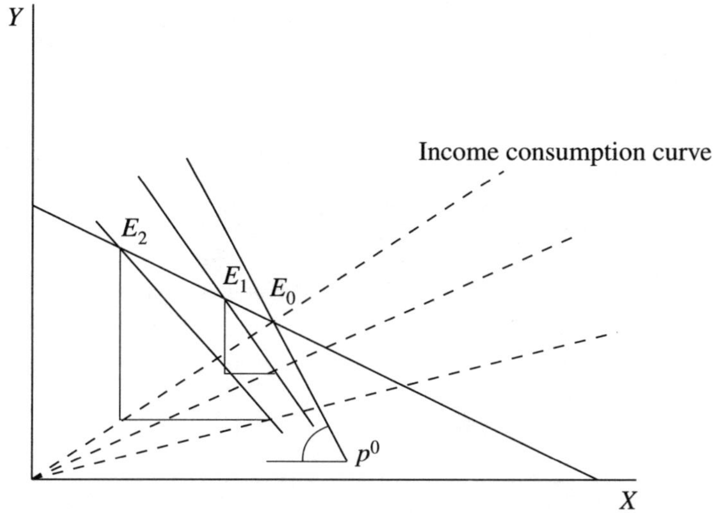

Figure 7.6 Equilibrium in autarky and under trade

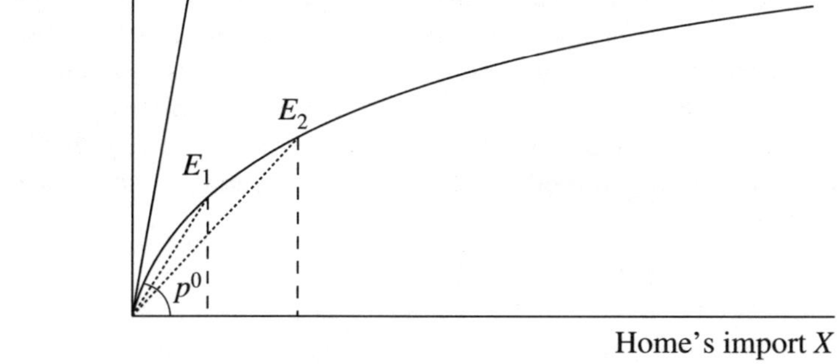

Figure 7.7 Home's trade offer curve

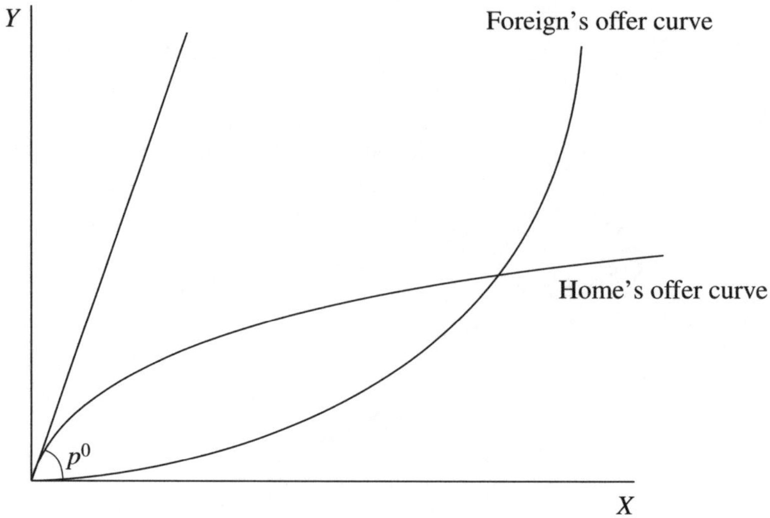

Figure 7.8 Superimposing Home's and Foreign's trade offer curves

procedure at $p^2 < p^1$, we obtain another trade triangle in Figure 7.7. Joining all the relevant points gives us Home's offer curve. Superimposing Foreign's offer curve in Figure 7.8, we obtain the free trade terms of trade. Notice that if w_x/w_y were given exogenously, as in Krugman (1996), the fact that Home is incompletely specialised would mean that the relative price would be the same as that under autarky. In our model, where the wage gap is endogenous, trade here leads to a decline in sector X for the country that becomes a net importer of the primary sector good without necessarily becoming completely specialised. Consequently, the number of jobs available in the primary sector declines. Since this acts to cause primary sector workers to value their jobs more as these jobs are now more scarce, the incentive wage w_x declines. This means that the relative price must fall even though the country remains incompletely specialised. The free trade terms of trade lies between Home's and foreign's autarkic relative prices.

More specifically, the autarkic relative price in Home is given by the following pair of equations obtained by replacing w_x with pea_x^{-1} in equations (7.34) and (7.37):

$$\frac{A}{a_y}\left[\left(\frac{a_x}{a_y}\right)^{-1} p^{1-\alpha} - p^{-\alpha}\right] = \frac{1}{g}\left[\frac{b}{(L_y/\overline{L})} + \rho\right], \tag{7.38}$$

$$p = \left(\frac{\alpha}{1-\alpha}\right)\left(\frac{a_x}{a_y}\right)\left[\frac{(L_y/\overline{L})}{1-(L_y/\overline{L})}\right]. \tag{7.39}$$

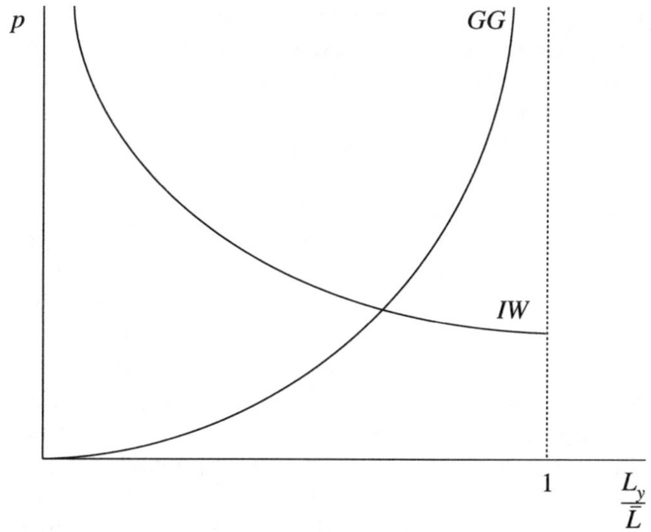

Figure 7.9 Equilibrium expressed in diagram with p

The equilibrium is depicted in Figure 7.9. A similiar pair of equations apply to the Foreign country. Suppose we assume that absolute productivities in the secondary sectors are equal across countries, that is, $a_y^{-1} = a_y^{*-1}$ but Foreign has comparative advantage in the primary sector good, that is, $a_x/a_y > a_x^*/a_y^*$. We allow the size of the labour force to differ across countries but everything else is identical across the two countries. Then it is clear that in autarky, p is higher in Home than in Foreign. Since p falls for Home under trade, it is clear that the primary sector shrinks. However, the wage gap also declines as workers hold on more tightly to their high-wage-premium jobs.

In the standard Ricardian model without the informational imperfections implied by a shirking story of the labour market, relative productivity differences across countries is the sole basis for trade. Differences in absolute productivities across countries will not lead to trade if relative productivities are the same. In other words, trade is based solely on comparative advantage and not absolute advantage. In the model here, suppose that relative productivities are the same in the two countries, that is, $a_x/a_y = a_x^*/a_y^*$, but Foreign is uniformly more productive than Home in the two sectors. In that case, observe from equations (7.38) and (7.39) as well as Figure 7.9 that, in autarky, the schedule *GG* is the same for both Home and Foreign. However, since, by assumption, a_y^{*-1} is higher than a_y^{-1} the *IW* schedule for Foreign will also lie below that of Home. Consequently, the autarkic relative price of the primary sector good, p, will actually be lower in Foreign – the more productive country – than in Home – the less productive country. Hence trade will occur despite identical relative productivities across countries. The intuition is as follows: in both countries, the same absolute wage differential is required to maintain worker discipline given any particular share of workers employed in the primary sector. In the high productivity country, the product wage that firms can afford to pay workers employed in the secondary sector is higher as, by assumption, absolute productivity across all sectors is higher than in the low productivity country. To achieve any given absolute differential between primary and secondary sector wage, therefore, requires a lower *relative* primary sector to secondary sector wage. With the relative primary sector to secondary sector wage being lower, competition leads to a relatively cheaper primary sector good in the high productivity country, which, therefore, ends up as the net-exporter of the primary sector good. Thus, contrary to popular fears that trade by the advanced country with developing economies will cause it to lose good jobs, the model predicts that under free trade the advanced country actually ends up being the net exporter of the primary sector good and so increases the number of good jobs under trade. Note that although this competitive model then implies that trade causes developing economies to lose high-wage jobs, in practice, the ability of developing countries to buy a wide range of differentiated consumer products from the developed economies would have the beneficial effects of improving the wage gap–good jobs trade-off studied in the earlier section.

7.5 CONCLUDING REMARKS

It is possible that the mechanism highlighted in this chapter – that international trade among industrial economies involving the exchange of differentiated goods leads both to an expansion of high-wage jobs as well as a decline in the wage gap – has not so far played a quantitatively important role in the US economy since the share of trade in America's GDP is still relatively small. Krugman (1995, p. 327) reports that the share was 4.7 per cent in 1960 and 11.4 per cent in 1994. Thus the loss of high-wage jobs and rising wage inequality between low-skilled and high-skilled workers as well as inequality among workers within narrowly defined skill categories (for example, among college graduates with one to ten years of work experience reported in Juhn, Murphy and Pierce, 1993) in the US economy in the last two decades or so have been attributed to domestic causes (see Krugman, 1996 for an expression of this view). On the other hand, some writers such as Bluestone and Harrison (1982) and Cohen and Zysman (1987) have linked the loss of high-wage jobs to international trade. Thinking in terms of a model of inter-industry trade, Katz and Summers (1989) have argued that America has, in fact, been a net exporter of the high-wage good. Hence inter-industry trade for America would actually expand the primary sector and increase the number of high-wage jobs. By the same token, America's trading partners would experience a loss of high-wage jobs although they experience a narrowing of the wage gap. This was also the implication of our competitive model studied in the preceding section.

One key contribution of this chapter has been to show that when trade is intra-industry in nature, which describes the bulk of the trade of industrial economies, all participating economies stand to gain in terms of the expansion of good jobs. At the same time, wage inequality, at least among identical workers, is reduced through trade. This result carries an implication for the rising share of intra-industry trade in total East Asian trade flows: such trade can lead to the creation of more good jobs without leading to a widening wage gap. Fields (1985) examined data on income inequality in the East Asian economies from the mid-sixties to the end of the seventies and concluded: 'The Gini coefficient of inequality in developing countries ranges from below 0.3 (low inequality) to above 0.6 (high inequality). By comparison, inequality is at low-to-moderate levels in the four Asian NICs.' (p. 351) In more recent work on income inequality in Taiwan, Fields and O'Hara Mitchell (1999) have documented that since 1980, Taiwan has experienced a slow but steady increase in family income inequality. Their analysis, however, uncovered some striking findings:

> The first surprising finding was that the inequality of labor earnings fell very slightly in Taiwan during this period of time. This means that *all* [emphasis in original] of the increase in family income inequality in Taiwan since 1980 is due to nonlabor sources and that various changes in Taiwan's labor market had almost exactly offsetting effects on labor earnings inequality. (p. 147)

Another noteworthy result of this chapter is that even when relative productivities are identical across two countries, the difference in absolute productivity levels can be the basis for international trade. Interestingly, the pattern of trade is such that the advanced country (with the higher productivity level) ends up being the net exporter of the high-wage good so that trade actually expands the number of good jobs, contrary to common fears that trade with poorer nations leads to a loss of good jobs. Even though inter-industry trade dominates the trade flows between the developed and developing countries, clearly worker-consumers in the latter must also benefit from being able to buy the wide range of differentiated products available from the advanced economies. Hence, in practice, they, too, would face an improved wage gap–good jobs trade-off as a result of trade.

NOTES

1. Another paper by Jones (1987) applies a similiar shirking model to the study of minimum wage legislation in a dual labour market.
2. Note that θ^{-1} is a measure of the degree of monopoly power.

8. International trade and wage inequality: The role of economies of scale and relative factor endowments

8.1 INTRODUCTION

Although the issue of wage inequality has held centre stage in policy discussions in recent years, it is arguable that it is not the inequality *per se* that is the major problem. In any market economy, a certain amount of wage inequality necessarily exists, which corresponds to an equilibrium wage premium that a skilled worker can earn over an unskilled worker, thus providing the needed incentive for the latter to acquire skills. Instead, it is the fact that rising wage inequality has been *accompanied by* absolute declines in real earnings of workers at the low end of the wage distribution that is a matter for serious policy concern. This is the view expressed, for example, by Feldstein (1998) who sees poverty among workers in the bottom decile or quintile as the real problem.

Whether the rise in wage dispersion corresponds to an absolute decline in real earnings or real gains for the bottom decile has, indeed, important social implications. For example, Freeman (1994) has linked the high rate of crime in the United States despite massive incarceration to the rise in earnings inequality accompanied by a fall in the real earnings of the less skilled. The fall in real earnings from work relative to the returns to crime such as from dealing in illegal drug business served to provide a job market push into crime. Phelps (1997) has also made a strong argument that the decline in net wages *relative* to median pay makes it impossible for low-skilled workers to support themselves and their families at decent standards and to have access to mainstream community support. The consequent marginalization of these workers creates a climate of despondency, which is apt to stimulate violence, crime and drug use.

In this regard, the experiences of the developed countries have been varied. In the sample of seventeen OECD countries studied in the *Employment Outlook* (OECD, 1993), wage inequality was found to have risen from the late seventies to the late eighties in twelve of them. (These twelve countries include Australia, Austria, Belgium, Canada, France, Japan, the Netherlands, Portugal, Spain, Sweden, the United Kingdom and the United States.) The rise in wage inequality, however, has corresponded to an absolute decline in real earnings of the last decile of workers in the United States, Canada and Australia but roughly steady or rising real wages for the bottom decile of workers in the others. In these latter countries, the rise of wage dispersion relative to the median was due more to gains by the top of the distribution of wage earnings as opposed to losses by the bottom, making wage inequality a less serious problem there than in the former group of countries.

By now, there is a vast literature that seeks to uncover the causes of the rise in wage inequality. Two main candidates stand out: skill-biased technological change and growing world trade. (As examples, see Katz and Murphy, 1992 and Cline, 1997.) In this chapter, we will hold technology fixed and examine the role that trade plays in influencing not only relative pay but also the absolute levels of real earnings of workers. In evaluating the role that trade plays in influencing the wage gap and the values of real earnings for unskilled workers, it has been common to adopt the two-good, two-factor and two-country Heckscher–Ohlin framework. In this framework, international trade decreases both the relative pay as well as the absolute pay of unskilled workers in the skilled labour abundant country via the Stolper–Samuelson channel. The use of such a framework, however, fails to take into account some very important facts highlighted by Krugman (1995) about the nature of world trade in the postwar era, in particular, the growth and dominance of intra-industry trade in differentiated intermediates among industrial countries and growing but nevertheless small amount of trade with low-wage countries. Krugman (1995, p. 327) reports that the average OECD country's trade share rose from 12.5 per cent in 1960 to 18.6 per cent in 1990. Although the growth of manufactured exports from low-wage, Newly Industrialising Countries (NICs) has been very rapid, they do not make up a very big share out of total OECD spending. Instead, a large component of the growth of trade experienced by OECD countries occurred among themselves and consisted mainly of intra-industry trade. Since any country's rewards to its factors of production must ultimately be determined in the *general equilibrium*, we need a multi-country model in which both economies of scale and relative factor endowments play a role (the former to motivate intra-industry trade and the latter to explain inter-industry trade).[1] The idea is that in order to properly evaluate the full impact that trade has on both relative and absolute real factor rewards of a European Union (EU) country, for example, we need a model in which both intra-EU trade and, say, EU-Asia trade occur. In the general equilibrium, French real wages are determined both by its intra-EU trade (which is predominantly intra-industry)[2] as well as its trade with Asia (which is largely but not solely inter-industry).[3]

When the presence of economies of scale is taken into account, the welfare of all types of workers can rise, even with differences in factor proportions. This point was originally made in Krugman (1981) in a model where differentiated consumer products enter into workers' utility functions exhibiting a 'love for variety' effect. That model, however, was constructed so as to leave the relative wage always equal to unity in both trading economies. This is a severe limitation when the interest is to study how differences in factor proportions interact with scale economies to determine both relative pay as well as absolute wage – we want, for our purposes, a model in which the relative wage is endogenous. This chapter will proceed to endogenously determine both relative and absolute wages in a multi-country model where inter-industry trade is based on differences in factor proportions and intra-industry trade in differentiated intermediates arises due to specialisation in production.

Krugman (1995, p. 339) argues that there remains substantial room for policy moves – harmonization of laws and institutions – to expand international trade among EU countries. This is the thinking underlying the '1992' initiative in Europe. The collapse of communism in Eastern Europe and the former Soviet Union (EESU) raises the question of what the prospects are for the formerly socialist economies to smoothly integrate into the world economy, and, in particular, into the economic bloc in Western Europe. This chapter argues that any realistic assessment of this question requires a multi-country framework that simultaneously incorporates intra-EU trade along with EU–EESU trade. An analysis based on a Heckscher–Ohlin interpretation of EU–EESU trade based upon differences in factor proportions alone would give a partial, and possibly misleading, answer. The presence of scale economies, and the extent of intra-industry trade among EU countries, must be taken into account in determining how trade with EESU countries is likely to affect the relative and absolute wages of unskilled workers in EU.

The chapter is organised as follows: We review the standard result in the Heckscher–Ohlin model that trade between a skilled labour abundant country and an unskilled labour abundant country widens the wage gap and reduces the unskilled real wage in the former in Section 8.2. In Section 8.3, we first analyse a closed economy exhibiting two sectors – a competitive constant-returns-to-scale sector and another sector that assembles a range of intermediate inputs produced by monopolistically competitive firms. Section 8.4 studies the impact of trade in such a model. Concluding remarks are contained in Section 8.5.

8.2 SKILLED AND UNSKILLED WORKERS IN HECKSCHER–OHLIN MODEL

The issue that has been of great importance in the US economy in the past decade and a half or so has to do with the relative role of trade versus technology in influencing the wage gap between skilled and unskilled workers. We will focus here on the role of trade and hold technology constant. We present here a model that has two types of workers – skilled and unskilled.

Firstly, let us consider an economy in autarky, called Home. We assume a fixed coefficient technology and full employment. There are two goods, good X being relatively skill-intensive and good Y relatively unskilled-intensive. Let a_{sx}, a_{ux} be the unit input–output coefficients of skilled and unskilled labour, respectively, in the production of good X. Correspondingly, a_{sy} and a_{uy} are the unit input–output coefficients of skilled and unskilled labour, respectively, in the production of good Y. We assume that $a_{sx}/a_{ux} > a_{sy}/a_{uy}$, that is, good X is skilled labour-intensive. It is convenient to let good Y be the numeraire. Then, competition requires that

$$p = w_s a_{sx} + w_u a_{ux}, \tag{8.1}$$

$$1 = w_s a_{sy} + w_u a_{uy}, \tag{8.2}$$

where w_s and w_u are the skilled and unskilled wages, respectively, and $p \equiv p_x/p_y$.

Competition for factors and free mobility across sectors ensures

$$L_{sx} + L_{sy} = \overline{L}_s, \tag{8.3}$$

$$L_{ux} + L_{uy} = \overline{L}_u, \tag{8.4}$$

where $\overline{L}_s$ is the fixed skilled labour force size and $\overline{L}_u$ is the unskilled labour force size. Dividing throughout by $\overline{L}_u$, we have

$$\frac{\overline{L}_s}{\overline{L}_u} = \frac{L_{sx}}{\overline{L}_u} + \frac{L_{sy}}{\overline{L}_u}, \tag{8.5}$$

$$1 = \frac{L_{ux}}{\overline{L}_u} + \frac{L_{uy}}{\overline{L}_u}. \tag{8.6}$$

Using the assumption that $a_{sx}/a_{ux} > a_{sy}/a_{uy}$ together with the relative total endowments, we construct a Bowley–Edgeworth box diagram in Figure 8.1.

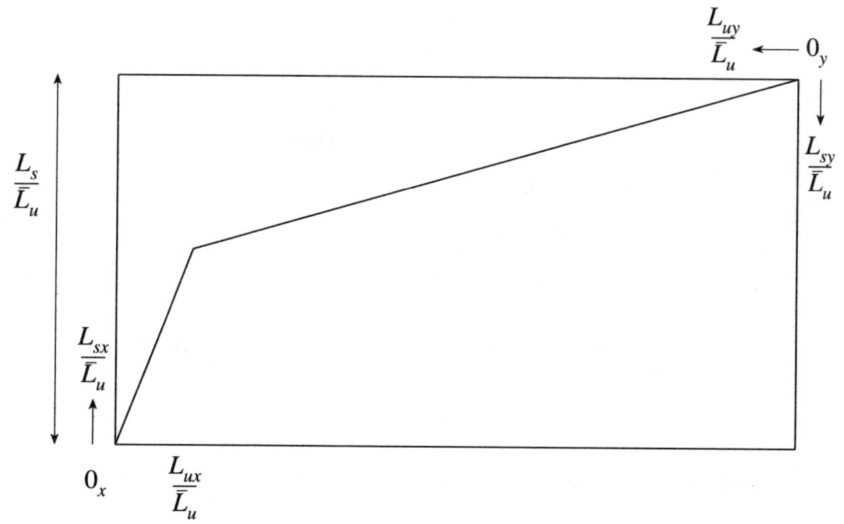

Figure 8.1 Bowley–Edgeworth box diagram

To solve for the relative wage, w_s/w_u, we bring in the demand conditions. Assuming a CES utility function, $[c_x^\theta + c_y^\theta]^{1/\theta}$, where $\sigma \equiv (1-\theta)^{-1}$, the share of total expenditure going to good X, b_x, is given by

$$b_x = \frac{p^{1-\sigma}}{1+p^{1-\sigma}}. \tag{8.7}$$

Notice that with $\sigma > 1$, b_x declines when p rises, where $p \equiv p_x/p_y$. For the goods market to clear, we have that the value of output is equal to the value of expenditure:

$$w_u L_{ux} + w_s L_{sx} = b_x[w_u \bar{L}_u + w_s \bar{L}_s]. \tag{8.8}$$

Solving for w_s/w_u, we have

$$\frac{w_s}{w_u} = \frac{b_x - (L_{ux}/\bar{L}_u)}{(L_{sx}/\bar{L}_u) - b_x(\bar{L}_s/\bar{L}_u)}. \tag{8.9}$$

From Figure 8.1, we can read off the values required to pin down w_s/w_u for given p in equation (8.9). As we increase p, w_s/w_u declines in the case where $\sigma > 1$, giving us the negatively-sloped schedule in Figure 8.2.

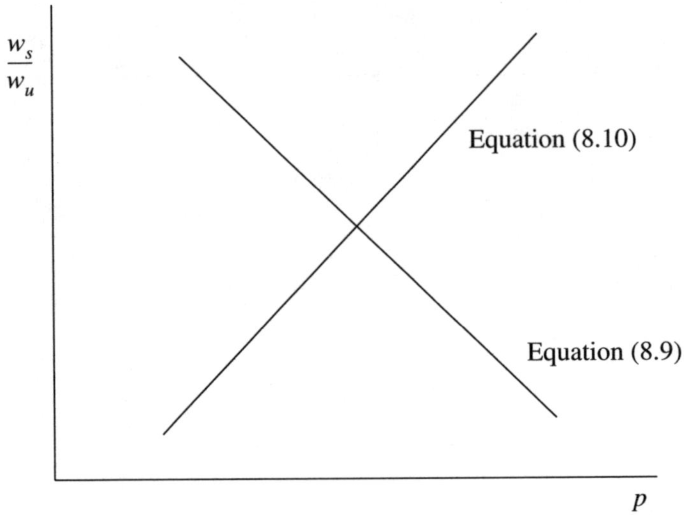

Figure 8.2 Equilibrium in case where σ>1

Using next the relationships for unit costs equal price, we have

$$p = \frac{a_{ux} + \left[\frac{w_s}{w_u}\right] a_{sx}}{a_{uy} + \left[\frac{w_s}{w_u}\right] a_{sy}}. \tag{8.10}$$

Under the assumption that good X is relatively skill-intensive, w_s/w_u increases as p increases. This is depicted as the upward-sloping schedule in Figure 8.2. Once p is pinned down, we can use the Lerner's diagram with unit value isoquants to show diagrammatically the solutions for w_s and w_u (see Figure 8.3).

Writing out explicitly an expression for w_s/w_u, we obtain:

$$\frac{w_s}{w_u} = \frac{b_x - \left[(\bar{L}_s/\bar{L}_u) - \left(\frac{a_{sy}}{a_{uy}}\right)\right]\left[\frac{a_{sx}}{a_{ux}} - \frac{a_{sy}}{a_{uy}}\right]^{-1}}{\left\{\left[1 - b_x\left(1 - \frac{a_{sy}/a_{uy}}{a_{sx}/a_{ux}}\right)\right](\bar{L}_s/\bar{L}_u) - \left(\frac{a_{sy}}{a_{uy}}\right)\right\}\left[1 - \left(\frac{a_{sy}/a_{uy}}{a_{sx}/a_{ux}}\right)\right]^{-1}}. \tag{8.11}$$

In autarky, the country that is relatively well-endowed with skilled labour has a lower w_s/w_u ratio. Trade raises w_s/w_u for this economy. Since p is increased under trade, inspection of Figure 8.3 shows that w_u declines while w_s rises. Clearly, the unskilled real wage in terms of good X also declines. It

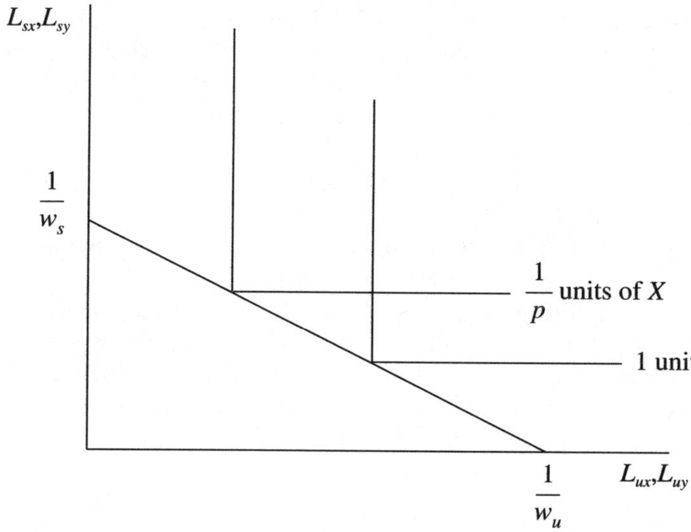

Figure 8.3 Lerner diagram

can be checked from Figure 8.3 that w_s rises by more than p rises. Consequently, the skilled real wage in terms of good X also rises.

This model produces the very stark result that free trade between a skilled labour abundant country and an unskilled labour abundant country leads to a worsened wage gap in the former and a narrower wage gap in the latter. Moreover, unskilled workers in the skilled labour abundant country suffer an absolute decline in their real wage earnings. As the introduction to this chapter makes clear, this model fails to take into account the dominance of intra-industry trade among the skilled labour abundant countries, a form of trade that leads to a rise in absolute wage earnings for all participants. Since factor rewards are determined in the general equilibrium, we need a multi-country model where both intra-industry trade and inter-industry trade occur in order to accurately assess the impact of trade on earnings.

8.3 THE CLOSED ECONOMY WITH SCALE ECONOMIES

We now introduce the production of differentiated intermediates by monopolistically competitive firms in a factor proportions model. It is convenient to first analyse the closed economy. There are two final goods in this single closed economy, good X and good Y. Good Y is produced by competitive firms that assemble together a range of intermediate inputs. Specialised intermediate inputs themselves are produced by monopolistically competitive firms. The production function is given by

$$Y=\left[\int_0^n m_j^{\mu} dj\right]^{\frac{1}{\mu}};\ 0<\mu<1, \tag{8.12}$$

where m_j is intermediate input j. To produce a unit of input j requires a set-up cost given in f_m units of skilled labour. (This set-up cost is often interpreted as the cost of hiring R & D workers, which we regard as skilled labour.) Denoting the return to skilled labour as w_s, the fixed cost is equal to $w_s f_m$. The variable factor is unskilled labour giving variable cost as $w_u \beta_m^{-1} m_j$, where w_u is the return to unskilled labour. Thus the maximisation problem solved by firm j is given by: Maximise

$$p_{mj} m_j - [w_s f_m + w_u \beta_m^{-1} m_j],$$

where p_{mj} is the price of the intermediate good j. Solving this problem, and using the fact of symmetry, gives

$$w_u = \mu p_m \beta_m. \tag{8.13}$$

Perfectly competitive firms in sector Y assemble the intermediate inputs to produce the final good Y. The condition that unit cost equals price gives

$$p_y=\left[\int_0^n p_{mj}^{\frac{-\mu}{1-\mu}} dj\right]^{\frac{-(1-\mu)}{\mu}}. \tag{8.14}$$

Under a symmetric equilibrium, we have

$$p_m = p_y n^{\frac{1-\mu}{\mu}}. \tag{8.15}$$

Substituting equation (8.15) into equation (8.13), we obtain

$$w_u = \mu \beta_m p_y n^{\frac{1-\mu}{\mu}}. \tag{8.16}$$

Free entry into and exit from the monopolistically competitive sector yields

$$m=\left[\frac{\mu}{1-\mu}\right]\left[\frac{w_s}{w_u}\right] f_m \beta_m. \tag{8.17}$$

The number of unskilled workers employed per monopolistically competitive firm is given by

$$l_{um} = \left[\frac{\mu}{1-\mu}\right]\left[\frac{w_s}{w_u}\right] f_m. \tag{8.18}$$

Note that the relative factor intensity used in the monopolistically competitive sector is given by

$$k_m \equiv \frac{L_{sm}}{L_{um}} = \frac{nf_m}{nl_{um}} = \frac{f_m}{l_{um}} = \left[\frac{1-\mu}{\mu}\right]\left[\frac{w_u}{w_s}\right], \tag{8.19}$$

where L_{sm} is skilled labour used in the intermediate input sector and L_{um} is unskilled labour used in the intermediate input sector.

Another competitive sector produces good X, using unskilled and skilled labour, $X = L_{ux}^{\eta} L_{sx}^{1-\eta}$, $0<\eta<1$, where L_{ux} is unskilled labour used in sector X and L_{sx} is skilled labour used in sector X. Perfect competition gives

$$w_u = \eta p_x k_x^{1-\eta}, \tag{8.20}$$

$$w_s = (1-\eta) p_x k_x^{-\eta}. \tag{8.21}$$

Dividing equation (8.20) by equation (8.21), we obtain

$$k_x \equiv \frac{L_{sx}}{L_{ux}} = \left[\frac{1-\eta}{\eta}\right]\left[\frac{w_u}{w_s}\right]. \tag{8.22}$$

If $\mu<\eta$ ($\mu>\eta$) the intermediate input sector is relatively skilled (unskilled) labour-intensive.

We assume that workers have identical Cobb–Douglas tastes given by $c_x^{\alpha} c_y^{1-\alpha}$, $0<\alpha<1$, and that full employment prevails. Letting $A \equiv \alpha^{\alpha}(1-\alpha)^{1-\alpha}$, we use the normalisation $p_x^{\alpha} p_y^{1-\alpha} \equiv 1$ so that $p_x = p^{1-\alpha}$ and $p_y = p^{-\alpha}$, where $p \equiv p_x/p_y$ is the relative price. Equating the wage levels of unskilled workers across the two sectors, we obtain

$$p = \frac{\mu \beta_m n^{\frac{1-\mu}{\mu}}}{\eta k_x^{1-\eta}}. \tag{8.23}$$

Since k_x is positively related to w_u/w_s, we see that p is increasing in n and decreasing in w_u/w_s. Substituting out for p_x in equations (8.20) and (8.21), and using equation (8.23), we obtain

$$w_u = \eta^{\alpha}[\mu\beta_m]^{1-\alpha} k_x^{\alpha(1-\eta)} n^{\frac{(1-\alpha)(1-\mu)}{\mu}}, \tag{8.24}$$

$$w_s = (1-\eta)\left[\frac{\mu\beta_m}{\eta}\right]^{1-\alpha} k_x^{-[(1-\alpha)+\alpha\eta]} n^{\frac{(1-\alpha)(1-\mu)}{\mu}}. \tag{8.25}$$

The adding up constraints are given by

$$\bar{L}_u = nl_{um} + L_{ux}, \tag{8.26}$$

$$\bar{L}_s = nf_m + L_{sx}, \tag{8.27}$$

where $\bar{L}_u$ and $\bar{L}_s$ are the endowments of unskilled and skilled workers, respectively. Using equations (8.26) and (8.27), we obtain

$$\frac{L_{ux}}{\bar{L}_u} = \frac{k_m - \left(\frac{\bar{L}_s}{\bar{L}_u}\right)}{k_m - k_x}, \tag{8.28}$$

$$n = \frac{\bar{L}_u\left[\left(\frac{\bar{L}_s}{\bar{L}_u}\right) - k_x\right]}{l_m\,[k_m - k_x]}. \tag{8.29}$$

Another condition needed to solve the model in autarky can be represented by the condition that the value of production in sector X is equal to the value of expenditure on good X. After some tedious steps, the condition can be expressed as

$$\frac{w_u}{w_s} = \zeta\left[\frac{\bar{L}_s}{\bar{L}_u}\right], \tag{8.30}$$

where $\zeta \equiv [\frac{\alpha\eta + (1-\alpha)\mu}{\alpha(1-\eta) + (1-\alpha)(1-\mu)}]$. As expected, the relative wage of low-skilled workers improves the greater the relative endowment of skilled workers. With the equilibrium (w_u/w_s) value determined, we can pin down n using equations (8.18), (8.19) and (8.22) in equation (8.29). Accordingly, we can infer the equilibrium values of w_u and w_s.

8.4 TRADE IN A MULTI-COUNTRY WORLD

Suppose that we are in a N-country world. We let 1 denote Home. Then country i is endowed with $\bar{L}_s^i \equiv \gamma^i \lambda^i \bar{L}_s^i$ and $\bar{L}_u^i \equiv (2-\gamma^i)\lambda^i \bar{L}^1$, where $i = 2,\ldots,N$. With these notations introduced by Lawrence and Spiller (1983), where $\lambda^i > 0$ is a measure of country i's size relative to Home and $0 < \gamma^i < 2$ is a measure of country i's factor proportions relative to Home, the world relative factor endowment is given by[4]

$$\frac{\sum_{i=1}^{N} \bar{L}_s^i}{\sum_{i=1}^{N} \bar{L}_u^i} = \left[\frac{1 + \sum_{i=2}^{N} \gamma^i \lambda^i}{1 + \sum_{i=2}^{N} (2-\gamma^i)\lambda^i}\right]\left[\frac{\bar{L}_s^1}{\bar{L}_u^1}\right].$$

Assuming identical tastes and technology across countries, the relative wage, under free trade, is given by

$$\left[\frac{w_u}{w_s}\right]_{\mathrm{FT}} = \zeta\left[\frac{1+\sum_{i=2}^{N}\gamma^i\lambda^i}{1+\sum_{i=2}^{N}(2-\gamma^i)\lambda^i}\right]\left[\frac{\bar{L}_s^1}{\bar{L}_u^1}\right], \tag{8.31}$$

where $[w_u/w_s]_{\mathrm{FT}}$ denotes the free trade relative wage. The total number of differentiated intermediate inputs produced in the world is given by

$$\sum_{i=1}^{N} n_{\mathrm{FT}}^i = \frac{[1+\sum_{i=2}^{N}(2-\gamma^i)\lambda^i]\left\{\left[\frac{1+\sum_{i=2}^{N}\gamma^i\lambda^i}{1+\sum_{i=2}^{N}(2-\gamma^i)\lambda^i}\right][\bar{L}_s^1/\bar{L}_u^1] - \left[\frac{1-\eta}{\eta}\right]\left[\frac{w_u}{w_s}\right]_{FT}\right\}\bar{L}_u^1}{\left[1-\left(\frac{\mu}{1-\mu}\right)\left(\frac{1-\eta}{\eta}\right)\right]f_m}. \tag{8.32}$$

Since our focus is on how trade affects the relative wage as well as the absolute real wage of unskilled workers, it is convenient to derive a measure of an unskilled worker's wage under free trade taken as a ratio to his autarkic wage.[5] For Home, this is given by

$$\left[\frac{w_u^{FT}}{w_u^{A}}\right]^1 = \left[\frac{1+\sum_{i=2}^{N}\gamma^i\lambda^i}{1+\sum_{i=2}^{N}(2-\gamma^i)\lambda^i}\right]^{\alpha(1-\eta)}\left[1+\sum_{i=2}^{N}\gamma^i\lambda^i\right]^{\frac{(1-\alpha)(1-\mu)}{\mu}}, \tag{8.33}$$

where the superscript 'FT' denotes free trade and 'A' denotes autarky. For country i other than Home, this is given by

$$\left[\frac{w_u^{FT}}{w_u^{A}}\right]^i = \left\{\left[\frac{1+\sum_{i=2}^{N}\gamma^i\lambda^i}{1+\sum_{i=2}^{N}(2-\gamma^i)\lambda^i}\right]\left[\frac{(2-\gamma^i)}{\gamma^i}\right]\right\}^{\alpha(1-\eta)}\left[\frac{1+\sum_{i=2}^{N}\gamma^i\lambda^i}{\gamma^i\lambda^i}\right]^{\frac{(1-\alpha)(1-\mu)}{\mu}}. \tag{8.34}$$

As an exercise, let us first consider a world in which all countries share the same relative factor endowments ($\gamma^i = 1$, $i = 2, \ldots, N$) and only country size differs. From equation (8.31), we check that trade leaves the relative wage unaffected for all trading nations. However, absolute real wages for both skilled and unskilled workers improve as a result of trade. From equations (8.33) and (8.34), the ratio between an unskilled worker's free trade wage to his autarkic wage simplifies to $[1+\sum_{i=2}^{N}\lambda^i]^{\frac{(1-\alpha)(1-\mu)}{\mu}}$ for Home and $[(1+\sum_{i=2}^{N}\lambda^i)/\lambda^i]^{\frac{(1-\alpha)(1-\mu)}{\mu}}$ for every other trading nation. It is clear that the larger is the size of trading partners, the greater will be the increase of real wage for any country that trade brings about.

Next, to study the influence of trade when factor proportions also matter, let us consider a special case where there are two industrial countries (denoted Home and DC), whose sizes may differ but whose factor proportions are identical, trading with a third low-wage, developing country (denoted LDC) that is relatively abundant in unskilled labour. How will free trade affect the wages of the unskilled workers in Home? Choosing the parameters $\alpha = 0.3$, $\mu = 0.3$, and $\eta = 0.7$ so that seventy per cent of household expenditure is spent on the good assembled from differentiated intermediates and the monopolistically competitive sector is skilled labour-intensive, the ratio $[w_u^{FT}/w_u^A]$ is equal to $[2+\gamma^{LDC}\lambda^{DC}]^{1.72}/[2+(2-\gamma^{LDC})\lambda^{LDC}]^{0.09}$ if we set the size of Home and DC equal. If $\gamma^{LDC} = 0.5$, so that the relative endowment of skilled to unskilled labour of the developing economy is only one-third of the industrial countries', the value of $[w_u^{FT}/w_u^A]$ is equal to 3.68 when $\lambda^{LDC} = 0.5$, 4.32 when $\lambda^{LDC} = 1$, and 5.00 when $\lambda^{LDC} = 1.5$.[6] Correspondingly, free trade causes the ratio of unskilled wage to skilled wage in Home to decline to a fraction of its autarkic value, which is 0.82 when $\lambda^{LDC} = 0.5$, 0.71 when $\lambda^{LDC} = 1$, and 0.65 when $\lambda^{LDC} = 1.5$. In the worst case, we see that even when trade causes the unskilled to skilled wage ratio to fall to 65 per cent of its autarkic value, the absolute unskilled real wage still rises by a factor of 1.5.

To take another example, if $\gamma^{LDC} = 0.01$, so that the relative endowment of skilled to unskilled labour of the developing country is now only 1/199 times that of the industrial countries', the value of $[w_u^{FT}/w_u^A]$ is equal to 2.99 when $\lambda^{LDC} = 0.5$, 2.93 when $\lambda^{LDC} = 1$, and 2.89 when $\lambda^{LDC} = 1.5$. Notice that the wage gains enjoyed by unskilled workers in the industrial countries as a result of trade do not rise monotonically with λ^{LDC}. The reason is that when λ^{LDC} rises, the expansionary effect on unskilled wages in the industrial countries due to an enlarged market size is offset by the larger influence exerted by the relative abundance of unskilled labor in LDC. More precisely, free trade causes the ratio of unskilled wage to skilled wage in the industrial countries to decline to a fraction of its autarkic value. This fraction is $[2+\gamma^{LDC}\lambda^{LDC}]/[2+(2-\gamma^{LDC})\lambda^{LDC}] < 1$, for $\gamma^{LDC} < 1$, and falls further as λ^{LDC} rises. When λ^{LDC} is 10 and $\gamma^{LDC} = 0.01$, relative unskilled wage falls to the fraction 0.096 of its autarkic value. Despite such a big fall in relative wage, absolute real unskilled wage rises by a factor of 2.72. Hence the presence of scale economies can more than offset the depressing effect of differences in factor proportions on low-skilled wages in the industrial countries under trade.[7]

8.5 CONCLUDING REMARKS

This chapter has proceeded under the neoclassical assumption of the labour market. Following the analysis in Chapter 4, it is straightforward to infer how trade based upon scale economies and differences in factor proportions will affect the equilibrium rate of unemployment. The essential insight is that trade affects a worker's work incentive – shirking, quitting or absenteeism. In a purely Heckscher–Ohlin interpretation of trade between a skilled-labour-abundant country and an unskilled-labour-abundant country, the work incentive among the unskilled workers in the former country will worsen. In general equilibrium, this is translated into a rise in the equilibrium rate of unemployment among the low-skilled there. The added wrinkle in this chapter is that in the presence of scale economies work incentives for both skilled and unskilled workers may rise under trade despite differences in factor proportions. Consequently, the natural rate of unemployment can decline, not only on average but separately for each class of workers.

NOTES

1. Davis (1995) has presented a model in which both intra-industry and inter-industry trade arise despite the absence of scale economies. Whether scale economies are, in fact, empirically important is still an unsettled question (see Krugman, 1994c). This chapter generates intra-industry trade via specialisation due to scale economies and shows that it plays a crucial role in generating the possibility that despite differences in relative factor endowments, both skilled and unskilled workers gain from trade.
2. Krugman (1995, p. 340) reports that EU countries have an average trade share of 28.0 per cent in 1990 and that over 60 per cent of their merchandise trade is with each other.
3. Chow and Kellman (1993) report that by the end of the eighties, the East Asian NICs – Hong Kong, Singapore, South Korea and Taiwan – made up more than 50 per cent of total manufactured exports of all developing countries. Over their sample period, 1965–90, intra-industry trade grew as a share of its total trade. By 1990, intra-industry trade constituted over 40 per cent of Singapore's trade with EU. The corresponding figures for Hong Kong, South Korea and Taiwan were 37.9 per cent, 27.9 per cent and 30.1 per cent, respectively.
4. Note that when $0<\gamma^i<1$ Home is relatively abundant in skilled labour compared to country *i*.
5. The analogous measure for a skilled worker is easily derived.
6. It is clear that the gains would be magnified if DC was larger than Home. To take a specific example, suppose that DC is four times as large as Home. If we take the case of $\lambda^{LDC}=1.5$, trade raises real earnings of unskilled workers in Home by a factor of 16.95.
7. In a computable general equilibrium model calibrated to the NAFTA arrangements, Brown, Deardorff and Stern (1992) incorporated economies of scale of the kind discussed here and obtained the result that real wages rise in Canada, Mexico and the US as a result of the trade agreement. In place of skilled and unskilled labour, they worked with capital and homogeneous labour. The prediction of the Heckscher–Ohlin model, without scale economies, is that real wages should fall in the US and Canada. In fact, scale economies played the role of a tide lifting all boats.

9. Wealth, labour force participation and trade

9.1 INTRODUCTION

Although the unemployment rate is often used as an indicator of labour-market conditions, it is sometimes argued that the amount of non-employment may actually provide more information about the state of the labour market. Non-employment or non-participation would include potential workers who choose not to seek employment and would, in official labour statistics, be counted as 'out of the labour force'. Declining labour-market opportunities that are reflected in declining take-home wages relative to workers' non-wage incomes would lead workers to choose not to work, or at least not to work all the time. Conversely, improving labour market conditions reflected in rising wages relative to workers' non-wage incomes would lead individuals who were formerly out of the labour force to rejoin the labour market. In this chapter, we use a neoclassical growth model to study how changes in workers' current and future wage earnings relative to their non-wage incomes affect their labour supply decisions. Here, all variation in employment takes the form of adjustment in equilibrium man-hours supplied. However, following Woodford (1994), the adjustment of equilibrium man-hours supplied could be interpreted as occurring at the extensive margin if we think of the representative agent as belonging to a large group, which pools together its resources and decides jointly on consumption and employment supply. Under the latter interpretation, the variation in total employment reflects individuals' decisions to participate in or withdraw from the labour force.

The model we develop in this chapter incorporates individual labour supply decisions in the one-sector Blanchardian framework of finitely-lived agents without bequest motives. Inter-temporal general equilibrium involves the simultaneous determination of the wage to non-wage income ratio, the real interest rate and the equilibrium amount of labour supply in the closed economy. In the case of a small open economy taking the world interest rate as given, the equilibrium amount of external debt is also endogenously determined. We apply the model to study two issues. First, we analyse the effects of a revenue-neutral shift towards an increased payroll tax rate and decreased VAT. In a closed economy, such a tax shift is shown to decrease labour force participation as the interest rate is driven up and labour market conditions worsen. In a small open economy open to international capital mobility, however, the increased decumulation of foreign assets erodes the negative effect of such a tax shift.[1] Finally, in a two-country world integrated via an international capital market, a revenue-neutral shift of the tax mix away from VAT towards higher payroll taxes in one country acts to raise world interest rate and so to contract employment in both countries.

We also apply the model to a study of the effects of an increase in the rate of human capital accumulation on real wages and labour force participation. In the small open economy that takes the world interest rate as given, we show that a rise in the rate of human capital accumulation raises the human wealth relative to non-human wealth ratio thus stimulating the supply of labour. The result we obtain throws light on two facts about the East Asian tigers that have been highlighted by Young (1995): In Hong Kong, Singapore, South Korea and Taiwan, there has been a very rapid increase in the labour force participation rate, which has occurred along with sharp increases in educational attainments since the mid-sixties. From 1966 to 1991, the labour force participation rate in Hong Kong rose from 38 to 49 per cent. In Singapore, South Korea and Taiwan over the period 1966 to 1990, the labour force participation rate rose from 27 to 51 per cent, 27 to 36 per cent and 28 to 37 per cent, respectively. Human capital accumulation in these economies has been very rapid. From 1966 to 1990/1991, the proportion of the labour force with a secondary education or more doubled in Hong Kong and Taiwan, tripled in South Korea and quadrupled in Singapore.

The chapter is organised as follows: In Sections 9.2 and 9.3, we study the effects of a change in the tax mix – a revenue-neutral shift from VAT to higher payroll taxes – in the closed and open economies, respectively. The effects of an increase in the pace of human capital accumulation is studied in Section 9.4. In Section 9.5, we also briefly discuss the role of wealth in determining the natural rate, as well as the influence trade has on jobs through the beneficial effects of international R&D spillovers. Concluding remarks are contained in Section 9.6.

9.2 TAX SHIFT IN THE CLOSED ECONOMY

We follow the treatment of Blanchard (1985) of finitely-lived agents with no bequest in a one-sector set-up. (See Phelps, 1994, chapter 16.) Agents derive utility from consumption and leisure, have finite lives and face an instantaneous probability of death ϱ that is constant throughout life.

Let $c(s, t)$ denote consumption at time t of an agent born at time s, $l(s, t)$ labour supply, $a(s, t)$ non-human wealth, and $h(s, t)$ human wealth. Also let $w^h(t)$ be the take-home real wage, $r(t)$ the real rate of interest, ρ the pure rate of time preference, and 1 is total available time. Consumption $c(s, t)$ and consumption expenditure $\hat{c}(s, t)$ are related by $\hat{c}(s, t) = c(s, t)/(1 - \tau_c)$, where τ_c is the *ad valorem* value-added tax rate. (This expenditure is the consumer's nominal outlay, including the part that goes to pay the tax, deflated by factor cost.) The household's product wage, calculated at factor cost, $w^h(t)$, that is, the nominal household wage deflated by the nominal price received by firms, is related to the firm's product wage, denoted $w^f(t)$, by $w^h(t) = w^f(t)/(1 + \tau_w)$, where τ_w is the *ad valorem* payroll tax rate.

In this notation, the agent maximises

$$\int_t^{\infty} [\log c(s, v) + \log(1 - l(s, v))] \exp^{-(\varrho+\rho)(v-t)} dv$$

subject to

$$\frac{da(s,t)}{dt} = [r(t) + \varrho]a(s, t) + w^h(t)l(s, t) - \hat{c}(s, t)$$

and a transversality condition that prevents agents from going indefinitely into debt. The solution to the agent's problem is given by

$$\hat{c}(s, t) = (\varrho + \rho)[h(s,t) + a(s, t)], \tag{9.1}$$

$$\frac{1 - l(s,t)}{\hat{c}(s,t)} = \frac{1}{w^h(t)}, \tag{9.2}$$

where human wealth is given by

$$h(s, t) = \int_t^{\infty} [l(s, v)w^h(v)] \exp^{-\int_t^v [r(v) + \varrho] dv} dv. \tag{9.3}$$

Normalising the population size to one, dropping the time index t and denoting aggregate variables by capital letters, we obtain

$$\hat{C} = (\varrho + \rho)[H + A], \tag{9.4}$$

$$\frac{1 - L}{\hat{C}} = \frac{1}{w^h}. \tag{9.5}$$

The dynamics are given by

$$\dot{H} = (r + \varrho)H - Lw^h, \tag{9.6}$$

$$\dot{A} = rA + Lw^h - \hat{C}, \tag{9.7}$$

$$\dot{\hat{C}} = (r - \rho)\hat{C} - \varrho(\varrho + \rho)A. \tag{9.8}$$

In a steady state, aggregate human wealth, H, equals $w^hL/(r+\varrho)$. Non-wage income per capita is given by $y^w = (r+\varrho)A$, which takes the form of annuity income, ϱA being the component called the actuarial dividend. Using these relations in equations (9.4) and (9.5), and rearranging, we obtain the steady-state labour supply relation in man-hours or the labour force participation rate:

$$L = \frac{1 - \left[\dfrac{\varrho + \rho}{r + \varrho}\right]\left[\dfrac{w^h}{y^w}\right]^{-1}}{1 + \left[\dfrac{\varrho + \rho}{r + \varrho}\right]}. \tag{9.9}$$

Notice from equation (9.9) that given r, labour supply, L, is increasing in the take-home wage to non-wage income ratio. A rise in the take-home wage relative to the individual's fall-back income – his non-wage income in other words – represents an improvement in labour-market conditions and encourages an increase in the supply of labour. In Figure 9.1, we show that an iso-interest labour supply schedule is positively sloped in the (L, w^h/y^w) plane. A decrease in r shifts the iso-interest labour supply schedule upwards and hence leftwards. We also note that in a steady state, equation (9.8) can be expressed as

$$r = \rho + \frac{\varrho}{1 + \left[\dfrac{w^h}{y^w}\right]L}. \tag{9.10}$$

This condition, which we can interpret as a capital–market equilibrium condition, is obtained by noting that in steady state, with $\dot{\hat{C}} = 0$, we have $r = \rho + [\varrho(\varrho+\rho)A/\hat{C}]$. Then, using equation (9.4) and the definitions of steady-state H and y^w, we obtain equation (9.10). In Figure 9.1, the iso-interest capital–market equilibrium locus is a rectangular hyperbola. A decrease in r shifts the hyperbola outwards and hence upwards, reflecting a rise in the human wealth to non-human wealth ratio. Notice from Figure 9.1 that given r, the intersection of the iso-interest labour supply schedule and the iso-interest capital–market equilibrium locus uniquely determines the equilibrium labour supply and the take-home wage to non-wage income ratio.

What is the effect of a decline in r on the equilibrium levels of L and w^h/y^w? As we have pointed out, the lower r shifts the iso-interest labour

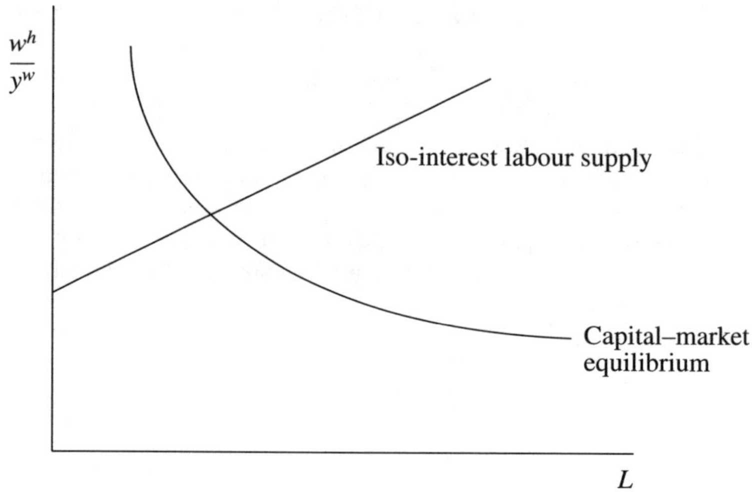

Figure 9.1 Iso-interest labour supply and capital–market equilibrium

supply schedule leftwards and hyperbola outwards. The take-home wage to non-wage income ratio unambiguously rises but what is the net effect on labour supply? To obtain an answer, note that from equation (9.10), we obtain r as a decreasing function of w^h/y^w and L, namely, $r = R(w^h/y^w, L)$, with $R_1 < 0$ and $R_2 < 0$. Substituting the function R for r in equation (9.9), we obtain an upward-sloping variable-interest-rate supply schedule denoted the S schedule in the $(L, w^h/y^w)$ plane that we illustrate in Figure 9.2 (see Appendix 9.1 for the derivative giving the slope of the S schedule). This implies that in Figure 9.1, a decrease in r shifts up the hyperbola by more than it shifts up the iso-interest labour supply schedule, implying that a lower interest rate stimulates L and raises w^h/y^w. Although at a given wage to non-wage income ratio, a decrease in r contracts labour supply, we discover that a decrease in r raises the wage to non-wage income ratio. Overall, the latter effect dominates and, consequently, a fall in the real interest rate acts to stimulate labour force participation.

To determine r endogenously, we need to add the labour-demand side of the model. Let us take the Cobb–Douglas production with η the capital-share parameter. Firms' optimal choice of labour and capital–labour ratio, $k \equiv (K/L)$, imply

$$w^f = (1-\eta)k^{\eta}, \tag{9.11}$$

$$r = \eta k^{-(1-\eta)}. \tag{9.12}$$

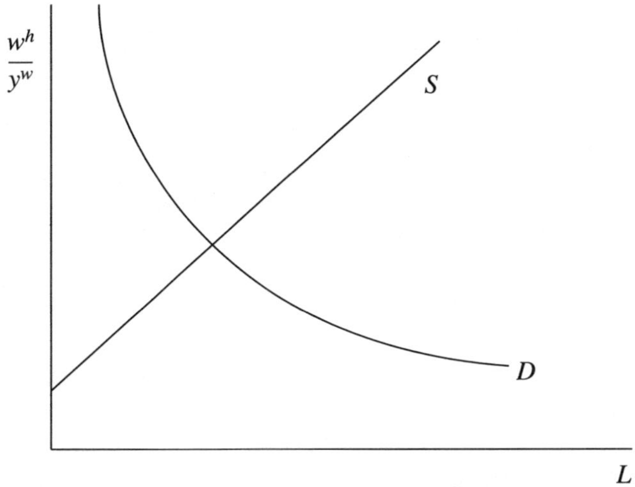

Figure 9.2 Variable-interest labour supply and demand

Hence, we obtain a sort of labour-demand relation:

$$\frac{w^h}{y^w} = \left\{(1+\tau_w)\left[\frac{\eta}{1-\eta} + \frac{\varrho[\phi(r)]^{1-\eta}}{1-\eta}\right]L\right\}^{-1}, \tag{9.13}$$

where the marginal product of capital condition in equation (9.12) is written $k = \phi(r)$, $\phi'(r) < 0$.

Equations (9.9), (9.10) and (9.13) give us three equations in the three unknowns: w^h/y^w, L, and r. Making the same substitution of the function R for r in equation (9.13), we obtain a downward-sloping variable-interest-rate demand schedule denoted the D schedule in Figure 9.2 (see Appendix 9.1 for the derivative giving the slope of the D schedule). At the intersection of the S and D schedules, we can draw a hyperbola (not shown) that would give the equilibrium real rate of interest.

The total tax revenue collected from payroll taxes and VAT is equal to $[\tau_w w^f L/(1+\tau_w)] + [\tau_c \hat{C}]$. Suppose that there is an increase in the payroll tax rate and a corresponding decline in the value-added tax rate τ_c that leaves total tax revenue unchanged. The effect of the tax shift is illustrated in Figure 9.3. The labour demand schedule shifts down, leading to a lower w^h/y^w and L. Passing through point B in Figure 9.3, we can draw an iso-interest capital–market equilibrium contour in the shape of a hyperbola (not shown) that gives a higher real rate of interest than the contour going through point A. In essence, the interest rate rises because the payroll tax hike tightens the supply of saving (deflated

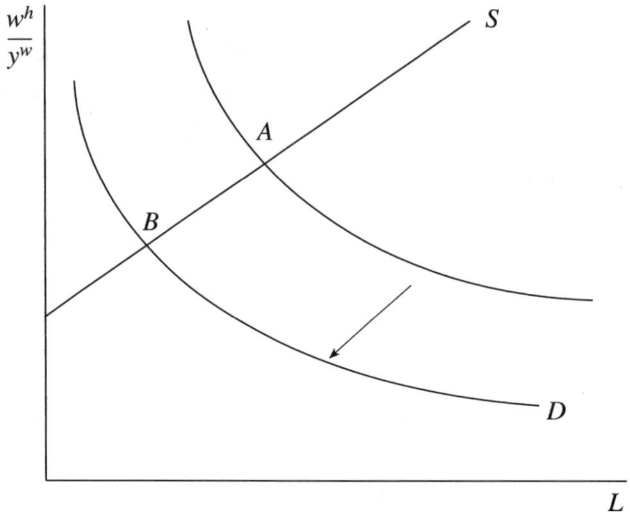

Figure 9.3 Revenue-neutral tax shift

by producers' price level). Labour force participation rate contracts because the payroll tax, in reducing the demand–wage relation to workers' non-wage incomes, induces a decline in the labour supplied. Although saving is decreased, causing non-wage incomes also to fall, the resulting rise of the interest rate prevents them from falling in proportion to the wage. Hence the decline in labour force participation has a permanent component.

9.3 TAX SHIFT IN OPEN ECONOMIES

In a small open economy whose interest rate is given by the world rate, we set $r = r^*$, where r^* is the exogenously given world interest rate. Observe from equation (9.10) that the wage-to-nonwage income ratio, w^h/y^w, is an implicit function of r^* at each L:

$$\frac{w^h}{y^w} = \Upsilon(r^* - \rho, L); \ \Upsilon_1 < 0, \ \Upsilon_2 < 0. \tag{9.14}$$

Using equation (9.14) in equation (9.9), we obtain a reduced-form supply relation or equilibrium labour force participation rate:

$$L = \frac{1 - \left[\frac{\varrho + \rho}{r^* + \varrho}\right][\Upsilon(r^* - \rho, L)]^{-1}}{1 + \left[\frac{\varrho + \rho}{r^* + \varrho}\right]}. \tag{9.15}$$

This equation uniquely determines the labour force participation rate. When the labour demand curve is shifted down by the increased payroll tax, the labour supply curve must sink ultimately by as much so as to return hours worked to its original level. This is accomplished through foreign asset decumulation, which erodes non-wage incomes.

In the small open economy, non-wage income is now given by $y^w = (r^* + \varrho)(K + F)$, where F is the amount of net foreign assets held per capita. The demand-side relationship in equation (9.13) is now modified to

$$\Upsilon(r^* - \rho, L) = \frac{(1 - \eta)[\phi(r^*)]^{\eta}}{(1 + \tau_w)\{(r^* + \varrho)[\phi(r^*)L + F]\}} \tag{9.16}$$

after using equation (9.14) and incorporating the open economy version of y^w. With L determined from equation (9.15), we see from equation (9.16) that an increase in τ_w leads to a decline in F that leaves the wage to non-wage income ratio invariant. The end result is the same wage share and labour force participation rate.

Extending the analysis to a two-country world with perfect international capital mobility is straightforward. We consider two initially identical economies called Home and Foreign, and suppose that a tax shift involving increased payroll taxation matched by a decline in the VAT rate in a revenue-neutral fashion occurs in Home. It is clear that such a tax shift raises the domestic interest rate in Home, resulting in capital outflow from Foreign. As foreigners accumulate foreign assets, their wage to non-wage income ratio declines resulting in reduced labour force participation. In terms of a diagram like Figure 9.2, the open-economy version of the D schedule (incorporating foreign assets as a component of non-human wealth) shifts down along an invariant S schedule. In Home, the D schedule also shifts down along an invariant S schedule. Although the tax shift leads to a decumulation of foreign assets by Home, the resulting higher world interest rate leads to a lower wage to non-wage income ratio and correspondingly lower labour force participation. Thus in a world with two large economies, the tax shift in one country, by pushing up the world interest rate, reduces labour force participation in both countries.

9.4 EFFECTS OF GROWTH

For simplicity, we now set τ_w and τ_c equal to zero. Following Frenkel and Razin (1996, chapter 12), we shall consider a simple steady-state balanced-growth model where the index of skill level grows exogenously at the rate of λ. In such a steady state, the aggregate per unit of effective human wealth, $\tilde{H}$, equals $\tilde{w}L/(r-\lambda+\varrho)$, where $\tilde{w}\equiv w/\Lambda$, Λ being the index of human capital. Effective non-wage income per capita using the growth adjusted interest rate is given by $\tilde{y}^w=(r-\lambda+\varrho)\tilde{A}$, where $\tilde{A}\equiv A/\Lambda$. Using the newly defined relations, $\tilde{H}$ and $\tilde{y}^w$, in equations (9.4) and (9.5), and rearranging, we obtain the steady-state labour supply relation in man-hours or the labour force participation rate:

$$L=\frac{1-\left[\dfrac{\varrho+\rho}{r-\lambda+\varrho}\right]\left[\dfrac{\tilde{w}}{\tilde{y}^w}\right]^{-1}}{1+\left[\dfrac{\varrho+\rho}{r-\lambda+\varrho}\right]}. \tag{9.17}$$

We also note that in a steady state with balanced growth, equation (9.8) can now be expressed as

$$r=\rho+\lambda+\frac{\varrho}{1+\left[\dfrac{\tilde{w}}{\tilde{y}^w}\right]L}. \tag{9.18}$$

This condition is obtained by noting that in steady state, with $\dot{\tilde{C}}=0$, we have $r=\rho+\lambda+[\varrho(\varrho+\rho)\tilde{A}/\tilde{C}]$, where $\tilde{C}=C/\Lambda$. Then, using equation (9.4) and the definitions of steady-state $\tilde{H}$ and $\tilde{y}^w$, we obtain equation (9.18).

Turning to the production side of the model, let us once again take the Cobb–Douglas production with η the capital-share parameter. Firms' optimal choice of labour and capital-labour ratio, $\tilde{k}\equiv K/(\Lambda L)$, imply

$$\tilde{w}=(1-\eta)\tilde{k}^{\eta}, \tag{9.19}$$

$$r=\eta\tilde{k}^{-(1-\eta)}. \tag{9.20}$$

Hence, we obtain a sort of labour-demand relation:

$$\frac{\tilde{w}}{\tilde{y}^w}=\left\{\left[\frac{\eta}{1-\eta}+\frac{[\varrho-\lambda][\phi(r-\lambda+\lambda)]^{1-\eta}}{1-\eta}\right]L\right\}^{-1}, \tag{9.21}$$

where the marginal product of capital condition is written $\tilde{k}=\phi(r-\lambda+\lambda)$, $\phi'(\cdot)<0$.

We can express $r-\lambda$ as a decreasing function of $\tilde{w}/\tilde{y}^w$ and L, namely,

$r-\lambda = R(\tilde{w}/\tilde{y}^w, L)$ with $R_1 < 0$ and $R_2 < 0$. Substituting the function R for $r-\lambda$, we obtain an upward-sloping variable-growth-adjusted-interest rate supply schedule in the $(L, \tilde{w}/\tilde{y}^w)$ plane. Making another substitution in the demand-side relation, we obtain a downward-sloping variable-growth-adjusted-interest-rate demand schedule for given λ. These are the D and S schedules in Figure 9.4.

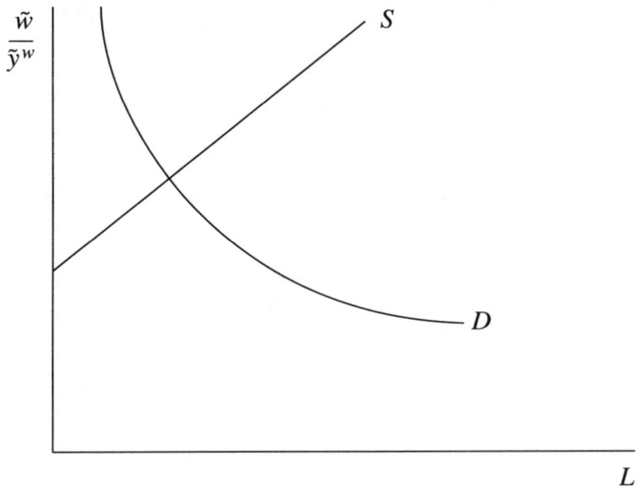

Figure 9.4 Variable-interest labour supply and demand

What is the effect of an increase in λ? It can be checked that this results in a rightward and hence upward shift of the D curve along an invariant S curve in Figure 9.4. Consequently, there is an expansion of labour force participation. Moreover, we are now left on a higher hyperbola, meaning a contour corresponding to a lower growth-adjusted rate of interest. Looking at the expression

$$r = \rho + \lambda + \frac{\varrho}{1 + \left[\frac{\tilde{w}}{\tilde{y}^w}\right] L},$$

we see that although r would be expected to rise on account of a higher λ, that rise is somewhat dampened by the stimulation of labour force participation along with an increase in the $\tilde{w}/\tilde{y}^w$ ratio. As a result, the growth-adjusted interest rate actually falls.

It is clear that in a small open economy, as in the case of the East Asian economies, with interest rate pinned down by the international capital market, the higher λ is translated fully into an expansion of labour force participation. Specifically, in a small open economy whose interest rate is given by the world rate, we set $r = r^*$, where r^* is the exogenously given world interest rate. In Figure 9.5, where we plot the variable-growth-adjusted-interest-rate labour supply schedule, the fact that $r - \lambda$ is known helps us pin down a specific hyperbola. Since the hyperbola is indexed to $r^* - \lambda$, it is clear that growth in a small open economy has the maximum impact on

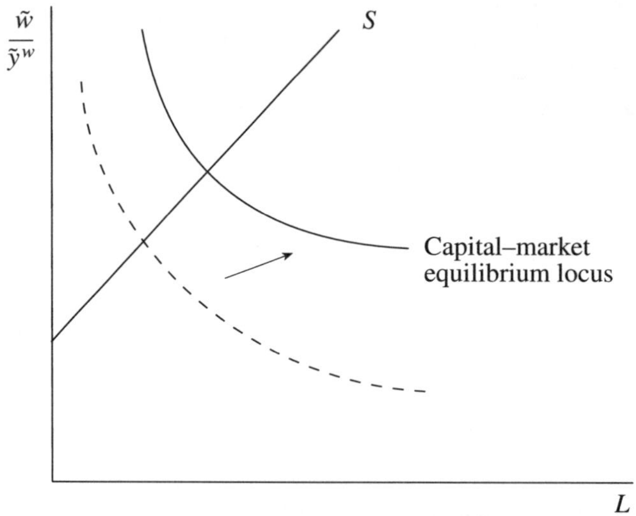

Figure 9.5 Growth in small open economy

stimulating labour force participation, as a higher rate of human capital accumulation leaves the domestic interest rate unchanged (since it has to be equal to the exogenously given r^*) but leads instead to an increase in external debt. The rise in human wealth relative to non-human wealth ratio implies an improvement in labour-market conditions, which stimulates labour supply. This provides an explanation for the sharp rise in labour force participation rate in the four East Asian economies of Hong Kong, Singapore, South Korea and Taiwan.

What about the effects of asymmetric growth in a two-country or two-region world? Suppose that Home experiences a rise in λ exclusively. How would this affect Foreign? It is clear that the increased growth rate in Home puts an upward pressure on the interest rate. This dampens somewhat the expansionary effect domestically. Abroad, however, there is no faster growth to ameliorate the effects of the rise in interest rate. Consequently, Foreign must experience a decrease in its labour force participation rate as a result of overseas growth.

9.5 WEALTH, TECHNOLOGICAL CATCH-UP, AND THE NATURAL RATE

While the focus of this chapter has been on the role of wealth on labour force participation, there is clearly also an influence that wealth has on the determination of the natural rate, especially over the long term. Firstly, it is plausible that as most citizens of a nation become more wealthy, earning income not simply from work but also increasingly also from holding of non-human assets such as consumer durables, real estate, and stocks, the wages that firms need to pay their employees to keep them as motivated as before or to stay as loyal to the firm as before at any *given* measure of labour market tightness increases. This adds to wage pressure so that along a given labour demand curve this acts to raise equilibrium unemployment. In the East Asian context, we can readily understand that in the early days of industrialisation – the sixties – when most citizens owned very little non-human assets, they recognised that their opportunities relied almost entirely upon their ability to hold on to a job. Thus, the pull upward of the wage that firms could afford to pay because they were able to sell labour-intensive goods into the world market had the maximum impact on jobs. The further upward pull of labour demand arising from the shift of the industrial structure towards more capital-intensive lines of production as firms produced higher value-added products and so could afford to pay higher wages later in the eighties and nineties had smaller impact on jobs as workers could fall back on more comfortable cushions in the event that they lost a job. This, it was suggested in Chapter 2, explained why in the eighties and nineties, Singapore's wages experienced sharp rises in concert with small changes in the unemployment rate. With the East Asian economies becoming wealthier, Ezra Vogel (1991, pp. 107–8) has observed:

> The public in these East Asian societies has begun demanding a greater voice in government . . . The winds of democracy have also been felt on the factory floor, as labor has begun to demand more rights. The changes have been most dramatic in South Korea, where days lost to strikes in 1987 were greater than they had been in the previous twenty-five years combined, but workers in Taiwan, Hong Kong, and Singapore have also begun to lose their docility.

There is another way in which a steady accumulation of wealth may lead to increased demands for a welfare state historically, in the US but possibly also in Europe. Abramovitz (1981, pp. 2–3), in his presidential address to the American Economic Association, has argued:

> The enlargement of the government's economic role, including its support of income minima, health care, social insurance, and the other elements of the welfare state, was, therefore – at least up to a point – not just a question of compassionate regards for the unfortunate, and not just a question of reducing inequalities of outcome and opportunity, though that is how people usually think of it. It was, and is – up to a point – a part of the productivity growth process itself.

As Europe recovered from the war-time destruction of capital, the next two decades or so – the fifties and sixties – of high growth could be a factor leading to a demand for many elements of the welfare state. In the framework of the endogenous natural rate theory, this would have had the effect of shifting up the wage curve, and so raising the natural rate. It is yet to be seen how the economic and socio-political factors would work themselves out in determining the system of social safety net in the East Asian countries as wealth catches up. The form it would take has an influence on the amount of joblessness that would prevail.

As we have alluded to before, there is a dynamic role that trade can play in influencing the natural rate of unemployment based upon the international spillover effects of R&D. This is supported by some empirical evidence that the degree of trade integration is positively associated with total factor productivity improvements (see Coe and Helpman, 1995; Bayoumi, Coe and Helpman, 1996; and Coe, Helpman and Hoffmaister, 1997). There are opportunities for learning from other countries about manufacturing techniques, organisational techniques and product market conditions in the normal course of business that are available through international trade and foreign direct investments. Also, international trade and investment provide opportunities for follower-countries to imitate foreign products and methods. For these and other reasons, Helpman (1997) argues that international trade is the main carrier of productivity gains. Because of the high degree of trade orientation of the East Asian economies, Coe, Helpman and Hoffmaister (1997) find that the size of the spillover effect of R&D undertaken in an advanced country on these economies is large. For example, they find that an addition of 100 dollars to the US domestic R&D capital stock raises Singapore's by 1 dollar, Brazil's by 77 cents, and Zimbabwe's by only 4 cents. An addition of 100 dollars to Japan's domestic R&D capital raises Singapore's by 1.5 dollars, Brazil's by 23 cents and Zimbabwe's by only 3 cents. Bayoumi, Coe and Helpman (1997) conclude that open trading policies of the type followed by the East Asian economies can benefit developing nations through facilitating technology transfer from industrial countries. In their work based upon an econometric model of the world economy, they show that expanding imports of manufactures in developing countries other than the East Asian economies of Hong Kong, Singapore, South Korea and Taiwan by 5 percentage points of GDP raises output by about 9 per cent in the long run, and consumption by 6 per cent. They infer from these results that part of the success of the East Asian economies over the last 20 years can be attributed to productivity improvements stemming from foreign R&D spillovers through trade.

In their study aimed at deriving quantitative estimates of these international R&D spillover effects for a group of 77 developing countries (see Coe, Helpman and Hoffmaister, 1997), the authors also find that a developing country's total factor productivity is larger the more educated is its labour force. If we accept the Nelson–Phelps (1966) hypothesis that higher education improves a worker's ability to follow and to understand new technological developments, it might be that both trade orientation as well as the steady increase in human capital accumulation both worked to hasten the pace of technological catch-up in the East Asian economies.

The view that there has been, to an important degree, a process of technological catch-up – one facilitated by trade and, at least in the case of Singapore and Taiwan, also by foreign direct investments – as the East Asian economies moved closer to the knowledge frontier defined by the advanced economies, suggests a mechanism through which trade lowers the natural rate and raises the job participation rate. The mechanism is one in which firms operating in the small open economies, faced with the prospects of rapid technological growth at exogenously given world real interest rates, would be induced to raise their hiring of new workers and so increase labour demand. On the side of employees' work incentives, with rapid productivity growth pulling up wages ahead of wealth, wage pressure would be correspondingly reduced. The result is a shrinking of the pool of unemployed.

9.6 CONCLUDING REMARKS

In this chapter, we have emphasised the role of labour-market conditions as measured by workers' take-home wages relative to their non-wage incomes in determining the supply of labour. We showed that a revenue-neutral tax shift from VAT to higher payroll taxes raises the interest rate and worsens labour-market conditions. As a result, the amount of non-employment rises. Here, the rise in non-employment takes the form of a decline in labour force participation. In Hoon and Phelps (1996), we showed that the tax shift also tends to raise the natural rate of unemployment. In a small open economy that takes the world interest rate as given, asset decumulation acts to offset the contractionary effect on employment of the tax shift. In a two-country world, however, the extent of asset decumulation by the country implementing the tax shift fails to restore the economy to the original take-home wage to non-wage income ratio as the world interest rate is pushed up. Instead, the higher real interest rate acts to reduce employment overseas as well.

Our analysis of growth uncovered the result that in the closed economy case as well as in the small open economy case, a faster pace of human capital accumulation acts to stimulate labour supply. In the closed economy case, faster growth leads to a rise in the wage to growth-adjusted non-wage income ratio. Hence, although the rate of interest is pushed up, it does not increase by the full extent of the rise in the rate of growth of human capital. So the growth-adjusted rate of interest actually falls. In the small open economy case, free international capital mobility ensures that the domestic interest rate is equal to the exogenously given world interest rate. Hence an increase in the rate of human capital accumulation has the full effect on expanding labour supply as higher growth leads to a rise in the human wealth to non-human wealth ratio. The implication of asymmetric growth in a two-country world is that the higher world interest rate caused by higher growth in one region of the world contracts labour supply overseas. We also discussed the role of wealth in determining the natural rate, as well as the influence trade has on jobs through the beneficial effects of international R&D spillovers.

NOTES

1. This analysis draws on Hoon and Phelps (1996).

APPENDIX 9.1

The respective slopes of the D and S schedules in Figure 9.1 are

$$\left.\frac{d\left(\frac{w^h}{y^w}\right)}{dL}\right|_D = \frac{-\left(\frac{w^h}{y^w}\right)L^{-1} - \left(\frac{w^h}{y^w}\right)^2 L(1+\tau_w)\varrho k^{-\eta}\phi' R_2}{1+\left(\frac{w^h}{y^w}\right)^2 L(1+\tau_w)\varrho k^{-\eta}\phi' R_1},$$

$$\left.\frac{d\left(\frac{w^h}{y^w}\right)}{dL}\right|_S = \frac{1 + \left[\frac{\varrho + \rho}{r + \varrho}\right] + \left[\frac{\varrho(\varrho + \rho)}{1 + \left(\frac{w^h}{y^w}\right)L}\right]}{\left[\frac{\varrho + \rho}{r + \varrho}\right]\left(\frac{w^h}{y^w}\right)^{-2}\left\{1 - \left[\frac{1}{\left(1 + \frac{r}{\varrho}\right)\left(1 + \left(\frac{w^h}{y^w}\right)^{-1} L^{-1}\right)}\right]\right\}},$$

where

$$R_1 = \frac{-\varrho L}{\left[1 + \left(\frac{w^h}{y^w}\right)L\right]^2},$$

$$R_2 = \frac{-\varrho\left(\frac{w^h}{y^w}\right)}{\left[1 + \left(\frac{w^h}{y^w}\right)L\right]^2}.$$

10. Trade, growth and unemployment in Ricardo's *Essay on Profits* model

10.1 INTRODUCTION

A major theme of this book has been that international trade enlarges market size and through this channel has salutary effects on real wages and jobs. In this chapter, we return to a classical model of trade, growth and unemployment and show how market size interacts with the Stolper–Samuelson effect to influence jobs and wages. It draws upon recent formalisations of Ricardo's ([1815] 1923) *Essay* model. Although the formalisation of Ricardo's theory of trade based principally on Chapter 7 of his *Principles* ([1817] 1911) is static, various authors such as Burgstaller (1986), Findlay (1974) and Maneschi (1983) have developed a dynamic trade model based upon Ricardo's ([1815] 1923) *Essay on Profits*. In the *Essay* model, the subsistence wage is treated as a parameter. If, following Leibenstein (1957), we treat the subsistence wage as a biologically determined wage that the workers require to be able to work, and we treat the labour force as a constant, we obtain a model that links trade and growth to employment expansion. Mokyr (1991, p. 189), looking at the Industrial Revolution, has suggested:

> In the final analysis, then, cheap labor could have been detrimental to industrialization through a variety of mechanisms. It could and probably did mean in some places that workers were underfed and possibly handicapped in other ways. Cheap labor could mean unmotivated, quarrelsome workers, poorly adapted to the discipline and rigor of factory and mining life. It meant poor labor relations, low morale, high turnover, and absenteeism. Cheap labor could mean that workers were illiterate, unskilled, and incapable of making the adjustments required by changing techniques.

Mokyr (1991, p. 186) also cited Adam Smith ([1776] 1937, p. 81), who thought that

> the wages of labour are the encouragement of industry, which like every other quality, improves in proportion to the encouragement it receives. A plentiful subsistence increases the bodily strength of the laborer . . . where wages are high,

accordingly, we shall always find the workmen more active, diligent, and expeditious, than where they are low.[1]

The chapter is organised as follows. In Section 10.2, we show in a competitive model that under free trade, the relatively land abundant country experiences a decline in its growth rate – correspondingly, a decline in the rate at which employment grows – as the relative price of the agricultural good rises under trade. When we introduce an intermediates good sector that produces a variety of fertilizer inputs in Section 10.3, giving rise in effect to increasing returns to scale, we show that intra-industry trade allows all participating countries to experience a rise in their growth rate. In that model, when both inter-industry trade as well as intra-industry trade take place, it is possible that trade raises the rate of employment expansion for the land abundant country as well despite a rise in the relative price of the agricultural good under trade.

10.2 THE COMPETITIVE MODEL

Following Findlay (1974), we think of a natural wage rate fixed in terms of corn, the agricultural good, there being an 'unlimited supply of labour' à la Arthur Lewis. The natural wage rate can be generated from the assumption that nutrition affects workers' productivity as suggested earlier. Then, if the effort function depends on the real wage measured in terms of the agricultural good, cost minimisation yields a rigid real wage. The time elapsing between the application of labour inputs and emergence of agricultural output is one period. Velvet, the luxury good, is produced with constant returns to scale and requires also one period of production.

Consider first the problem of the velvet producer. His production function is given by $V_t = aL_{vt-1}$, where V_t is the output of velvet and L_{vt-1} is labour allocated to velvet production at the beginning of period $t-1$. The maximisation problem facing the velvet producer is: Maximise

$$\frac{p_t a L_{vt-1}}{1+r_t} - wL_{vt-1}$$

by choosing L_{vt-1}, where p_t is the relative price of velvet (in terms of corn), w is the natural wage and r_t is the profit rate. The solution yields

$$\frac{p_t a}{w} = 1 + r_t. \tag{10.1}$$

Turning now to the problem of the agricultural producer, his production function is given by $C_t = T^{1-b}L_{ct-1}^{b}$, where $0<b<1$. Here, C_t is corn output,

T is land, and L_{ct-1} is the labour allocation to the corn sector. The agricultural producer solves the problem: Maximise

$$\frac{T^{1-b}L^{b}_{ct-1}}{1+r_t} - wL_{ct-1}$$

by choosing L_{ct-1}. The solution yields

$$\frac{bT^{1-b}L^{-(1-b)}_{ct-1}}{w} = 1 + r_t. \tag{10.2}$$

Equating, we obtain

$$p_t = \frac{bT^{1-b}}{aL^{1-b}_{ct-1}}, \tag{10.3}$$

so that p_t is decreasing in L_{ct-1}. From equation (10.1), this implies that r_t is decreasing in L_{ct-1}.

We have now solved the optimisation problems of each producer. The solution of the complete model requires that we also specify the adding-up constraint on labour allocation as well as the condition of market clearing for either the corn or velvet market. We will choose to clear the velvet market, making the assumption that only landlords demand velvet and, in particular, they spend all their income on velvet. Thus, for the velvet market to clear we require

$$(1-b)T^{1-b}L^{b}_{ct-1} = p_t aL_{vt-1}, \tag{10.4}$$

where the left-hand side of the equation gives us the total rent accruing to the landlords in period t and the right-hand side gives the supply of velvet. The adding-up constraint on labour allocation is

$$L_{vt-1} + L_{ct-1} = L_{t-1}. \tag{10.5}$$

Solving, we obtain

$$p_t = D\left[\frac{T}{L_{t-1}}\right]^{1-b}, \tag{10.6}$$

where

$$D \equiv \frac{\left[(1-b)b^{\frac{b}{1-b}} + b^{\frac{1}{1-b}}\right]^{1-b}}{a}.$$

Notice that we can write

$$r_t = \frac{p_t a - w}{w}.$$

Starting with an initial wage fund, the economy grows. However, as more labour is employed, the relative price of velvet gradually declines. Consequently, the rate of profit, and hence the rate at which labour is employed declines. In the long run, we reach a stationary state, where the additional employment of labour grinds to a halt.

Notice that for a given wage fund, L_{t-1}, the relative price of velvet is higher for the country with the larger supply of arable land. Free trade, therefore, implies that the land scarce country becomes a net exporter of velvet. Since the free trade price of velvet rises from the autarkic value, that country experiences a rise in the rate of profit, and hence, the rate of employment creation. Thus trade for the land scarce country acts as an engine generating faster growth in employment. The converse occurs for the land abundant country.

10.3 THE MODEL WITH INTERNAL INCREASING RETURNS TO SCALE

We introduce an intermediate (fertilizer) input sector to an otherwise Findlay (1974) model.[2] Fertilizer inputs are differentiated intermediates produced under increasing returns to scale. The scale economies are internal to firms as in Ethier (1982). The market structure that emerges is that of Dixit–Stiglitz monopolistic competition in the intermediate goods sector. The intermediate goods sector is able to produce any of a large number of inputs that enter symmetrically into the production function of the agricultural good. The total number of intermediates actually produced (which is to be determined endogenously) is assumed to be large, although small relative to the number of potential inputs. All fertilizer inputs are presumed to be produced with the same production function, exhibiting rising average products and constant marginal products. With symmetry built into the problem, we are assured that all manufacturing goods actually produced will be produced in the same quantity and sold at the same price.

There is a natural wage rate fixed in terms of corn, the agricultural good. The production of intermediates is assumed to be instantaneous, whereas the time elapsing between the application of labour inputs and fertilizer inputs in the corn sector is one period. Velvet, the luxury good, is produced with constant returns to scale and requires also one period for production. Thus, we abstract from the difficulties of unequal periods of production of the two final goods.

Consider first the problem of the velvet producer. His production function is given by $V_t = aL_{vt-1}$, where V_t is the output of velvet and L_{vt-1} is the labour allocated to velvet production at the beginning of period $t-1$. The maximisation problem facing the velvet producer is: Maximise

$$\frac{p_t a L_{vt-1}}{1+r_t} - wL_{vt-1}$$

by choosing L_{vt-1}, where p_t is the relative price of velvet (in terms of corn), w is the natural wage and r_t is the profit rate. The solution yields

$$p_t a = 1 + r_t \tag{10.7}$$

upon normalisation by setting $w \equiv 1$.

Turning now to the problem of the agricultural producer, his production function is given by $C_t = T^{1-b-e} L^b_{ct-1} \int_0^{n_{t-1}} m^e_{it-1} di$, where b and e are positive constants, and $b+e$ lies between zero and one. Here, C_t is corn output, T is land, L_{ct-1} is the labour allocation to the corn sector, m_{it-1} is the quantity of the ith intermediate input, and n_{t-1} is the number of intermediates available to the agricultural producer. Using the fact of symmetry, we can simplify the production function to $C_t = T^{1-b-e} L^b_{ct-1} n_{t-1} m^e_{t-1}$.

In solving his optimisation problem, the corn producer treats the number of intermediates as given (being determined in the economy-wide general equilibrium). Notice that with n_{t-1} given, the production function of the agricultural good is Cobb–Douglas, exhibiting diminishing returns to labour, as well as intermediate inputs. However, in the process of growth, the number of intermediates rises, serving as a type of positive externality, giving in effect increasing returns in agriculture.

The agricultural producer solves the problem: Maximise

$$\frac{T^{1-b-e} L^b_{ct-1} n_{t-1} m^e_{t-1}}{1+r_t} - L_{ct-1} - q_{t-1} n_{t-1} m_{t-1}$$

by choosing L_{ct-1} and m_{t-1}, where q_{t-1} is the relative price of the intermediate input. Solving our problem yields

$$bL^{-(1-b)}_{ct-1} n_{t-1} m^e_{t-1} = 1 + r_t, \tag{10.8}$$

$$\frac{eL^b_{ct-1} m^{-(1-e)}_{t-1}}{q_{t-1}} = 1 + r_t, \tag{10.9}$$

upon another normalisation setting $T \equiv 1$.

Now, consider the problem facing the typical fertilizer input producer. He solves the problem: Maximise

$$q_{t-1} m_{t-1} - (g + hm_{t-1})$$

by choosing m_{t-1}, where $g+hm_{t-1}\equiv L_{\mathrm{mt}-1}$ gives us the labour required to produce m_{t-1} units of the intermediate. Here, g is the fixed cost (in labour units), while h^{-1} gives us the constant marginal physical product of labour. The typical intermediate good producer behaves in a monopolistically competitive manner, with free entry in the intermediate good industry so that zero profits are achieved at each point.

To derive the demand function for a typical intermediate input, we eliminate L_{ct-1} in equations (10.8) and (10.9) to obtain

$$q_{t-1}=\frac{em_{t-1}^{-(1-b-e)/(1-b)}}{(1+r_t)^{1/(1-b)}(bn_{t-1})^{-b/(1-b)}}.$$

With a substitution, the maximisation problem facing the typical fertilizer input producer can be rewritten as: Maximise

$$\frac{em_{t-1}^{-(1-b-e)/(1-b)}}{(1+r_t)^{1/(1-b)}(bn_{t-1})^{-b/(1-b)}}-(g+hm_{t-1})$$

by choosing m_{t-1}. Solution of our problem yields

$$\frac{e^2m_{t-1}^{-(1-b-e)/(1-b)}}{(1-b)(1+r_t)^{1/(1-b)}(bn_{t-1})^{-b/(1-b)}}=h. \tag{10.10}$$

With free entry into the intermediate good industry, we also require the zero-profit condition, which we write as

$$m_{t-1}=\frac{g}{q_{t-1}-h}. \tag{10.11}$$

We have now solved the optimisation problems of each producer. The solution of the complete model requires also that we specify the full-employment of labour condition, as well as the condition of market clearing for either the corn or the velvet market. We will choose to clear the velvet market, making the assumption that only landlords demand velvet and, in particular, they spend all their income on velvet. Thus for the velvet market to clear we require

$$(1-b-e)L_{ct-1}^{b}n_{t-1}m_{t-1}^{e}=p_taL_{vt-1}, \tag{10.12}$$

where the left-hand side of equation (10.12) gives us the rent accruing to the landlords in period t and the right-hand side gives the supply of velvet.

The full-employment of labour condition can be written as

$$n_{t-1}(g+hm_{t-1})+L_{vt-1}+L_{ct-1}=L_{t-1}. \tag{10.13}$$

We now have seven independent equations to solve for seven variables in the closed economy: r_t, p_t, L_{vt-1}, L_{ct-1}, q_{t-1}, m_{t-1}, and n_{t-1}. We turn next to solving the model.

To solve the closed economy model, we first rewrite equation (10.10) as

$$\frac{e^2 m_{t-1}^{-(1-e)} L_{ct-1}^{b}}{(1-b)(1+r_t)} = h,$$

recalling the definition of L_{ct-1} from equations (10.8) and (10.9). Using this equation and equation (10.9), we obtain, after some cancellation of terms,

$$q_{t-1} = \frac{h(1-b)}{e}. \tag{10.14}$$

Thus we find that the relative price of the intermediate is a constant, being inversely related to the marginal physical product of labour in the intermediate good sector (h^{-1}).

Substituting equation (10.14) into equation (10.11), we obtain the quantity of each intermediate that is produced, which is a constant and positively related to the marginal physical productivity of labour:

$$m_{t-1} = \frac{ge}{h(1-b-e)}. \tag{10.15}$$

Eliminating q_{t-1} in equations (10.9) and (10.11), we obtain

$$\frac{eL_{ct-1}^{b} m_{t-1}^{e}}{1+r_t} = g + hm_{t-1}.$$

Using this equation and equation (10.8), we obtain

$$L_{ct-1} = \frac{bn_{t-1}(g + hm_{t-1})}{e}. \tag{10.16}$$

From equation (10.15), we know that m_{t-1} is a constant. Thus, equation (10.16) predicts that L_{ct-1}/n_{t-1} is a constant. With economic growth, both the labour allocation to the corn sector as well as the number of differentiated intermediates increase at the same rate.

Substituting equation (10.16) into equation (10.13), we obtain

$$(1 + eb^{-1})L_{ct-1} + L_{vt-1} = L_{t-1}. \tag{10.17}$$

Combining equations (10.12), (10.16) and (10.17), we obtain an implicit function of L_{ct-1} (recalling that m_{t-1} is already solved) and p_t:

$$\frac{e(1-b-e)L_{ct-1}^{1+b} m_{t-1}^{e}}{b(g + hm_{t-1})} = p_t a[L_{t-1} - (1 + eb^{-1})L_{ct-1}]. \tag{10.18}$$

Further combining equations (10.7), (10.8) and (10.16), we obtain an equation relating p_t and L_{ct-1}:

$$p_t = \frac{em^e_{t-1}L^b_{ct-1}}{a(g+hm_{t-1})}. \tag{10.19}$$

With two equations in two unknowns (L_{ct-1} and p_t), we can use equations (10.18) and (10.19) to solve for L_{ct-1}:

$$L_{ct-1} = bL_{t-1}. \tag{10.20}$$

With L_{ct-1} determined, we can solve for n_{t-1} from equation (10.16):

$$n_{t-1} = \frac{eL_{t-1}}{g+hm_{t-1}}. \tag{10.21}$$

Notice that both L_{ct-1} and n_{t-1} are proportional to L_{t-1}. Since total labour in the economy grows at the rate of profit (assuming that all profits are reinvested), we have the result that the number of differentiated intermediates grows at the economy-wide profit rate, r_t.

To determine L_{vt-1}, we make use of equation (10.17) to obtain

$$L_{vt-1} = (1-b-e)L_{t-1}. \tag{10.22}$$

The labour allocated to the velvet sector is also proportional to the total labour force. To determine the economy-wide rate of profit, we combine equations (10.9), (10.14) and (10.15) to yield

$$1+r_t = \frac{b^b e^{1+e}(1-b-e)^{1-e}L^b_{t-1}}{(1-b)h^e g^{1-e}}. \tag{10.23}$$

Finally, given equation (10.23), equation (10.7) yields the relative price of velvet, p_t. All variables in the system are thus completely determined.

In this model, with a sufficiently large initial wage fund, there is long-run sustained growth in this economy. The proof of this result follows quite simply from equation (10.23). With some simple notation, we rewrite equation (10.23) as

$$1+r_t = \Phi L^b_{t-1},$$

where

$$\Phi \equiv \frac{b^b e^{1+e}(1-b-e)^{1-e}}{(1-b)h^e g^{1-e}}$$

is a constant. Given an initial wage fund that is sufficiently large in size, r_t is positive. Then, $L_t = (1+r_t)L_{t-1}$. Accordingly, we have

$$1+r_{t+1}=\Phi L_t^b=\Phi(1+r_t)^b L_{t-1}^b=(1+r_t)^{1+b}.$$

In general, the growth rate in period $t+j$ is given by $1+r_{t+j}=(1+r_t)^{(1+b)j}$. Apparently, $1+r_{t+1}$ is greater than $1+r_t$ so long as $r_t>0$, a condition which we assume holds. In general, $1+r_{t+j}>1+r_{j-1}$.

To see why there is sustained growth in this economy, it is useful to focus on equation (10.8), which gives us the condition that labour in agriculture has to be applied to the point where the present discounted value of the marginal product of labour should be equal to the natural wage rate. Rearranging equation (10.8), we may write

$$r_t=bL_{ct-1}^{-(1-b)}n_{t-1}m_{t-1}^e-1.$$

In order to enjoy long-run sustained growth it is necessary that the marginal product of agricultural labour should not decline in the process of growth. From our equation above, it is apparent that, for *given* m_{t-1} and n_{t-1}, there will indeed be diminishing marginal product of agricultural labour. From equation (10.15) we know that a fixed quantity of each differentiated intermediate is applied to agriculture. What keeps the marginal productivity of agricultural labour from declining is the fact that the number of intermediates being applied increases in the process of growth so that labour cooperates with a wider range of intermediates. This, in effect, raises the marginal product of agricultural labour as the economy grows. To see this, we rewrite the marginal product of agricultural labour as

$$T^{1-b-e}b\left(\frac{L_{ct-1}}{n_{t-1}}\right)^{-(1-b)}m_{t-1}^e n_{t-1}^b,$$

where we write out T explicitly. We note from equations (10.15) and (10.16) that m_{t-1} and L_{ct-1}/n_{t-1} are constants. The only term that varies is n_{t-1}, the number of differentiated intermediates. In particular, n_{t-1} grows at the rate of profit.

Notice also the effect of pure intra-industry trade. Suppose that there are two countries with the same land–labour ratio. Then, no inter-industry trade occurs. However, there will be an international exchange of differentiated intermediates. Consequently, the profit rate in each country rises upon opening up to trade. When we allow the land–labour ratio to differ across the two countries, the land scarce country must unambiguously face an increase in the profit rate both because the relative price of corn moves in its favour but also because it now faces a wider range of intermediate inputs. The crucial new result in the presence of scale economies is that even the land abundant country can experience a rise in the profit rate under international trade since the enlarged market size can offset the adverse shift of the relative price.

NOTES

1. Mokyr (1991, p. 186), however, suggested: 'What Smith seems to be describing, however, is an upward-sloping supply curve of labor, which makes people work *more* [emphasis in original] if the wage is higher. The question is, however, what makes people work *better* [emphasis in original] or harder per unit of time?'
2. This analysis draws upon Hoon (1993).

11. A synthesis

This book has been motivated by a desire to build a theory which is general-equilibrium in its approach but yet allows one to study how the economic forces that operate in the global economy affect a nation's long-term unemployment and wage performance. In undertaking this enterprise, the book makes a departure from the conventional treatment of unemployment in the international economics literature. By focusing on the determinants of the natural rate of unemployment, the theory places an emphasis on real (as opposed to monetary) factors in accounting for long-run movements in wages and unemployment. The theory is micro-foundation based, being built up from optimisation problems solved by decision-making workers and firms. The crucial new element that is introduced to standard full-employment trade models is the informational asymmetric problem arising from the difficulty that firms have in monitoring the effort levels of workers. In the absence of bonding solutions, due, say, to capital–market imperfections, firms use wages as an incentive device. In general equilibrium, endogenous job rationing arises. The incentive-compatible wage generally rises as the equilibrium rate of unemployment declines giving, in effect, an upward-sloping wage curve in the employment rate–real wage plane. A demand–wage relation can be juxtaposed against the wage curve to determine the natural rate of unemployment, whose position in the Marshallian employment–wage diagram depends on the details of the production conditions and market structure.

What are the principal lessons that have been derived from the analysis conducted in this book? In the view of this author, the insights derived can be summarised in the following points:

1. At the most basic level, the integration of a country into the world trading system affects the position of both the wage curve as well as the demand–wage relation and consequently affects real wages and the amount of joblessness. In the simple Ricardian model with fixed technological coefficients, the real export wage is unaffected by trade. However, as goods imported can be purchased at a lower relative price compared to autarky, the real consumption wage is increased. Consequently, this relaxes the no-shirking constraint and, taken by itself, acts to lower the natural rate. When we consider a monopolistically com-

petitive world, where workers exhibit the Dixit–Stiglitz 'love-for-variety' preferences, there is an additional gain from being able to purchase a larger number of differentiated products from an enlarged market in a global economy. As the utility level rises with a larger number of varieties at any given real wage, workers value their jobs more under trade. Through this channel, there is a further rightward shift of the wage curve.

The demand–wage relation is also affected by international trade. In the pure Heckscher–Ohlin model, whether the real demand wage is increased or decreased by integration into the global economy depends upon the relative factor abundance of the country concerned. Trade raises the real demand wage of the relatively labour abundant country but reduces it in the relatively labour scarce country. In the latter, the decline in the real demand wage more than offsets the rightward shift of the wage curve so that trade actually raises the natural rate of the relatively labour scarce country. Two other channels, both operative in a non-competitive world, however, work to shift up the real demand wage relation. In a set-up with oligopolistic competition, international trade acts to reduce the size of the price–marginal cost mark-up and consequently increases the real demand wage. In the monopolistically competitive world of free entry and exit with intermediates produced by firms facing downward-sloping demand curves, the marginal productivity of workers depends upon the size of the international market. With international increasing returns to scale, the marginal contribution of an employed worker is higher under trade due to trade in intermediate inputs. Consequently, the real demand wage again rises as a result of trade.

2. In the trading world envisaged here, the gains from international trade are likely to be greater for smaller nations. A particularly stark characterisation of the international distribution of the gains from trade comes from the Ricardian model with a large country and many small countries. Under trade, the large country is incompletely specialised while all the small countries are completely specialised. In that case, the international terms of trade are given by the autarkic relative price of the large country and trade leads to gains for all the small trading nations, including a decline in their natural rate of unemployment. The large country is, however, unaffected by trade; its real wage and equilibrium unemployment remain unchanged. When we take into account economies of scale that are internal to the firm arising in the context of monopolistic competition, it is clear once again that indirect utilities of employed workers are far higher under trade compared to autarky for those living in smaller countries. Thus the incentive effect of trade tends to be greater for workers in the smaller trading nations.

3. In conventional trade models exhibiting an exogenous natural rate, we are apt to conclude that there is little basis for arguing that protectionism, even when practised on a large scale, as occurred in the interwar years when international trade collapsed, cannot lead to massive joblessness. The perspective developed in this book suggests a channel through which protectionism can, indeed, lead to a worldwide collapse in output and rise in unemployment as occurred in the interwar years. While the *cause* of the Great Depression in the United States is unlikely to be due to the implementation of the Smoot–Hawley tariffs, trade being such a small share of US GDP in 1929, the setting up of tariff barriers by the largest economy in the world at the time and the accompanying retaliatory trade barriers put up by the other economies led to a collapse of world trade. In the framework developed here, the fragmentation of markets and the removal of the gains from trade must shift upwards the wage curve and downwards the aggregate labour demand curve, with the end result that the collapse of world trade must be accompanied by a rise in equilibrium unemployment. Such a perspective does away with any role for Keynesian effective demand but relies on real supply-side factors to understand the link between trade and the volume of joblessness.

   Consider the effects of protection by a large country in the Ricardian world made up of a large incompletely specialised country and many small completely specialised trading nations. For simplicity, suppose that all the small countries export the same good. Let the large country impose a unilateral tariff on its import from all the small trading nations. Assuming that the large country remains incompletely specialised under protection, the domestic relative price must continue to be equal to the original autarkic price given by the ratio of productivities of the import and export goods. This implies that the international terms of trade move against all the small trading nations by an amount which depends on the size of the tariff. Since the adverse terms of trade reduce the real purchasing power of workers in the small trading nations, hence reducing the value of holding a job in these countries, the result of protection is to raise the equilibrium rate of unemployment abroad. In the protecting country, as the domestic relative price is unchanged, there is no effect on the natural rate if we assume that the tariff revenue collected is redistributed to all workers regardless of their employment status.
4. Economic effects of disturbances in one country are propagated to other trading economies via the international terms of trade. When a group of individual countries trade a lot among themselves, a primary shock in one country can have strong repercussions on the other

trading nations. One principal result we obtained in Chapter 3 is that the rise of payroll taxes required to finance generous unemployment benefits in one country raises the natural rate not only in that country but also in its trading partners via a deterioration in the latter's terms of trade. The collapse of the Berlin Wall, in enlarging the labour force size of the integrated Germany, leads to a rise in Germany's natural rate but reduces the equilibrium rate of unemployment in the other European Union countries as the latter's terms of trade improve.

5. What are the effects of a technological catch-up by developing countries on their own equilibrium unemployment rate and on the job prospects of the developed countries? If we view the developing countries as individually small nations existing alongside a large country (say, the OECD) in the Ricardian set-up, it is clear that a one-time level increase in productivity in the small countries lowers their own natural rate but leaves job prospects unaffected in the large country. If we view the group of developing countries as one large region, however, a permanent one-time level increase in productivity of workers in that region has salutary effects on its trading partners who experience a decline in their natural rate and a rise in their real consumption wage when that growth occurs solely in the export sector. We saw this in the two-country Ricardian world with both countries being completely specialised. There, the improvement in the productivity of workers employed in the export sector must improve foreign welfare though it is possible that the growth may be immiserising. The immiserisation is typified by a rise in the natural rate of the growing country. Results may change when growth is confined not just to the export sector but occurs more generally throughout the economy. When growth takes the form of a general increase in the level of Harrod-neutral technical progress in both sectors of the relatively labour abundant country in the two-country Heckscher–Ohlin model, we showed that the relatively capital abundant trading partner experiences a terms of trade improvement. However, via the Stolper–Samuelson effect, there is, overall, a rise in the natural rate of unemployment in the trading partner despite the terms of trade improvement unless the capital abundant country is completely specialised in the production of the capital-intensive good. In the case of complete specialisation, the natural rate in the capital abundant country is lowered just as the Ricardian model predicts.
6. In a dual labour market model, we showed in Chapter 7 that when trade is intra-industry in nature, which describes the bulk of world trade, all participating economies stand to gain in terms of the expansion of high-wage-premium primary sector jobs. At the same time, wage inequality among identical workers – those working in the

primary sector earning a wage premium over those equally qualified but working in the secondary sector – is reduced through trade. This result turns on its head the popular supposition that globalisation must widen the wage gap. We also showed in Chapter 7 that when relative productivities are identical across two countries, the difference in absolute productivity levels can be the basis for international trade. Interestingly, the pattern of trade is such that the advanced country (with the higher productivity level) ends up being the net exporter of the high-wage good so that trade actually expands the number of good jobs contrary to common fears that trade with poorer nations will lead to a loss of good jobs.

7. Declining labour-market opportunities that are reflected in rising wages relative to workers' non-wage incomes lead workers to choose not to work, or at least not to work all the time. Conversely, improving labour-market conditions reflected in rising wages relative to workers' non-wage incomes would lead individuals who were formerly out of the labour force to rejoin the labour market. In Chapter 9, we used a neoclassical growth model to study how changes in workers' current and future wage earnings relative to their non-wage incomes affect their labour supply decisions. We analysed the effects of a revenue-neutral shift towards an increased payroll tax rate and decreased VAT. In a closed economy, such a tax shift decreases labour force participation as the interest rate is driven up and labour-market conditions worsen. In a small open economy open to international capital mobility, however, the increased decumulation of foreign assets erodes the negative effect of such a tax shift. Finally, in a two-country world integrated via an international capital market, a revenue-neutral shift of the tax mix away from VAT towards higher payroll taxes in one country acts to raise the world interest rate and so to contract employment in both countries. We also applied the model to study the effects of an increase in the rate of human capital accumulation on real wages and labour force participation. In the small open economy that takes the world interest rate as given, we showed that a rise in the rate of human capital accumulation raises the human wealth relative to non-human wealth ratio thus stimulating the supply of labour. This result throws light on the rising labour force participation rate that occurred in the East Asian economies, which occurred along with sharp increases in educational attainments since the mid-sixties.
8. There is some empirical evidence that the degree of trade integration is positively associated with total factor productivity improvements (see Coe and Helpman, 1995; Bayoumi, Coe and Helpman, 1996; and Coe, Helpman and Hoffmaister, 1997). In the words of Bayoumi, Coe and

Helpman (1996, pp. 25–6),

> [O]pen trading policies of the type followed by the NIEs [Hong Kong, Singapore, South Korea and Taiwan] can benefit developing nations through facilitating technology transfer from industrial countries. Expanding imports of manufactures in developing countries other than the NIEs by 5 percentage points of GDP – roughly equivalent to the increase that has occurred in these regions between 1992 and 1995 – raises output by about 9 percent in the long run, and consumption by 6 percent. These results indicate that part of the success of the NIEs over the last 20 years can be attributed to productivity improvements stemming from foreign R&D spillovers through trade. Other factors that have boosted growth in these countries include rapid increases in labor and capital input (Young, 1995).

If we accept the view that there has been, to an important degree, a process of technological catch-up – one facilitated by trade and, at least in the case of Singapore and Taiwan, also by foreign direct investments – as the East Asian economies moved closer to the knowledge frontier defined by the advanced economies, we see another mechanism through which trade lowers the natural rate. The mechanism is one in which firms operating in the small open economies, faced with the prospects of rapid technological growth at exogenously given world real interest rates, would be induced to raise their hiring of new workers and so increase labour demand. On the side of employees' work incentives, with rapid productivity growth pulling up wages ahead of wealth, wage pressure would be correspondingly reduced. The result is a shrinking of the pool of unemployed.

9. A study by Rodrik (1997) based on international cross-sectional data has argued that in economies subject to external risks as a result of trade opening, government consumption spending, especially income transfers, has been especially high. Rodrik interprets this finding to mean that economies that have been open to trade have found it necessary to develop a welfare state partly as an insurance against external shocks. Within the endogenous natural rate framework developed here, the rise of the welfare state, through its disincentive effects on work, would end up raising the equilibrium rate of unemployment. It is not apparent though that all open economies need necessarily choose a social insurance system that would weaken job attachments and lead to higher joblessness. The Singapore case provides a counter-example. There, no simultaneous increase in welfare spending as the economy opened up to foreign trade and investment has been observed. Instead, the setting up of the Central Provident Fund, a fully-funded social security system, is a key pillar of the government social policy. Under

this scheme, monthly contributions are made by both employers and employees to the workers' social security accounts only when the workers are employed, the savings being allowed to be drawn out for specified purposes such as to cover medical expenses. Being fully funded, the scheme does not have work disincentive effects found in unemployment benefit schemes. The bulk of government expenditures instead goes to public investment activities.

10. Garnaut (1996), looking at the East Asian growth experience, has shown that each country's export-oriented growth was initially built upon the rapid expansion of relatively labour-intensive exports, especially garments and textiles but over time a wider range of simple products. The export of relatively labour-intensive goods in exchange for goods intensive in the use of capital and raw materials was important to the establishment of growth momentum at first in Japan and Hong Kong, and then successively in Taiwan, South Korea, Singapore and Malaysia, Thailand, China, Indonesia and most recently Vietnam and the Philippines. He notes that the continued rapid expansion of exports of relatively labour-intensive goods from relative newcomers to the East Asian growth process was accommodated increasingly not from increased total imports of inter-regional markets in advanced countries (although these did grow considerably), but through increased exports to the higher-income East Asian economies whose comparative advantage had shifted away from relatively labour-intensive commodities. Hence there is potential today for the newly emerging low-income economies to undergo the sort of labour market developments through integration into the world economy that the East Asian economies underwent in the sixties and seventies, without causing adverse movements in jobs and wages in the high-income countries. This is predicated upon greater intra-industry trade as a share of world trade, allowing the richer nations to enjoy higher real incomes due to the benefits of trade based on scale economies, and so become better able to absorb the exports of the poorer nations based upon sale of the relatively labour-intensive good without suffering wage declines and increased joblessness.

References

Abramovitz, M. (1981), 'Welfare quandaries and productivity concerns', *American Economic Review*, 71, March, 1–17.

Allison, C. and D. Ringold (1996), *Labour Markets in Transition in Central and Eastern Europe: 1989–1995*, World Bank Technical Paper No. 352, Washington, DC: The World Bank.

Balassa, B. (1989), 'Outward orientation', in H. Chenery and T. N. Srinivasan (eds), *Handbook of Development Economics*, Vol. 2, Amsterdam: North-Holland.

Baldwin, R. E. (1971), 'Determinants of the commodity structure of US trade', *American Economic Review*, 6, March, 126–46.

Bayoumi, T., D. T. Coe and E. Helpman (1996), 'R&D spillovers and global growth', *NBER Working Paper Series*, No. 5628, Cambridge, Mass.

Ben-David, D. (1993), 'Equalizing exchange: Trade liberalization and income convergence', *Quarterly Journal of Economics*, 108, 653–79.

Bhagwati, J. N. and V. H. Dehejia (1994), 'Freer trade and wages of the unskilled: Is Marx striking again?', in J. N. Bhagwati and M. Kosters (eds), *Trade and Wages: Leveling Wages Down?*, Washington, DC: American Enterprise Institute.

Blanchard, O. J. (1985), 'Debts, deficits, and finite horizons', *Journal of Political Economy*, 93, April, 223–47.

Blinder, A. (1988), 'The challenge of high unemployment', *American Economic Review: Papers and Proceedings*, 78, May, 1–15.

Bluestone, B. and B. Harrison (1982), *The Deindustrialization of America*, New York: Basic Books.

Brecher, R. A. (1974), 'Optimal commercial policy for a minimum-wage economy', *Journal of International Economics*, 4, 139–49.

Brenner, M. H. (1987), 'Economic change, alcohol consumption and heart disease mortality in nine industrialized countries', *Social Science & Medicine*, 25, 119–32.

Brown, D. K., A. V. Deardorff, and R. M. Stern (1992), 'A North American free trade agreement: Analytical issues and a computational assessment', *World Economy*, 15, 11–29.

Bulow, J. and L. Summers (1986), 'A theory of dual labor markets with application to industrial policy, discrimination, and Keynesian unemployment', *Journal of Labor Economics*, 4, 376–414.

Burgstaller, A. (1986), 'Unifying Ricardo's theories of growth and comparative advantage', *Economica*, 53, 467–82.

Calvo, G. A. (1979), 'Quasi-Walrasian models of unemployment', *American Economic Review: Papers and Proceedings*, 69, May, 102–8.

Capie, F. H. (1994), *Tariffs and Growth: Some Illustrations from the World Economy 1850–1940*, Manchester and New York: Manchester University Press.

Casella, A. (1996), 'On standards and trade: A review of simple results', in J. N. Bhagwati and R. Hudec (eds), *Fair Trade and Harmonization: Prerequisites for Free Trade?*, Cambridge, Mass.: MIT Press.

Chow, P. C. Y. and M. H. Kellman (1993), *Trade – The Engine of Growth in East Asia*, New York: Oxford University Press.
Clark, A. E. and A. J. Oswald (1994), 'Unhappiness and unemployment', *Economic Journal*, 104, 648–59.
Cline, W. R. (1997), *Trade and Income Distribution*, Washington, DC: Institute for International Economics.
Coe, D. T. and E. Helpman (1995), 'International R&D spillovers', *European Economic Review*, 39, 859–87.
Coe, D. T., E. Helpman and A. W. Hoffmaister (1997), 'North–South R&D spillovers', *Economic Journal*, 107, 134–49.
Cohen, S. and J. Zysman (1987), *Manufacturing Matters*, New York: Basic Books.
Collins, S. M. and Rodrik, D. (1991), *Eastern Europe and the Soviet Union in the World Economy*, Washington, DC: Institute for International Economics.
Commission of the European Communities (1993), *Growth, Competitiveness, Employment: The Challenges and Ways Forward into the 21st Century – White Paper*, Luxembourg: Office for Official Publications of the European Communities.
Cooper, R. N. and János Gács (eds) (1997), *Trade Growth in Transition Economies: Export Impediments for Central and Eastern Europe*, Cheltenham: Edward Elgar.
Copeland, B. R. (1989), 'Efficiency wages in a Ricardian model of international trade', *Journal of International Economics*, 27, 221–44.
Davis, D. R. (1995), 'Intra-industry trade: A Heckscher–Ohlin–Ricardo approach', *Journal of International Economics*, 39, 201–26.
Department of Statistics (1988), *Singapore Input–Output Tables 1988*, Singapore: Singapore National Printers.
Doeringer, P. and M. Piore (1971), *Internal Labor Markets and Manpower Analysis*, Lexington, MA: D.C. Heath.
Ellis, H. S. and L. Metzler (eds) (1950), *Readings in the Theory of International Trade*, Homewood, Illinois: Richard D. Irwin, Inc.
Ethier, W. (1982), 'National and international returns to scale in the modern theory of international trade', *American Economic Review*, 72, 389–405.
Feldstein, M. S. (1998), 'Income inequality and poverty', *NBER Working Paper Series*, No. 6770, Cambridge, Mass.
Fields, G. S. (1984), 'Employment, income distribution and economic growth in seven small open economies', *Economic Journal*, 94, March, 74–83.
Fields, G. S. (1985), 'Industrialization and employment in Hong Kong, Korea, Singapore and Taiwan', in W. Galenson (ed.), *Trade, Foreign Investment and Economic Growth in the Newly Industrializing Countries*, Wisconsin, Madison: University of Wisconsin Press.
Fields, G. S. and J. C. O'Hara Mitchell (1999), 'Changing income inequality in Taiwan: A decomposition analysis', in G. R. Saxonhouse and T. N. Srinivasan (eds), *Development, Duality, and the International Economic Regime: Essays in Honor of Gustav Ranis*, Ann Arbor: University of Michigan Press.
Findlay, R. (1974), 'Relative prices, growth and trade in a simple Ricardian system', *Economica*, 41, 1–13.
Freeman, R. B. (1994), 'Crime and the job market', *NBER Working Paper Series*, No. 4910, Cambridge, Mass.
Frenkel, J. and A. Razin (1996), *Fiscal Policies and Growth in the World Economy*, 3rd edition, Cambridge, Mass.: MIT Press.
Garnaut, R. (1996), *Open Regionalism and Trade Liberalization: An Asia-Pacific*

Contribution to the World Trade System, Singapore: Institute of Southeast Asian Studies and Sydney: Allen & Unwin.

Hall, R. E. and C. Jones (1999), 'Why do some countries produce so much more output per worker than others?', *Quarterly Journal of Economics*, 114, 83–116.

Harrison, A. E. (1994), 'Productivity, imperfect competition, and trade reform', *Journal of International Economics*, 36, 53–73.

Helpman, E. (1997), 'R&D and productivity: The international connection', *NBER Working Paper Series*, No. 6101, Cambridge, Mass.

Helpman, E. and P. R. Krugman (1989), *Trade Policy and Market Structure*, Cambridge, Mass.: MIT Press.

Hoon, H. T. (1990), *Market Structure, Trade Theory and Equilibrium Unemployment*, PhD dissertation submitted to Columbia University in the City of New York.

Hoon, H. T. (1991), 'Comparative advantage and the equilibrium rate of unemployment', *Economics Letters*, 37, November, 299–304.

Hoon, H. T. (1993), 'Improvements in agriculture in Ricardo's *Essay on Profits*', *The Manchester School*, 61, 425–38.

Hoon, H. T. (1994), 'The impact of intraindustry trade on the natural rate of unemployment in two simple models', *Open Economies Review*, 5, 29–46.

Hoon, H. T. (2000a), 'Adjustment of wages and equilibrium unemployment in a Ricardian global economy', *Journal of International Economics*, forthcoming.

Hoon, H. T. (2000b), 'General-equilibrium implications of international product-market competition for jobs and wages', *Oxford Economic Papers*, forthcoming.

Hoon, H. T. and E. S. Phelps (1992), 'Macroeconomic shocks in a dynamized model of the natural rate of unemployment', *American Economic Review*, 82, September, 889–900.

Hoon, H. T. and E. S. Phelps (1996), 'Payroll taxes and VAT in a labor-turnover model of the "natural rate"', *International Tax and Public Finance*, 3, 369–83.

Hoon, H. T. and E. S. Phelps (1997), 'Growth, wealth and the natural rate: Is the jobs crisis a growth crisis?', *European Economic Review* (Papers and Proceedings), 41, 549–57.

Hoon, H. T. and H. L. Kee (1998), 'Factors shaping Singapore's wages and unemployment and the role of the NWC', in C. Y. Lim and R. Chew (eds), *Wages and Wages Policies: Tripartism in Singapore*, Singapore: World Scientific.

Hoon, H. T. and K. W. Ho (1999), 'Production fragmentation, jobs and wages in Singapore: The role of MNCs', paper presented at the international conference on Global Production: Specialization and Trade, Hong Kong, October.

Hsieh, C. T. (1998), 'What explains the Industrial Revolution in East Asia? Evidence from factor markets', Working Paper, University of California, Berkeley, January.

Jones, S. (1987), 'Minimum wage legislation in a dual labor market', *European Economic Review*, 31, 1229–46.

Juhn, C., K. Murphy, and B. Pierce (1993), 'Wage inequality and the rise in returns to skill', *Journal of Political Economy*, 101, 410–42.

Kates, N., B. S. Grieff, and D. Q. Hagen (1990), *The Psychosocial Impact of Job Loss*, Washington, DC: American Psychiatric Press.

Katz, L. F. (1986), 'Efficiency wage theories: A partial evaluation', in S. Fischer (ed.), *NBER Macroeconomics Annual*, Cambridge, Mass.: MIT Press.

Katz, L. and L. Summers (1989), 'Industry rents: Evidence and implications', *Brookings Papers on Economic Activity: Microeconomics*, 209–290.

Katz, L. F. and K. M. Murphy (1992), 'Changes in relative wages, 1963–1987: Supply and demand factors', *Quarterly Journal of Economics*, 107, February, 35–78.

Keynes, J. M. (1920), *The Economic Consequences of the Peace*, London: Macmillan.

Kimball, M. (1994), 'Labor-market dynamics when unemployment is a worker discipline device', *American Economic Review*, 84, September, 1045–59.

Krueger, A. (1983), *Trade and Employment in Developing Countries: Synthesis and Conclusions*, Chicago: University of Chicago Press.

Krugman, P. R. (1979), 'Increasing returns, monopolistic competition, and international trade,' *Journal of International Economics*, 9, November, 469–79.

Krugman, P. R. (1981), 'Intraindustry specialization and the gains from trade', *Journal of Political Economy*, 89, 959–74.

Krugman, P. R. (1994a), *The Age of Diminished Expectations: US Economic Policy in the 1990s*, 3rd edition, Cambridge, Mass.: MIT Press.

Krugman, P. R. (1994b), 'The myth of Asia's miracle', *Foreign Affairs*, 73, November/December.

Krugman, P. R. (1994c), 'Empirical evidence on the new trade theories: The current state of play', in *New Trade Theories: A Look at the Empirical Evidence*, CEPR conference report, London.

Krugman, P. R. (1995), 'Growing world trade: Causes and consequences', *Brookings Papers on Economic Activity*, 1, 327–77.

Krugman, P. R. (1996), 'Domestic distortions and the deindustrialization hypothesis', in R. Feenstra, G. Grossman and D. Irwin (eds), *The Political Economy of Trade: Papers in Honor of Jagdish Bhagwati*, Cambridge, Mass.: MIT Press.

Lawrence, C. and P. T. Spiller (1983), 'Product diversity, economies of scale, and international trade', *Quarterly Journal of Economies*, 98, 63–83.

Lawrence, R. Z. and M. J. Slaughter (1993), 'Trade and US wages: Giant sucking sound or small hiccup?', *Brookings Papers on Economic Activity*, 2, 161–210.

Layard, R., S. Nickell, and R. Jackman (1991), *Unemployment: Macroeconomic Performance and the Labour Market*, New York: Oxford University Press.

Leamer, E.E. and J. Levinsohn (1995), 'International trade theory: The evidence', in G. Grossman and K. Rogoff (eds), *Handbook of International Economics*, Vol. 3, Amsterdam: North Holland.

Lee, T. Y. (1987), 'Economic stabilization policies in Singapore', in P. B. Rana and F. A. Alburo (eds), *Economic Stabilization Policies in ASEAN Countries*, Singapore: ASEAN Economic Research Unit and Institute of Southeast Asian Studies.

Leibenstein, H. (1957), *Economic Backwardness and Economic Growth*, New York: John Wiley.

Leontief, W. (1954), 'Domestic production and foreign trade: the American capital position re-examined', *Economia Internazionale*, 7, 3–32, reprinted in R. E. Caves and H. G. Johnson (eds) (1968), *Readings in International Economics*, Homewood, Illinois: Richard D. Irwin, Inc.

Levinsohn, J. (1993), 'Testing the imports-as-market-discipline hypothesis', *Journal of International Economics*, 35, 1–22.

Lewis, W. A. (1949), *Economic Survey: 1919–1939*, London: George Allen and Unwin.

Lim, C. Y. (1998), 'NWC: Targets and goals', in C. Y. Lim and R. Chew (eds), *Wages and Wages Policies: Tripartism in Singapore*, Singapore: World Scientific.

Lindbeck, A. and D. Snower (1988), *The Insider–Outsider Theory of Employment and Unemployment*, Cambridge, Mass.: MIT Press.
Maneschi, A. (1983), 'Dynamic aspects of Ricardo's international trade theory', *Oxford Economic Papers*, 35, 67–80.
Markusen, J. R. (1981), 'Trade and the gains from trade with imperfect competition', *Journal of International Economics*, 11, 531–51.
Matusz, S. J. (1996), 'International trade, the division of labour, and unemployment', *International Economic Review*, 37, February, 71–84.
McDonald, I. and R. M. Solow (1981), 'Wage bargaining and employment', *American Economic Review*, 71, December, 896–908.
Mokyr, J. (1991), 'Dear labor, cheap labor, and the Industrial Revolution', in P. Higonnet, D. S. Landes and H. Rosovsky (eds), *Favorites of Fortune: Technology, Growth, and Economic Development since the Industrial Revolution*, Cambridge, Mass.: Harvard University Press.
Mortensen, D. and C. Pissarides (1998), 'Job reallocation, employment fluctuations and unemployment', mimeo., Northwestern University and London School of Economics.
Nelson, R. R. and E. S. Phelps (1966), 'Investment in humans, technological diffusion, and economic growth', *American Economic Review*, 56, March, 69–75.
Nelson, R. R. and H. Pack (1999), 'Firm competencies, technological catch-up, and the Asian miracle', in G. R. Saxonhouse and T. N. Srinivasan (eds), *Development, Duality, and the International Economic Regime: Essays in Honor of Gustav Ranis*, Ann Arbor: University of Michigan Press.
Obstfeld, M. and K. Rogoff (1995), 'Exchange rate dynamics redux', *Journal of Political Economy*, 103, June, 624–60.
OECD (1993), *Employment Outlook*, July, Paris.
Oswald, A. J. (1997), 'Happiness and economic performance', *Economic Journal*, 107, November, 1815–31.
Phelps, E. S. (1968), 'Money–wage dynamics and labor-market equilibrium', *Journal of Political Economy*, 76, August, Part 2, 678–711.
Phelps, E.S. (1991), '1992 Europe as a unified customer market', in G. R. Faulhaber and G. Tamburini (eds), *European Economic Integration*, Dordrecht: Kluwer Academic Publishers.
Phelps, E. S. (1994), *Structural Slumps: The Modern-Equilibrium Theory of Unemployment, Interest, and Assets*, Cambridge, Mass.: Harvard University Press.
Phelps, E. S. (1997), *Rewarding work: How to restore participation and self-support to free enterprise*, Cambridge, Mass.: Harvard University Press.
Piriyarangsan, K. (1999), 'Children as losers in economic development: Policies and strategies to promote the best interests of children in East and Southeast Asia', paper presented at Manila Social Forum organised by the Asian Development Bank and the World Bank, Manila, Philippines, 9–12 November.
Ricardo, D. ([1815] 1923), 'Essay on the influence of a low price of corn on the profits of stock', reprinted in E. C. K. Gonner (ed.) *Economic Essays*, London: G. Bell and Sons, Ltd.
Ricardo, D. ([1817] 1911), *Principles of Political Economy and Taxation*, Everyman's Library edition, London: J. M. Dent & Sons Ltd.
Robinson, J. (1947), 'Beggar-my-neighbour remedies for unemployment', *Essays on the Theory of Employment*, 2nd ed., Part III, Chapter 2, Oxford: Basil Blackwell, reprinted in H. S. Ellis and L. Metzler (eds) (1950), *Readings in the Theory of International Trade*, Homewood, Illinois: Richard D. Irwin, Inc.

Rodrik, D. (1988), 'Imperfect competition, scale economies, and trade policy in developing countries', in R. E. Baldwin (ed.), *Trade Policy Issues and Empirical Analysis*, Chicago: University of Chicago Press.
Rodrik, D. (1997), 'Trade, social insurance, and the limits of globalization', *NBER Working Paper Series*, No. 5905, Cambridge, Mass.
Rodrik, D. (1999), *The New Global Economy and Developing Countries: Making Openness Work*, Washington, DC: Overseas Development Council.
Romer, C. D. and D. H. Romer (1998), 'Monetary policy and the well-being of the poor', *NBER Working Paper Series*, No. 6793, Cambridge, Mass.
Salant, W. A. (1941), 'Foreign trade policy in the business cycle', *Public Policy*, Volume II, Cambridge, Mass., pp. 209–31, reprinted in H. S. Ellis and L. Metzler (eds) (1950), *Readings in the Theory of International Trade*, Homewood, Illinois: Richard D. Irwin, Inc.
Salop, S. C. (1979), 'A model of the natural rate of unemployment', *American Economic Review*, 69, March, 117–25.
Sen, A. K. (1999), *Development as Freedom*, New York: Alfred A. Knopf.
Shapiro, C. and J. E. Stiglitz (1984), 'Equilibrium unemployment as a worker-discipline device', *American Economic Review*, 74, June, 434–44.
Smith, A. (1776), *Wealth of Nations*, reprinted in (1937), New York.
Stolper, W. F. and P. A. Samuelson (1941), 'Protection and real wages', *Review of Economic Studies*, 9, November, 58–73, reprinted in H. S. Ellis and L. Metzler (eds) (1950), *Readings in the Theory of International Trade*, Homewood, Illinois: Richard D. Irwin, Inc.
Teh, K. P. and T. Shanmugaratnam (1992), 'Exchange rate policy: Philosophy and conduct over the past decade', in L. Low and M. H. Toh (eds), *Public Policies in Singapore: Changes in the 1980s and Future Signposts*, Singapore: Times Academic Press.
Vogel, E. F. (1991), *The Four Little Dragons: The Spread of Industrialization in East Asia*, Cambridge, Mass.: Harvard University Press.
Woodford, M. (1994), 'Review of Structural Slumps', *Journal of Economic Literature*, 32, December, 1784–815.
Young, A. (1992), 'A tale of two cities: Factor accumulation and technical change in Hong Kong and Singapore', *NBER Macroeconomics Annual*, Cambridge, Mass.: MIT Press.
Young, A. (1995), 'The tyranny of numbers: Confronting the statistical realities of the East Asian growth experience', *Quarterly Journal of Economics*, 110, August, 641–80.

Index